Date Due

SOUTHAMPTON

SHAKESPEARE'S

VENUS AND ADONIS, LUCRECE

822

AND OTHER POEMS

EDITED, WITH NOTES

BY

WILLIAM J. ROLFE, Litt.D.

FORMERLY HEAD MASTER OF THE HIGH SCHOOL
CAMBRIDGE, MASS.

ILLUSTRATED

1437

NEW YORK ·:· CINCINNATI ·:· CHICAGO

AMERICAN BOOK COMPANY

PREFACE

SHAKESPEARE'S *Poems* (aside from the *Sonnets*) have received comparatively slight attention from his biographers and editors. They have been often omitted from editions of his works, and when included have seldom been adequately discussed and annotated. Of separate editions Wyndham's (see p. 27 below) seems to me the only one of any critical value.

I have attempted to treat them with the same thoroughness as the plays. The early readings are given with sufficient fulness for the purposes of all classes of students ; and the same is true of the introduction and the notes, in which I have aimed to supply the deficiencies of other editors.

The text is given without expurgation. The *Lucrece* needs none, and the *Venus and Adonis* does not admit of it without serious mutilation. Of course these poems will never be read in secondary schools or Shakespeare clubs.

In *The Passionate Pilgrim* the pieces which are certainly not Shakespeare's are transferred from the text to the notes. Most of the others are of doubtful authenticity, but I give Shakespeare the benefit — if benefit it be — of the doubt. *A Lover's Complaint* and *The Phœnix and the Turtle* are now generally conceded to be his.

5

CONTENTS

ARMS OF SOUTHAMPTON

DEATH OF LUCRECE

INTRODUCTION TO SHAKESPEARE'S POEMS

THE HISTORY OF THE POEMS

Venus and Adonis was first published in quarto form, in 1593, with the following title-page: —

VENVS | AND ADONIS | *Vilia miretur vulgus: mihi flauus Apollo | Pocula Castalia plena ministret aqua.* | LONDON | Imprinted by Richard Field, and are to be sold at | the signe of the white Greyhound in | Paules Church-yard. | 1593.

The book is printed with remarkable accuracy, and doubtless from the author's manuscript.

A second quarto edition was published in 1594, the title-page of which differs from that of the first only in the date.

A third edition in octavo form (like all the subsequent editions) was issued in 1596 from the same printing-office " for Iohn Harison."

A fourth edition was published in 1599, with the following title-page (as given in Edmonds's reprint): —

VENVS | AND ADONIS. | *Vilia miretur vulgus: mihi flauus Apollo | Pocula Castalia plena ministret aqua.* | Imprinted at London for William Leake, dwel- | ling in Paules Churchyard at the signe of | the Greyhound. 1599.

This edition was not known until 1867, when a copy of it was discovered at Lamport Hall in Northamptonshire by Mr. Charles Edmonds, who issued a fac-simile reprint in 1870. It was evidently printed from the third edition. Mr. Edmonds says : " A few corrections are introduced, but they bear no proportion to the misprints."

Of the fifth edition a single copy is in existence (in the Bodleian Library), lacking the title-page, which has been restored in manuscript with the following imprint : " LONDON | Printed by I. H. | for Iohn Harrison | 1600." The date may be right, but, according to Halliwell-Phillipps and Edmonds, the publisher's name must be wrong, as Harrison had assigned the copyright to Leake four years previous. The Cambridge editors assumed in 1866 that this edition (the 4th of their numbering in 1866, but 5th in the ed. of 1893) was printed from that of 1596 ; but it is certain, since the discovery of the 1599 ed., that it must have been based on that.

Of the text they say: "It contains many erroneous readings, due, it would seem, partly to carelessness and partly to wilful alteration, which were repeated in later eds."

Two new editions were issued in 1602, and others in 1617 and 1620. In 1627, an edition (of which the only known copy is in the British Museum) was published in Edinburgh. In the Bodleian Library there is a unique copy of an edition wanting the title-page but catalogued with the date 1630; also a copy of another edition, published in 1630 (discovered since the Cambridge ed. of 1866 appeared).[1] A thirteenth edition was printed in 1636, "to be sold by Francis Coules in the Old Baily without Newgate."

The first edition of *Lucrece* was published in quarto in 1594, with the following title-page : —

LVCRECE. | LONDON. | Printed by Richard Field, for Iohn Harrison, and are | to be sold at the signe of the white Greyhound | in Paules Churh-yard.   1594.

The running title is "The Rape of Lvcrece." The Bodleian Library has two copies of this edition which differ in some important readings, indicating that it was corrected while passing through the press.

A second edition appeared in 1598, a third in 1600,

---

[1] *Bibliographical Contributions*, edited by J. Winsor, Librarian of Harvard University: No. 2, *Shakespeare's Poems* (1879). This Bibliography of the earlier editions of the Poems contains much valuable and curious information concerning their history, the extant copies, reprints, etc.

and a fourth in 1607, all in octavo and all "for Iohn Harrison " (or " Harison ").

In 1616, the year of Shakespeare's death, the poem was reprinted with his name as "newly revised ; " but " as the readings are generally inferior to those of the earlier editions, there is no reason for attaching any importance to an assertion which was merely intended to allure purchasers " (Cambridge ed.).   The title-page of this edition reads thus : —

THE | RAPE | OF | *LVCRECE.* | By | M^r. *William Shakespeare.* | Newly Reuised. | LONDON : | Printed by *T. S.* for *Roger Iackson,* and are | to be solde at his shop neere the Conduit | in Fleet-street. 1616.

A sixth edition, also printed for Jackson, was issued in 1624.

The fifth and sixth editions differ considerably in their readings from the first four, in which there are no important variations.

A seventh edition appeared in 1632, and an eighth in 1655.

A Lover's Complaint was first printed, so far as we know, in the first edition of the *Sonnets,* which appeared in 1609.   It was probably not reprinted until it was included in the *Poems* of 1640, mentioned below.

The Passionate Pilgrim was first published in 1599, with the following title-page : —

THE | PASSIONATE | PILGRIME. | *By W. Shake-*

speare. | *AT LONDON* | Printed for W. Iaggard, and are | to be sold by W. Leake, at the Grey- | hound in Paules Church-yard. | 1599.

In the middle of sheet C is a second title: —

SONNETS | To sundry notes of Musicke. | *AT LONDON* | Printed for W. Iaggard, and are | to be sold by W. Leake, at the Grey- | hound in Paules Church-yard. | 1599.

The book was reprinted in 1612, together with some poems by Thomas Heywood, the whole being attributed to Shakespeare. The title at first stood thus: —

THE | PASSIONATE | PILGRIME. | or | *Certaine Amorous Sonnets,* | betweene Venus *and* Adonis, | *newly corrected and aug-* | mented. | *By W. Shakespere.* | The third Edition. | Whereunto is newly ad- | ded two Loue-Epistles, the first | from *Paris* to *Hellen*, and | *Hellens* answere backe | againe to *Paris.* | Printed by W. Iaggard. | 1612.

The Bodleian copy of this edition contains the following note by Malone: "All the poems from Sig. D. 5 were written by Thomas Heywood, who was so offended at Jaggard for printing them under the name of Shakespeare that he has added a postscript to his *Apology for Actors,* 4to, 1612, on this subject; and Jaggard in consequence of it appears to have printed a new title-page to please Heywood, without the name of Shakespeare in it. The former title-page was no doubt intended to be cancelled, but by some inadvertence they were both prefixed to this copy and I have retained them as a curiosity." The corrected title-page is substantially as above, omitting " *By W. Shakespere.*"

It will be observed that this is called the *third* edition; but no other between 1599 and 1612 is known to exist.

In 1640 most of the *Sonnets,* all the poems of *The Passionate Pilgrim, A Lover's Complaint, The Phœnix and the Turtle,* the lines " Why should this a desert be," etc. (*A. Y. L.* iii. 2. 133 fol.), and " Take, O take those lips away," etc. (*M. for M.* iv. 1. 1 fol.), with some translations from Ovid and sundry other poems falsely ascribed to Shakespeare, were published in a volume with the following title : —

POEMS : | WRITTEN | BY | WIL. SHAKE-SPEARE. | Gent. | Printed at *London* by *Tho. Cotes,* and are | to be sold by *Iohn Benson,* dwelling in | S^t. *Dunstan's* Church-yard. 1640.

The first complete edition of Shakespeare's Poems, including the Sonnets, was issued (according to Lowndes, *Bibliographer's Manual*) in 1709, with the following title:

A Collection of Poems, in Two Volumes; Being all the Miscellanies of Mr. *William Shakespeare,* which were Publish'd by himself in the Year 1609, and now correctly Printed from those Editions. The First Volume contains, I. VENUS AND ADONIS. II. The Rape of LUCRECE. III. The Passionate Pilgrim. IV. Some Sonnets set to sundry Notes of Musick. The Second Volume contains One Hundred and Fifty Four Sonnets, all of them in Praise of his Mistress. II. A Lover's

theatres
in Londo
then wrot
it was pr
The *L*
promised
and, as I
turity tha
tion." It
a youthfu
date.
A Love
Lucrece, b
precision.
The Sh
were of c
was publi
Lost mus t
Venus an
have been
the long
much eas
cannot su
The Ph
speare's, a

The st
Metamorp

in 1567; but Shakespeare was doubtless familiar with it in the original Latin, which he had read in the Stratford grammar school, and to which he probably recurred in Field's edition after he came to London. In the poem he does not follow Ovid very closely.

That poet " relates, shortly, that Venus, accidentally wounded by an arrow of Cupid's, falls in love with the beauteous Adonis, leaves her favourite haunts and the skies for him, and follows him in his huntings over mountains and bushy rocks, and through woods. She warns him against wild boars and lions. She and he lie down in the shade on the grass — he without pressure on her part; and there, with her bosom on his, she tells him, with kisses, the story of how she helped Hippomenes to win the swift-footed Atalanta, and then, because he was ungrateful to her (Venus), she excited him and his wife to defile a sanctuary by a forbidden act, for which they were both turned into lions. With a final warning against wild beasts, Venus leaves Adonis. He then hunts a boar, and gets his death-wound from it. Venus comes down to see him die, and turns his blood into a flower — the *anemone*, or wind-flower, short-lived, because the winds (*anemoi*), which give it its name, beat it down,[1] so slender is it. Other authors give Venus the enjoyment which Ovid and Shakespeare deny her, and bring Adonis back from Hades to be with her " (Furnivall).

[1] Pliny (bk. i. c. 23) says it never opens but when the wind is blowing.

The main incidents of the *Lucrece* were doubtless
familiar to Shakespeare from his school-days ; and they
had been used again and again in poetry and prose.
" Chaucer had, in his *Legende of Good Women*, told the
story of Lucrece, after those of Cleopatra, Dido, Thisbe,
Ypsiphile, and Medea, ' As saythe Ovyde and Titus
Lyvyus ' (Ovid's *Fasti*, ii. 741 ; *Livy*, i. 57, 58): the
story is also told by Dionysius Halicarnassensis, iv. 72,
and by Diodorus Siculus, Dio Cassius, and Valerius
Maximus.   In English it is besides in Lydgate's *Falles
of Princes*, iii. 5, and in Wm. Painter's *Palace of Pleasure*, 1567, vol. i. fol. 5–7, where the story is very shortly
told : the heading is ' Sextus Tarquinius ravisheth Lucrece, who bewailyng the losse of her chastitie, killeth
her self.'   The story is not in the Rouen edition, 1603,
of Boaistuau and Belleforest's *Histoires Tragiques*, 7
vols. 12mo ; or the Lucca edition, 1554, of the *Novelle*
of Bandello, 3 parts ; or the Lyons edition, 1573, of the
Fourth Part.   Painter's short *Lucrece* must have been
taken by himself from one of the Latin authors he cites
as his originals at the end of his preface.   In 1568, was
entered on the Stat. Reg. A, lf. 174, a receipt for 4*d*.
from Jn. Alde ' for his lycense for prynting of a ballett,
the grevious complaynt of Lucrece ' (Arber's *Transcript*,
i. 379) ; and in 1570 the like from ' James Robertes,
for his lycense for the pryntinge of a ballett intituled
The Death of Lucryssia ' (Arber's *Transcript*, i. 416).
Another ballad of the legend of Lucrece was also
printed in 1576, says Warton (*Variorum* ed. of 1821,

xx. 100). Chaucer's simple, short telling of the story in 206 lines — of which 95 are taken up with the visit of Collatyne and Tarquynyus to Rome, before Shakspere's start with Tarquin's journey thither alone — cannot of course compare with Shakspere's rich and elaborate poem of 1855 lines, though, had the latter had more of the earlier maker's brevity, it would have attained greater fame " (Furnivall).

The story of *A Lover's Complaint*, so far as we know, was original with Shakespeare.

GENERAL COMMENTS ON THE POEMS

The breadth of Shakespeare's literary tastes and aspirations in the 'prentice period of his career is shown by the fact that, just when his reputation as an actor and a dramatist was becoming established, he published two long narrative poems, *Venus and Adonis* and *Lucrece*.

The *Venus and Adonis* was dedicated to the young Earl of Southampton, apparently without his permission, as the poet begins by saying, " I know not how I shall offend in dedicating my unpolished lines to your lordship." He adds a " vow to take advantage of all idle hours " till he can honour his patron " with some graver labour." This promise doubtless refers to the *Lucrece* which he also dedicates to Southampton, and in terms implying that he does it with the earl's permission : " The warrant I have of your honourable disposition, not the worth of my untutored lines, makes it

assured of acceptance. What I have done is yours;
what I have to do is yours; being part in all I have,
devoted yours."

Southampton was not quite twenty when the *Venus
and Adonis* was dedicated to him, having been born
October 6th, 1573.   He was entered at St. John's Col-
lege, Cambridge, on December 11, 1585, just after he
was twelve; he took his degree of Master of Arts before
he was sixteen, on June 6, 1589; and soon after entered
at Gray's Inn, London.   He was a ward of Lord Burgh-
ley.   He became a favourite of Queen Elizabeth's, but
lost her favour, in 1595, for making love to Elizabeth
Vernon (Essex's cousin), whom he married later, in
1598.   All his life he was a liberal patron of men of
letters.   He was particularly interested in the drama.
In 1599 we find a reference to him as "going to plays
every day."   It may be added that later in life he was
engaged in schemes for colonization in America.   "He
helped to equip expeditions to Virginia, and was treas-
urer of the Virginia Company.   The map of the country commemorates his labours as a colonial pioneer. In
his honour were named Southampton Hundred, Hampton River, and Hampton Roads in Virginia " (Sidney
Lee).

In the dedication of *Venus and Adonis* Shakespeare
calls the poem "the first heir of my invention"— that
is, the first product of his imagination.   It is a question whether this means that it was written before any
of the plays, or that it was his first distinctively *literary*

work, plays being then regarded as not belonging to "invention," or literature properly so called. Knight and some others take the expression in its literal sense. Knight, for instance, says: " We regard the *Venus and Adonis* as the production of a very young man, improved, perhaps, considerably in the interval between its first composition and its publication, but distinguished by peculiarities which belong to the wild luxuriance of youthful power, — such power, however, as few besides Shakspere had ever possessed."

Baynes remarks: " All the facts and probabilities of the case seem to me to indicate that the *Venus and Adonis*, as Shakespeare's earliest considerable effort, must have been produced at Stratford some years before his departure for London. With regard to the internal evidence in support of this view, Mr. Collier says: ' A young man so gifted would not, and could not, wait until he was five or six and twenty before he made considerable and most successful attempts at poetical composition; and we feel morally certain that *Venus and Adonis* was in being anterior to Shakespeare's quitting Stratford. It bears all the marks of youthful vigour, of strong passion, of luxuriant imagination, together with a force and originality of expression which betoken the first efforts of a great mind, not always well regulated in its taste. It seems to have been written in the open air of a fine country like Warwickshire, possessing all the freshness of the recent impression of natural objects; and we will go so far as to say that we do not think even Shakespeare himself could have produced it, in the form it bears, after he had reached the age of forty.' In relation to the last point I should be disposed to go further still, and say that it is very unlikely that Shakespeare either could or would have produced such a poem after he had found in the drama the free use of both his hands — the means of dealing effectively with action as well as passion."

But Shakespeare in London did not forget — with his love of nature he could not forget — his "woody Warwickshire;" and in London there were many large gardens, and the suburbs were distinctly rural. The Theatre and the Curtain, just outside the walls, were "in the fields," and wild flowers could be gathered almost at the door of the playhouse. Shakespeare, moreover, was a poet when he began to be a dramatist, and the semi-lyrical character of large portions of his earliest plays, as well as the delight in nature which they show, has been often pointed out by the critics. The poems, like these plays, abound in *reminiscences* of country life, but it is not necessary to suppose that they, any more than the plays, were actually written amid the scenes of country life.

In 1592 the theatres were closed from July to December on account of the plague, and as the *Venus and Adonis* was entered for publication in April, 1593, it is quite certain that it must have been mainly or wholly written during that half-year when the poet's interest was more or less diverted from dramatic composition into other literary channels. There is a striking allusion to the pestilence in the poem (505–510): —

> " Long may they kiss each other for this cure!
> O, never let their crimson liveries wear!
> And as they last, their verdure still endure,
> To drive infection from the dangerous year!
> That the star-gazers, having writ on death,
> May say the plague is banish'd by thy breath."

The allusion may have been immediately suggested by the practice of strewing rooms with rue and other strong-smelling herbs as a means of preventing infection. The reference to the astrologers, predicting death by their horoscopes, is also in keeping with the fatal season.

The critics of the eighteenth century were inclined to disparage Shakespeare's poems. Malone, in his concluding remarks upon the *Venus and Adonis* and *Lucrece*, says: "We should do Shakspeare injustice were we to try them by comparison with more modern and polished productions, or with our present idea of poetical excellence." Knight, after quoting this, observes: "This was written in the year 1780 — the period which rejoiced in the 'polished productions' of Hayley and Miss Seward, and founded its 'idea of poetical excellence' on some standard which, secure in its conventional forms, might depart as far as possible from simplicity and nature, to give us words without

thought, arranged in verses without music. It would
be injustice indeed to Shakspere to try the *Venus and
Adonis* and *Lucrece* by such a standard of 'poetical
excellence.' But we have outlived that period."

Coleridge was the first to do justice to the merits of
the *Venus and Adonis*. He remarks: " It is throughout
as if a superior spirit, more intuitive, more intimately
conscious, even than the characters themselves, not
only of every outward look and act, but of the flux and
reflux of the mind in all its subtlest thoughts and feelings, were placing the whole before our view ; himself
meanwhile unparticipating in the passions, and actuated
only by that pleasurable excitement which had resulted
from the energetic fervour of his own spirit in so vividly
exhibiting what it had so accurately and profoundly
contemplated. . . . His Venus and Adonis seem at
once the characters themselves, and the whole representation of those characters by the most consummate
actors. You seem to be *told* nothing, but to see and
hear everything. Hence it is, that, from the perpetual
activity of attention required on the part of the reader,
— from the rapid flow, the quick change, and the play-
ful nature of the thoughts and images, — and, above all,
from the alienation, and, if I may hazard such an expression, the utter *aloofness* of the poet's own feelings
from those of which he is at once the painter and the
analyst, — that though the very subject cannot but
detract from the pleasure of a delicate mind, yet
never was poem less dangerous on a moral account."

Elsewhere the same critic has observed that, " in the *Venus and Adonis*, the first and most obvious excellence is the perfect sweetness of the versification ; its adaptation to the subject ; and the power displayed in varying the march of the words without passing into a loftier and more majestic rhythm than was demanded by the thoughts, or permitted by the propriety of preserving a sense of melody predominant." This self-controlling power of " varying the march of the words without passing into a loftier and more majestic rhythm " is perhaps one of the most signal instances of Shakespeare's consummate mastery of his art, even as a very young man.

Dowden says of the *Venus and Adonis* and the *Lucrece* : " Each is an artistic *study ;* and they form companion studies — one of female lust and boyish coldness, the other of male lust and womanly chastity. Coleridge noticed ' the utter aloofness of the poet's own feelings from those of which he is at once the painter and the analyst ;' but it can hardly be admitted that this aloofness of the poet's own feelings proceeds from a dramatic abandonment of self. The subjects of these two poems did not call and choose their poet ; they did not possess him and compel him to render them into art. Rather the poet expressly made choice of the subjects, and deliberately set himself down before each to accomplish an exhaustive study of it. . . . And for a young writer of the Renascence, the subject of Shakspere's earliest poem was a splendid one — as voluptuous and unspiritual as that of a classical picture of Titian. It included two figures containing inexhaustible pasture for the fleshly eye, and delicacies and dainties for the sensuous imagination of the Renascence — the enamoured Queen of Beauty, and the beautiful, disdainful boy. It afforded occasion for endless exercises and variations on the themes, Beauty, Lust, and Death. In holding the subject before his imagination, Shakspere is perfectly cool and collected. He has made choice of the subject, and he is interested in doing his duty by it in the most thorough way a young poet can; but he remains unimpassioned — intent wholly upon getting down the right colours and lines upon his canvas."

Furnivall says: "From whatever source came the impulse to take from Ovid the heated story of the heathen goddess's lust, we cannot forbear noticing how through this stifling atmosphere Shakspere has blown the fresh breezes of English meads and downs. *A Midsummer-Night's Dream* itself is not fuller of evidence of Shakspere's intimate knowledge of, and intense delight in, country scenes and sights, whether shown in his description of horse and hounds, or in closer touches, like that of the hush of wind before the rain; while such lines as those about the eagle flapping, 'shaking its wings' over its food, send us still to the Zoological Gardens to verify. Two lines (*V. and A.* 707, 708) there are, reflecting Shakspere's own experience of life — his own early life in London possibly — which we must not fail to note; they are echoed in *Hamlet*: —

> 'For misery is trodden on by many,
> And being low, never reliev'd by any.'

'Twas a lesson plainly taught by the Elizabethan days, and the Victorian preach it too. It has been the fashion lately to run down the *Venus* as compared with Marlowe's *Hero and Leander*. Its faults are manifest. It shows less restraint and training than the work of the earlier-ripened Marlowe; but to me it has a fulness of power and promise of genius enough to make three Marlowes. . . . Of possession and promise in Shakspere's first poem, we have an intense love of nature, and a conviction (which never left him) of her sympathy with the moods of men; a penetrating eye; a passionate soul; a striving power of throwing himself into all he sees, and reproducing it living and real to his reader; a lively fancy, command of words, and music of verse; these wielded by a shaping spirit that strives to keep each faculty under one control, and guide it while doing its share of the desired whole."

Mr. George Wyndham (1898),[1] in his *Poems of Shakespeare*, is right in declaring that Shakespeare handles his theme with due regard for beauty and "disregard for all that disfigures beauty," and, like Coleridge, defends the poem from the charge of immorality. He

---

[1] Some of my readers may not know that the author of this admirable edition of the *Poems* is the Rt. Hon. George Wyndham, chief secretary for Ireland in 1900 and a cabinet minister in 1902.

says : " Shakespeare portrays an amorous encounter
through its every gesture ; yet, unless in some dozen
lines where he glances aside, like any Mediæval, at a
gaiety not yet divorced from love, his appeal to Beauty
persists from first to last ; and nowhere is there an
appeal to Lust.   The laughter and sorrow of the
poem belong wholly to the faery world of vision and
romance, where there is no sickness, whether of senti-
ment or of sense.   And both are rendered by images,
clean-cut as in antique gems, brilliantly enamelled
as in mediæval chalices, numerous and interwoven
as in Moorish arabesques ; so that their incision,
colour, and rapidity of development, apart even
from the intricate melodies of the verbal medium in
which they live, tax the faculty of artistic apprecia-
tion to a point where it begins to participate in the
asceticism of artistic creation.   ' As little can a mind
thus roused and awakened be brooded on by mean and
indistinct emotion as the low, lazy mist can creep upon
the surface of a lake while a strong gale is driving it
onward in waves and billows : ' — Thus does Coleridge
resist the application to shift the venue of criticism on
this poem from the court of Beauty to the court of
Morals, and upon that subject little more can be said.
How wilful it is to discuss the moral bearing of an in-
vitation couched by an imaginary goddess in such
imaginative terms as these : —

> Bid me discourse, I will enchant thine ear,
> Or, like a fairy, trip upon the green,

> Or, like a nymph, with long dishevell'd hair,
> Dance on the sands, and yet no footing seen!' . . .

"When Venus says, 'Bid me discourse, I will enchant thine ear,' she instances yet another peculiar
excellence of Shakespeare's lyrical art, which shows in
this poem, is redoubled in *Lucrece*, and in the *Sonnets*
yields the most perfect examples of human speech : —

> 'Touch but my lips with those fair lips of thine,
> Though mine be not so fair, yet are they red. . . .
> Art thou ashamed to kiss ? Then wink again,
> And I will wink; so shall the day seem night.'

These are the fair words of her soliciting, and Adonis's
reply is of the same silvery quality : —

> 'If love have lent you twenty thousand tongues,
> And every tongue more moving than your own,
> Bewitching like the wanton mermaid's songs,
> Yet from mine ear the tempting tune is blown.'

And, as he goes on : —

> 'Lest the deceiving harmony should run
> Into the quiet closure of my breast ; '

you catch a note prelusive to the pleading altercation
of the *Sonnets*. It is the discourse in *Venus and Adonis*
and *Lucrece* which renders them discursive. Indeed
they are long poems, on whose first reading Poe's
advice, never to begin at the same place, may wisely
be followed. You do well, for instance, to begin at
stanza 136 —

> ['With this, he breaketh from the sweet embrace
> Of those fair arms which bound him to her breast,

> And homeward through the dark laund runs apace,
> Leaves Love upon her back deeply distress'd.
>   Look, how a bright star shooteth from the sky,
>   So glides he in the night from Venus' eye.'] —

in order to enjoy the narrative of Venus's vain pursuit,
with your senses unwearied by the length and sweetness of her argument. The passage hence to the end
is in the true romantic tradition: stanzas 140 and
141 —

> ['She marking them begins a wailing note
> And sings extemporally a woeful ditty:
> How love makes young men thrall and old men dote;
> How love is wise in folly, foolish-witty.
>   Her heavy anthem still concludes in woe,
>   And still the choir of echoes answer so.
>
> Her song was tedious and outwore the night,
> For lovers' hours are long, though seeming short;
> If pleased themselves, others, they think, delight
> In such-like circumstance, with such-like sport;
>   Their copious stories oftentimes begun
>   End without audience and are never done.']

are as clearly forerunners of Keats as 144 —

> ['Venus salutes him with this fair good-morrow:
> "O thou clear god, and patron of all light,
> From whom each lamp and shining star doth borrow
> The beauteous influence that makes him bright,
>   There lives a son that suck'd an earthly mother,
>   May lend thee light, as thou dost lend to others."'] —

is the child of Chaucer. The truth of such art con-
sists in magnifying selected details until their gigantic

shapes, edged with a shadowy iridescence, fill the whole
field of observation. Certain gestures of the body,
certain moods of the mind, are made to tell with the
weight of trifles during awe-stricken pauses of delay."

The three sonnets on the story of Venus and Adonis
in *The Passionate Pilgrim* are generally regarded by
the critics as preliminary studies for the poem; but it
is doubtful whether Shakespeare wrote them. If they
are his it is singular that they were not included in the
1609 edition of the *Sonnets* with the two sonnets (153,
154) on the same subject. Their authenticity may also
be questioned from the fact that in one of them the
author ridicules Adonis (" He rose and ran away — ah,
fool too froward!") for not yielding to the wiles of
Venus. In Shakespeare's poem it is to be noted that
nothing like this occurs. In the line (578), " The poor
fool prays her that he may depart," the context proves
that "fool" is used in a sympathetic pitying way; as
" poor fool " is in at least eight passages in the plays —
so also " good fool " and " pretty fool." The behaviour
of Adonis is indirectly approved by the poet, while that
of Venus is, again and again, directly condemned; as,
for instance, in lines 555–558 : —

> " Her face doth reek and smoke, her blood doth boil,
>   And careless lust stirs up a desperate courage ;
>   Planting oblivion, beating reason back,
>   Forgetting shame's pure blush and honour's wrack."

Adonis himself is eloquent in his denunciations of her
sensuality and her sophistry (787 fol.), and Shake-

speare speaks through him as truly as in the 129th
sonnet: —

> " ' What have you urged that I cannot reprove ?
> The path is smooth that leadeth on to danger:
> I hate not love, but your device in love,
> That lends embracements unto every stranger.
>> You do it for increase ; O strange excuse,
>> When reason is the bawd to lust's abuse !
>
> ' Call it not love, for Love to heaven is fled,
> Since sweating Lust on earth usurp'd his name ;
> Under whose simple semblance he hath fed
> Upon fresh beauty, blotting it with blame,
>> Which the hot tyrant stains and soon bereaves,
>> As caterpillars do the tender leaves.
>
> ' Love comforteth like sunshine after rain,
> But Lust's effect is tempest after sun ;
> Love's gentle spring doth always fresh remain,
> Lust's winter comes ere summer half be done ;
>> Love surfeits not, Lust like a glutton dies ;
>> Love is all truth, Lust full of forged lies.' "

It is significant, moreover, that the goddess is not successful in her lustful wooing, as other authors (except
Ovid) represent, bringing Adonis back from Hades to
be with her.

That the poem was considered somewhat objectionable even in Shakespeare's day is evident from certain
contemporaneous references to it. Halliwell-Phillipps
quotes *A Mad World my Masters*, 1608: " I have con-
vay'd away all her wanton pamphlets, as Hero and
Leander, Venus and Adonis ; " and Sir John Davies,

who in his *Papers Complaint* (found in his *Scourge of Folly*, 1610) makes "Paper" admit the superlative excellence of Shakespeare's poem, but at the same time censure its being "attired in such bawdy geare." It is also stated that "the coyest dames in private read it for their closset-games." In *The Dumbe Knight*, 1608, the lawyer's clerk refers to it as "maides philosophie;" and the stanza beginning with line 229 ("'Fondling,' she saith, 'since I have hemm'd thee here,'" etc.) is quoted both in that play and in Heywood's *Fayre Mayd of the Exchange*, 1607.

The greater maturity shown in the *Lucrece*, though published only a year after *Venus and Adonis*, certainly tends to support the theory that the latter was largely written some years before its publication, though probably not completed until 1592. Knight, indeed, goes so far as to say: "There is to our mind the difference of eight or even ten years in the aspect of these poems — a difference as manifest as that which exists between *Love's Labour's Lost* and *Romeo and Juliet*." Coleridge remarks: "The *Venus and Adonis* did not perhaps allow the display of the deeper passions. But the story of Lucretia seems to favour, and even demand, their intensest workings. And yet we find in *Shakespeare's* management of the tale neither pathos nor any other *dramatic* quality. There is the same minute and faithful imagery as in the former poem, in the same vivid colours, inspirited by the same impetuous vigour of thought, and diverging and contracting with the same

activity of the assimilative and of the modifying faculties ; and with a yet larger display, a yet wider range
of knowledge and reflection ; and, lastly, with the same
perfect dominion, often *domination*, over the whole
world of language."

Baynes, in his comments on " the profounder ethical
and reflective aspects " of the two poems, observes : " It
may justly be said that if Shakespeare follows Ovid in
the narrative and descriptive part of his work, in the
vivid picturing of sensuous passion, he is as decisively
separated from him in the reflective part, the higher
purpose and ethical significance of the poems. The
underlying subject in both is the same, the debasing
nature and destructive results of the violent sensuous
impulses, which in antiquity so often usurped the name
of love, although in truth they have little in common
with the nobler passion. The influence of fierce inordinate desire is dealt with by Shakespeare in these
poems in all its breadth as affecting both sexes, and in
all its intensity as blasting the most sacred interests
and relationships of life. In working out the subject,
Shakespeare shows his thorough knowledge of its seductive outward charm, of the arts and artifices, the
persuasions and assaults, the raptures and languors of
stimulated sensual passion. In this he is quite a match
for the erotic and elegiac poets of classic times, and
especially of Roman literature. He is not likely therefore in any way to undervalue the attraction or the
power of what they celebrate in strains so fervid and

rapturous. But, while contemplating the lower passion steadily in all its force and charm, he has at the same time the higher vision which enables him to see through and beyond it, the reflective insight to measure its results, and to estimate with remorseless accuracy its true worth. It is in this higher power of reflective insight, in depth and vigour of thought as well as feeling, that Shakespeare's earliest efforts are marked off even from the better works of those whom he took, if not as his masters, at least as his models and guides. He was himself full of rich and vigorous life, deepened by sensibilities of the rarest strength and delicacy; and in early youth had realized, in his own experience, the impetuous force of passionate impulses. But his intellectual power no less than the essential depth and purity of his nobler emotional nature would effectually prevent his ever becoming ' soft fancy's slave.'

"In the very earliest poem we have from Shakespeare's pen this higher note of the modern world is clearly sounded — the note that 'Love is Lord of all,' and that love is something infinitely higher and more divine than the lawless vagrant passion which in pagan times passed under that name. To the modern mind, while the latter is blind, selfish, and often brutal in proportion to its strength, the former is full of sympathy and self-abnegation, of an almost sacred ardour and gentleness, humility and devotion, the very heart and crown of life."

Further on, after quoting the stanzas (787 fol.) given

above, in which Adonis reproaches Venus for her sensuality, Baynes remarks : " In this reproof of the pagan goddess of love, the higher note of the modern world is struck fully and clearly. It is repeated with tragic emphasis in the *Lucrece*, deepened in the *Sonnets*, and developed through all the gracious range of higher female characters in the dramas. Nowhere indeed is the vital difference in the social axes of the ancient and modern world more vividly seen, than in the contrast between the Lesbias, Delias, and Corinnas of Roman poetry, and the Mirandas, Portias, and Imogens of Shakespeare's dramas. In the one we have the monotonous ardours and disdains, the gusts and glooms, the tricks and artifices belonging to the stunted life of lower impulse ; in the other, the fadeless beauty and grace, the vivacity and intelligence, the gentleness and truth of perfect womanhood."

Mr. Verity (" Henry Irving " edition), on the other hand, says : " Whereas *Lucrece* is intensely didactic, *Venus and Adonis* is no less intensely non-moral — not immoral, but unmoral. If *Lucrece* gives us the ' criticism of life ' theory of literature at its keenest, *Venus and Adonis* shows us the ' art for art's sake ' doctrine in the furthest possible development of that idea. . . . It is the purest paganism, a deification of erotic impulse which Catullus himself could not have surpassed. . . . There can be no place for the preacher here ; we cannot take very seriously the morality that flows from the pretty protesting lips of the blushing boy. . . . The poem is, as far as I can understand it, a study in sensuous effects; a series of stanzas in which morality and the ethical element that we usually look for in literature, especially English literature, are wholly absent."

But why should we not take the morality of Adonis as seriously as that of the 129th *Sonnet?* The tone of the stanzas quoted on p. 32 above is identical with that of the Sonnet. If the latter is more intense, it is only because it expresses the remorse of one who has yielded to the temptations of lust, while Adonis has resisted them, though the allurements of the goddess are so seductive and so persistent that they " might well have warm'd old Saturn."

"Lucrece," as the critic adds, " is perfectly different. Here the poet is at once an artist and a preacher; his achievement, if not his aim, is purely didactic. For no more terrible picture was ever drawn of the utter desolation and ruin wrought by unbridled, unreasoning impulse. Each phase of the passion is anatomized with the pitiless detail of minute realism. Simple enough in its beginning, the story works up with a gradual *crescendo* of horror to its tragic climax, and when the end comes no one, not the dullest of prosaicists, can be blind to the poet's purpose."

All this is true, but it is also substantially true of the other poem except for the lack there of the tragic element. The " minute realism " is the same in both — though in some details more minute in the earlier poem — and in both the " didactic " purpose, if we call it so, is equally clear. Shakespeare is seldom personally a " preacher," being generally content (as always in the plays) to let his characters speak for him ; but Adonis preaches no less truly than Lucrece, and with equally " sound doctrine," though the presentation of it is naturally and necessarily modified by the situation and circumstances. If *Venus and Adonis* is " the deification of erotic impulse," it is in no sense its defence or palliation, but, like *Lucrece*, its absolute and emphatic damnation.

Aside from *Venus and Adonis*, *Lucrece*, and the *Sonnets* (which will be discussed in another volume), the only poems ascribed to Shakespeare which are quite certainly his are *A Lover's Complaint* and *The Phœnix and the Turtle*.

A Lover's Complaint was first published with the *Sonnets* in 1609. There is no external evidence for determining when it was written, but the internal evidence of style and treatment indicates that it was later than *Lucrece*. It is in the same seven-lined stanza as that poem, and shows a " marked decrease in the use of antithesis and verbal paradox, and so far points to a refinement in taste ; " but there is nothing in the treatment of the subject — the lament of a girl who has been betrayed by a deceitful youth — which shows any noteworthy advance in other respects. The Spenserian flavour of the poem has been often noted by the critics. Malone remarks that it reads like a challenge to Spenser on his own ground. As Mr. Verity says, " it has much of Spenser's stately pathos and sense of physical beauty, and exquisite verbal melody." It appears to be an early exercise in the style of that poet, whose *Complaints: containing Sundry Small Poems of the World's Vanity* was published in 1591. These opening lines of *The Ruins of Time* in that volume have been compared with those of *A Lover's Complaint:*—

> "A woman sitting sorrowfully wailing,
> Rending her yellow locks like wiry gold,
> About her shoulders carelessly down trailing,
> And streams of tears from her fair eyes forth railing;
> In her right hand a broken rod she held,
> Which towards heaven she seemed on high to weld."

The Phœnix and the Turtle must have been written before 1601, when it was printed with Chester's *Love's Martyr* and ascribed to Shakespeare.

Malone had no doubt of the genuineness of the poem, but a few of the recent critics have been less confident of its authorship. Grant White says: "There is no other external evidence that these verses are Shakespeare's than their appearance with his signature in a collection of poems published in London while he was living there in the height of his reputation. The style, however, is at least a happy imitation of his, especially in the bold and original use of epithet." Dowden, in his *Primer* (1878), says: "That it is his seems in a high degree doubtful;" but, some years later, in a letter to the present writer, he said that he had no longer any doubt that the poem is Shakespeare's.

There is one point in favour of this view which apparently has been overlooked by the critics ; namely, that Chester's book was not a publisher's piratical venture, like *The Passionate Pilgrim*, but the reputable work of a gentleman who would hardly have ventured to insult his patron to whom he dedicates it, by palming off anonymous verses as the contribution of a well-known poet of the time, who was residing in London in 1601 when it appeared.

Ralph Waldo Emerson, in the preface to his *Parnassus* (1875), remarks : " I should like to have the Academy of Letters propose a prize for an essay on Shakespeare's poem, *Let the bird of loudest lay*, and the *Threnos* with which it closes, the aim of the essay being to explain, by a historical research into the poetic myths and tendencies of the age in which it was written, the frame and allusions of the poem. I have not seen Chester's *Love's Martyr* and 'the Additional Poems' (1601) in which it appeared. Perhaps that book will suggest all the explanation this poem requires. To unassisted readers, it would appear to be a lament on the death of a poet, and of his poetic mistress. But the poem is so quaint, and charming in diction, tone, and allusions, and in its perfect metre and harmony, that I would gladly have the fullest illustration yet attainable. I consider this piece a good example of the rule that there is a poetry for bards proper, as well as a poetry for the world of readers. This poem, if published for the first time, and without a known author's name, would find no general reception. Only the poets would save it."

Halliwell-Phillipps says: "It was towards the close of the present year, 1600, or at some time in the following one, that Shakespeare, for the first and only time, came forward in the avowed character of a philosophical writer." After giving an account of Chester's book, he adds: "The contribution of the great dramatist is a remarkable poem in which he makes a notice of the obsequies of the phœnix and turtle-dove subservient to the delineation of spiritual union. It is generally thought that Chester himself intended a personal allegory, but, if that be the case, there is nothing to indicate that Shakespeare participated in the design, nor even that he had endured the punishment of reading *Love's Martyr*."

VENUS AND ADONIS

TO THE

RIGHT HONOURABLE HENRY WRIOTHESLEY,

EARL OF SOUTHAMPTON AND BARON OF TICHFIELD

RIGHT HONOURABLE,

I know not how I shall offend in dedicating my unpolished lines to your Lordship, nor how the world will censure me for choosing so strong a prop to support so weak a burthen: only if your Honour seem but pleased, I account myself highly praised, and vow to take advantage of all idle hours till I have honoured you with some graver labour. But if the first heir of my invention prove deformed, I shall be sorry it had so noble a godfather, and never after ear so barren a land, for fear it yield me still so bad a harvest. I leave it to your honourable survey, and your Honour to your heart's content, which I wish may always answer your own wish and the world's hopeful expectation.

Your Honour's in all duty,

WILLIAM SHAKESPEARE.

VENUS AND ADONIS

EVEN as the sun with purple-colour'd face
Had ta'en his last leave of the weeping morn,
Rose-cheek'd Adonis hied him to the chase;
Hunting he lov'd, but love he laugh'd to scorn.
    Sick-thoughted Venus makes amain unto him,
    And like a bold-fac'd suitor gins to woo him.

' Thrice fairer than myself,' thus she began,
' The field's chief flower, sweet above compare,
Stain to all nymphs, more lovely than a man,
More white and red than doves or roses are,   10
    Nature that made thee, with herself at strife,
    Saith that the world hath ending with thy life.

' Vouchsafe, thou wonder, to alight thy steed,
And rein his proud head to the saddle-bow;

If thou wilt deign this favour, for thy meed
A thousand honey secrets shalt thou know.
    Here come and sit, where never serpent hisses,
    And being set I 'll smother thee with kisses,

' And yet not cloy thy lips with loath'd satiety,
But rather famish them amid their plenty,   20
Making them red and pale with fresh variety,
Ten kisses short as one, one long as twenty ;
    A summer's day will seem an hour but short,
    Being wasted in such time-beguiling sport.'

With this she seizeth on his sweating palm,
The precedent of pith and livelihood,
And, trembling in her passion, calls it balm,
Earth's sovereign salve to do a goddess good ;
    Being so enrag'd, desire doth lend her force
    Courageously to pluck him from his horse.   30

Over one arm the lusty courser's rein,
Under her other was the tender boy,
Who blush'd and pouted in a dull disdain,
With leaden appetite, unapt to toy ;
    She red and hot as coals of glowing fire,
    He red for shame, but frosty in desire.

The studded bridle on a ragged bough
Nimbly she fastens — O, how quick is love ! —
The steed is stalled up, and even now
To tie the rider she begins to prove ;   40

Backward she push'd him, as she would be thrust,
And govern'd him in strength, though not in lust.

So soon was she along as he was down,
Each leaning on their elbows and their hips;
Now doth she stroke his cheek, now doth he frown,
And gins to chide, but soon she stops his lips,
    And kissing speaks, with lustful language broken,
    ' If thou wilt chide, thy lips shall never open.'

He burns with bashful shame, she with her tears
Doth quench the maiden burning of his cheeks;   50
Then with her windy sighs and golden hairs
To fan and blow them dry again she seeks.
    He saith she is immodest, blames her miss;
    What follows more she murthers with a kiss.

Even as an empty eagle, sharp by fast,
Tires with her beak on feathers, flesh, and bone,
Shaking her wings, devouring all in haste,
Till either gorge be stuff'd or prey be gone,
    Even so she kiss'd his brow, his cheek, his chin,
    And where she ends she doth anew begin.   60

Forc'd to content, but never to obey,
Panting he lies and breatheth in her face;
She feedeth on the steam as on a prey,
And calls it heavenly moisture, air of grace,
    Wishing her cheeks were gardens full of flowers,
    So they were dew'd with such distilling showers.

Look how a bird lies tangled in a net,
So fasten'd in her arms Adonis lies;
Pure shame and awed resistance made him fret,
Which bred more beauty in his angry eyes.   70
    Rain added to a river that is rank
    Perforce will force it overflow the bank.

Still she entreats, and prettily entreats,
For to a pretty ear she tunes her tale;
Still is he sullen, still he lowers and frets,
'Twixt crimson shame and anger ashy-pale.
    Being red, she loves him best; and being white,
    Her best is better'd with a more delight.

Look how he can, she cannot choose but love;
And by her fair immortal hand she swears   80
From his soft bosom never to remove
Till he take truce with her contending tears,
    Which long have rain'd, making her cheeks all wet;
    And one sweet kiss shall pay this countless debt.

Upon this promise did he raise his chin,
Like a divedapper peering through a wave,
Who, being look'd on, ducks as quickly in;
So offers he to give what she did crave,
    But when her lips were ready for his pay,
    He winks and turns his lips another way.   90

Never did passenger in summer's heat
More thirst for drink than she for this good turn.

Her help she sees, but help she cannot get;
She bathes in water, yet her fire must burn.
   'O, pity,' gan she cry, 'flint-hearted boy!
   'T is but a kiss I beg; why art thou coy?

'I have been woo'd, as I entreat thee now,
Even by the stern and direful god of war,
Whose sinewy neck in battle ne'er did bow,
Who conquers where he comes in every jar;   100
   Yet hath he been my captive and my slave,
   And begg'd for that which thou unask'd shalt have.

'Over my altars hath he hung his lance,
His batter'd shield, his uncontrolled crest,
And for my sake hath learn'd to sport and dance,
To toy, to wanton, dally, smile, and jest,
   Scorning his churlish drum and ensign red,
   Making my arms his field, his tent my bed.

'Thus he that overrul'd I oversway'd,
Leading him prisoner in a red-rose chain;   110
Strong-temper'd steel his stronger strength obey'd,
Yet was he servile to my coy disdain.
   O, be not proud, nor brag not of thy might,
   For mastering her that foil'd the god of fight!

'Touch but my lips with those fair lips of thine, —
Though mine be not so fair, yet are they red, —
The kiss shall be thine own as well as mine.
What seest thou in the ground? hold up thy head.

Look in mine eye-balls, there thy beauty lies;
Then why not lips on lips, since eyes in eyes?   120

' Art thou asham'd to kiss? then wink again,
And I will wink; so shall the day seem night.
Love keeps his revels where there are but twain;
Be bold to play, our sport is not in sight.
 These blue-vein'd violets whereon we lean
 Never can blab, nor know not what we mean.

' The tender spring upon thy tempting lip
Shows thee unripe, yet mayst thou well be tasted.
Make use of time, let not advantage slip;
Beauty within itself should not be wasted.   130
 Fair flowers that are not gather'd in their prime
 Rot and consume themselves in little time.

' Were I hard-favour'd, foul, or wrinkled-old,
Ill-nurtur'd, crooked, churlish, harsh in voice,
O'erworn, despised, rheumatic and cold,
Thick-sighted, barren, lean and lacking juice,
 Then mightst thou pause, for then I were not for thee;
 But having no defects, why dost abhor me?

' Thou canst not see one wrinkle in my brow;
Mine eyes are gray and bright and quick in turning;
My beauty as the spring doth yearly grow;   141
My flesh is soft and plump, my marrow burning;
 My smooth moist hand, were it with thy hand felt,
 Would in thy palm dissolve, or seem to melt.

' Bid me discourse, I will enchant thine ear,
Or, like a fairy, trip upon the green,
Or, like a nymph, with long dishevell'd hair,
Dance on the sands, and yet no footing seen ;
   Love is a spirit all compact of fire,
    Not gross to sink, but light, and will aspire.   150

' Witness this primrose bank whereon I lie ;
These forceless flowers like sturdy trees support me ;
Two strengthless doves will draw me through the sky,
From morn till night, even where I list to sport me.
   Is love so light, sweet boy, and may it be
    That thou shouldst think it heavy unto thee ?

' Is thine own heart to thine own face affected ?
Can thy right hand seize love upon thy left ?
Then woo thyself, be of thyself rejected,
Steal thine own freedom and complain on theft.   160
   Narcissus so himself himself forsook,
    And died to kiss his shadow in the brook.

' Torches are made to light, jewels to wear,
Dainties to taste, fresh beauty for the use,
Herbs for their smell, and sappy plants to bear ;
Things growing to themselves are growth's abuse.
   Seeds spring from seeds and beauty breedeth beauty ;
    Thou wast begot, to get it is thy duty.

' Upon the earth's increase why shouldst thou feed
Unless the earth with thy increase be fed ?   170

1437

By law of nature thou are bound to breed,
That thine may live when thou thyself art dead;
   And so, in spite of death, thou dost survive,
   In that thy likeness still is left alive.'

By this the love-sick queen began to sweat,
For where they lay the shadow had forsook them,
And Titan, tired in the mid-day heat,
With burning eye did hotly overlook them,
   Wishing Adonis had his team to guide,
   So he were like him and by Venus' side.   180

And now Adonis, with a lazy spright,
And with a heavy, dark, disliking eye,
His lowering brows o'erwhelming his fair sight,
Like misty vapours when they blot the sky,
   Souring his cheeks, cries 'Fie, no more of love!
   The sun doth burn my face; I must remove.'

'Ay me,' quoth Venus, 'young and so unkind?
What bare excuses mak'st thou to be gone!
I'll sigh celestial breath, whose gentle wind
Shall cool the heat of this descending sun.   190
   I'll make a shadow for thee of my hairs;
   If they burn too, I'll quench them with my tears.

'The sun that shines from heaven shines but warm,
And, lo, I lie between that sun and thee.
The heat I have from thence doth little harm,
Thine eye darts forth the fire that burneth me;

And were I not immortal, life were done
Between this heavenly and earthly sun.

'Art thou obdurate, flinty, hard as steel,
Nay, more than flint, for stone at rain relenteth? 200
Art thou a woman's son, and canst not feel
What 't is to love? how want of love tormenteth?
  O, had thy mother borne so hard a mind,
  She had not brought forth thee, but died unkind!

'What am I, that thou shouldst contemn me this?
Or what great danger dwells upon my suit?
What were thy lips the worse for one poor kiss?
Speak, fair; but speak fair words, or else be mute.
  Give me one kiss, I 'll give it thee again,
  And one for interest, if thou wilt have twain. 210

'Fie, lifeless picture, cold and senseless stone,
Well-painted idol, image dull and dead,
Statue contenting but the eye alone,
Thing like a man, but of no woman bred!
  Thou art no man, though of a man's complexion;
  For men will kiss even by their own direction.'

This said, impatience chokes her pleading tongue,
And swelling passion doth provoke a pause;
Red cheeks and fiery eyes blaze forth her wrong;
Being judge in love, she cannot right her cause; 220
  And now she weeps, and now she fain would speak,
  And now her sobs do her intendments break.

Sometimes she shakes her head and then his hand,
Now gazeth she on him, now on the ground;
Sometimes her arms infold him like a band;
She would, he will not in her arms be bound;
   And when from thence he struggles to be gone,
   She locks her lily fingers one in one.

'Fondling,' she saith, 'since I have hemm'd thee here
Within the circuit of this ivory pale,   230
I 'll be a park, and thou shalt be my deer;
Feed where thou wilt, on mountain or in dale.
   Graze on my lips; and if those hills be dry,
   Stray lower, where the pleasant fountains lie.

'Within this limit is relief enough,
Sweet bottom-grass and high delightful plain,
Round rising hillocks, brakes obscure and rough,
To shelter thee from tempest and from rain.
   Then be my deer, since I am such a park;
   No dog shall rouse thee, though a thousand bark.'

At this Adonis smiles as in disdain,   241
That in each cheek appears a pretty dimple.
Love made those hollows, if himself were slain,
He might be buried in a tomb so simple;
   Foreknowing well, if there he came to lie,
   Why, there Love liv'd and there he could not die.

These lovely caves, these round enchanting pits,
Open'd their mouths to swallow Venus' liking.

Being mad before, how doth she now for wits?
Struck dead at first, what needs a second striking? 250
   Poor queen of love, in thine own law forlorn,
   To love a cheek that smiles at thee in scorn!

Now which way shall she turn? what shall she say?
Her words are done, her woes the more increasing;
The time is spent, her object will away,
And from her twining arms doth urge releasing.
   'Pity,' she cries, 'some favour, some remorse!'
   Away he springs and hasteth to his horse.

But, lo, from forth a copse that neighbours by,
A breeding jennet, lusty, young, and proud, 260
Adonis' trampling courser doth espy,
And forth she rushes, snorts, and neighs aloud;
   The strong-neck'd steed, being tied unto a tree,
   Breaketh his rein, and to her straight goes he.

Imperiously he leaps, he neighs, he bounds,
And now his woven girths he breaks asunder;
The bearing earth with his hard hoof he wounds,
Whose hollow womb resounds like heaven's thunder;
   The iron bit he crushes 'tween his teeth,
   Controlling what he was controlled with. 270

His ears up-prick'd; his braided hanging mane
Upon his compass'd crest now stand on end;
His nostrils drink the air, and forth again,
As from a furnace, vapours doth he send;

His eye, which scornfully glisters like fire,
Shows his hot courage and his high desire.

Sometime he trots, as if he told the steps,
With gentle majesty and modest pride ;
Anon he rears upright, curvets, and leaps,
As who should say 'Lo, thus my strength is tried,   280
    And this I do to captivate the eye
    Of the fair breeder that is standing by ! '

What recketh he his rider's angry stir,
His flattering ' Holla,' or his ' Stand, I say ? '
What cares he now for curb or pricking spur ?
For rich caparisons or trapping gay ?
    He sees his love, and nothing else he sees,
    For nothing else with his proud sight agrees.

Look, when a painter would surpass the life,
In limning out a well-proportion'd steed,   290
His art with nature's workmanship at strife,
As if the dead the living should exceed,
    So did this horse excel a common one
    In shape, in courage, colour, pace, and bone.

Round-hoof'd, short-jointed, fetlocks shag and long,
Broad breast, full eye, small head, and nostril wide,
High crest, short ears, straight legs and passing strong,
Thin mane, thick tail, broad buttock, tender hide, —
    Look, what a horse should have he did not lack,
    Save a proud rider on so proud a back.   300

Sometime he scuds far off, and there he stares ;
Anon he starts at stirring of a feather ;
To bid the wind a base he now prepares,
And whether he run or fly they know not whether ;
  For through his mane and tail the high wind sings,
  Fanning the hairs, who wave like feather'd wings.

He looks upon his love and neighs unto her,
She answers him as if she knew his mind ;
Being proud, as females are, to see him woo her,
She puts on outward strangeness, seems unkind,   310
  Spurns at his love and scorns the heat he feels,
  Beating his kind embracements with her heels.

Then, like a melancholy malcontent,
He vails his tail that, like a falling plume,
Cool shadow to his melting buttock lent;
He stamps and bites the poor flies in his fume.
  His love, perceiving how he is enrag'd,
  Grew kinder, and his fury was assuag'd.

His testy master goeth about to take him,
When, lo, the unback'd breeder, full of fear,   320
Jealous of catching, swiftly doth forsake him,
With her the horse, and left Adonis there;
  As they were mad, unto the wood they hie them,
  Out-stripping crows that strive to over-fly them.

All swoln with chafing, down Adonis sits,
Banning his boisterous and unruly beast ;

And now the happy season once more fits
That love-sick Love by pleading may be blest,
  For lovers say the heart hath treble wrong
  When it is barr'd the aidance of the tongue.   330

An oven that is stopp'd, or river stay'd,
Burneth more hotly, swelleth with more rage.
So of concealed sorrow may be said;
Free vent of words love's fire doth assuage,
  But when the heart's attorney once is mute
  The client breaks, as desperate in his suit.

He sees her coming, and begins to glow,
Even as a dying coal revives with wind,
And with his bonnet hides his angry brow,
Looks on the dull earth with disturbed mind,   340
  Taking no notice that she is so nigh,
  For all askance he holds her in his eye.

O, what a sight it was, wistly to view
How she came stealing to the wayward boy!
To note the fighting conflict of her hue,
How white and red each other did destroy!
  But now her cheek was pale, and by and by
  It flash'd forth fire, as lightning from the sky.

Now was she just before him as he sat,
And like a lowly lover down she kneels;   350
With one fair hand she heaveth up his hat,
Her other tender hand his fair cheek feels;

His tenderer cheek receives her soft hand's print,
As apt as new-fallen snow takes any dint.

O, what a war of looks was then between them!
Her eyes petitioners to his eyes suing;
His eyes saw her eyes as they had not seen them;
Her eyes woo'd still, his eyes disdain'd the wooing;
　　And all this dumb play had his acts made plain
　　With tears, which, chorus-like, her eyes did rain.　360

Full gently now she takes him by the hand,
A lily prison'd in a gaol of snow,
Or ivory in an alabaster band;
So white a friend engirts so white a foe.
　　This beauteous combat, wilful and unwilling,
　　Show'd like two silver doves that sit a-billing.

Once more the engine of her thoughts began:
' O fairest mover on this mortal round,
Would thou wert as I am, and I a man,
My heart all whole as thine, thy heart my wound;　370
　　For one sweet look thy help I would assure thee,
　　Though nothing but my body's bane would cure
　　　　thee.'

' Give me my hand,' saith he, ' why dost thou feel it?'
' Give me my heart,' saith she, ' and thou shalt have it;
O, give it me, lest thy hard heart do steel it,
And being steel'd, soft sighs can never grave it.
　　Then love's deep groans I never shall regard,
　　Because Adonis' heart hath made mine hard.'

'For shame,' he cries, 'let go, and let me go;
My day's delight is past, my horse is gone,   380
And 't is your fault I am bereft him so.
I pray you hence, and leave me here alone;
    For all my mind, my thought, my busy care,
    Is how to get my palfrey from the mare.'

Thus she replies: 'Thy palfrey, as he should,
Welcomes the warm approach of sweet desire.
Affection is a coal that must be cool'd;
Else, suffer'd, it will set the heart on fire.
    The sea hath bounds, but deep desire hath none;
    Therefore no marvel though thy horse be gone.   390

'How like a jade he stood, tied to the tree,
Servilely master'd with a leathern rein!
But when he saw his love, his youth's fair fee,
He held such petty bondage in disdain;
    Throwing the base thong from his bending crest,
    Enfranchising his mouth, his back, his breast.

'Who sees his true-love in her naked bed,
Teaching the sheets a whiter hue than white,
But, when his glutton eye so full hath fed,
His other agents aim at like delight?   400
    Who is so faint that dares not be so bold
    To touch the fire, the weather being cold?

'Let me excuse thy courser, gentle boy;
And learn of him, I heartily beseech thee,

To take advantage on presented joy;
Though I were dumb, yet his proceedings teach thee.
　　O, learn to love! the lesson is but plain,
　　And once made perfect, never lost again.'

'I know not love,' quoth he, 'nor will not know it,
Unless it be a boar, and then I chase it;　　410
'T is much to borrow, and I will not owe it;
My love to love is love but to disgrace it;
　　For I have heard it is a life in death,
　　That laughs and weeps, and all but with a breath.

'Who wears a garment shapeless and unfinish'd?
Who plucks the bud before one leaf put forth?
If springing things be any jot diminish'd,
They wither in their prime, prove nothing worth;
　　The colt that's back'd and burden'd being young
　　Loseth his pride and never waxeth strong.　　420

'You hurt my hand with wringing; let us part,
And leave this idle theme, this bootless chat.
Remove your siege from my unyielding heart;
To love's alarms it will not ope the gate.
　　Dismiss your vows, your feigned tears, your flattery;
　　For where a heart is hard they make no battery.'

'What! canst thou talk?' quoth she, 'hast thou a
　　　　tongue?
O, would thou hadst not, or I had no hearing!
Thy mermaid's voice hath done me double wrong;
I had my load before, now press'd with bearing;　　430

Melodious discord, heavenly tune harsh-sounding,
Ear's deep-sweet music, and heart's deep-sore
    wounding.

'Had I no eyes but ears, my ears would love
That inward beauty and invisible;
Or were I deaf, thy outward parts would move
Each part in me that were but sensible;
    Though neither eyes nor ears, to hear nor see,
    Yet should I be in love by touching thee.

'Say, that the sense of feeling were bereft me,
And that I could not see, nor hear, nor touch,   440
And nothing but the very smell were left me,
Yet would my love to thee be still as much;
    For from the stillitory of thy face excelling
    Comes breath perfum'd that breedeth love by
        smelling.

'But, O, what banquet wert thou to the taste,
Being nurse and feeder of the other four!
Would they not wish the feast might ever last,
And bid Suspicion double-lock the door,
    Lest Jealousy, that sour unwelcome guest,
    Should, by his stealing in, disturb the feast?'   450

Once more the ruby-colour'd portal open'd,
Which to his speech did honey passage yield;
Like a red morn, that ever yet betoken'd
Wrack to the seaman, tempest to the field,

Sorrow to shepherds, woe unto the birds,
Gusts and foul flaws to herdmen and to herds.

This ill presage advisedly she marketh;
Even as the wind is hush'd before it raineth,
Or as the wolf doth grin before he barketh,
Or as the berry breaks before it staineth,   460
    Or like the deadly bullet of a gun,
    His meaning struck her ere his words begun.

And at his look she flatly falleth down,
For looks kill love and love by looks reviveth;
A smile recures the wounding of a frown,
But blessed bankrupt, that by love so thriveth!
    The silly boy, believing she is dead,
    Claps her pale cheek, till clapping makes it red;

And all amaz'd brake off his late intent,
For sharply he did think to reprehend her,   470
Which cunning love did wittingly prevent —
Fair fall the wit that can so well defend her!
    For on the grass she lies as she were slain,
    Till his breath breatheth life in her again.

He wrings her nose, he strikes her on the cheeks,
He bends her fingers, holds her pulses hard,
He chafes her lips; a thousand ways he seeks
To mend the hurt that his unkindness marr'd.
    He kisses her; and she, by her good will,
    Will never rise, so he will kiss her still.   480

The night of sorrow now is turn'd to day;
Her two blue windows faintly she upheaveth,
Like the fair sun, when in his fresh array
He cheers the morn and all the earth relieveth;
    And as the bright sun glorifies the sky,
    So is her face illumin'd with her eye,

Whose beams upon his hairless face are fix'd,
As if from thence they borrow'd all their shine.
Were never four such lamps together mix'd,
Had not his clouded with his brow's repine;   490
    But hers, which through the crystal tears gave light,
    Shone like the moon in water seen by night.

'O, where am I?' quoth she, 'in earth or heaven,
Or in the ocean drench'd, or in the fire?
What hour is this? or morn or weary even?
Do I delight to die, or life desire?
    But now I liv'd, and life was death's annoy;
    But now I died, and death was lively joy.

'O, thou didst kill me; kill me once again!
Thy eyes' shrewd tutor, that hard heart of thine,   500
Hath taught them scornful tricks and such disdain
That they have murther'd this poor heart of mine;
    And these mine eyes, true leaders to their queen,
    But for thy piteous lips no more had seen.

'Long may they kiss each other for this cure!
O, never let their crimson liveries wear!

And as they last, their verdure still endure,
To drive infection from the dangerous year!
  That the star-gazers, having writ on death,
    May say the plague is banish'd by thy breath.   510

'Pure lips, sweet seals in my soft lips imprinted,
What bargains may I make, still to be sealing?
To sell myself I can be well contented,
So thou wilt buy and pay and use good dealing;
  Which purchase if thou make, for fear of slips
    Set thy seal-manual on my wax-red lips.

'A thousand kisses buys my heart from me;
And pay them at thy leisure, one by one.
What is ten hundred touches unto thee?
Are they not quickly told and quickly gone?   520
  Say, for non-payment that the debt should double,
    Is twenty hundred kisses such a trouble?'

'Fair queen,' quoth he, 'if any love you owe me,
Measure my strangeness with my unripe years.
Before I know myself, seek not to know me;
No fisher but the ungrown fry forbears.
  The mellow plum doth fall, the green sticks fast,
    Or being early pluck'd is sour to taste.

'Look, the world's comforter, with weary gait,
His day's hot task hath ended in the west;   530
The owl, night's herald, shrieks, "'T is very late;"
The sheep are gone to fold, birds to their nest,

And coal-black clouds that shadow heaven's light
Do summon us to part and bid good night.

'Now let me say "Good night," and so say you;
If you will say so, you shall have a kiss.'
'Good night,' quoth she, and, ere he says 'Adieu,'
The honey fee of parting tender'd is.
 Her arms do lend his neck a sweet embrace;
 Incorporate then they seem, face grows to face: 540

Till, breathless, he disjoin'd, and backward drew
The heavenly moisture, that sweet coral mouth,
Whose precious taste her thirsty lips well knew,
Whereon they surfeit, yet complain on drouth.
 He with her plenty press'd, she faint with dearth,
 Their lips together glued, fall to the earth.

Now quick desire hath caught the yielding prey,
And glutton-like she feeds, yet never filleth;
Her lips are conquerors, his lips obey,
Paying what ransom the insulter willeth, 550
 Whose vulture thought doth pitch the price so high
 That she will draw his lips' rich treasure dry;

And having felt the sweetness of the spoil,
With blindfold fury she begins to forage;
Her face doth reek and smoke, her blood doth boil,
And careless lust stirs up a desperate courage;
 Planting oblivion, beating reason back,
 Forgetting shame's pure blush and honour's wrack.

Hot, faint, and weary, with her hard embracing,
Like a wild bird being tam'd with too much handling,
Or as the fleet-foot roe that 's tir'd with chasing,   561
Or like the froward infant still'd with dandling,
   He now obeys, and now no more resisteth,
    While she takes all she can, not all she listeth.

What wax so frozen but dissolves with tempering,
And yields at last to every light impression?
Things out of hope are compass'd oft with venturing,
Chiefly in love, whose leave exceeds commission;
   Affection faints not like a pale-fac'd coward,
    But then wooes best when most his choice is froward.

When he did frown, O, had she then gave over,   571
Such nectar from his lips she had not suck'd.
Foul words and frowns must not repel a lover;
What though the rose have prickles, yet 't is pluck'd.
   Were beauty under twenty locks kept fast,
    Yet love breaks through and picks them all at last.

For pity now she can no more detain him;
The poor fool prays her that he may depart.
She is resolv'd no longer to restrain him;
Bids him farewell, and look well to her heart,   580
   The which, by Cupid's bow she doth protest,
    He carries thence incaged in his breast.

'Sweet boy,' she says, 'this night I 'll waste in sorrow,
For my sick heart commands mine eyes to watch.

Tell me, Love's master, shall we meet to-morrow?
Say, shall we? shall we? wilt thou make the match?'
  He tells her, no; to-morrow he intends
  To hunt the boar with certain of his friends.

'The boar!' quoth she; whereat a sudden pale,
Like lawn being spread upon the blushing rose,   590
Usurps her cheek; she trembles at his tale,
And on his neck her yoking arms she throws.
  She sinketh down, still hanging by his neck,
  He on her belly falls, she on her back.

Now is she in the very lists of love,
Her champion mounted for the hot encounter.
All is imaginary she doth prove,
He will not manage her, although he mount her;
  That worse than Tantalus' is her annoy,
  To clip Elysium and to lack her joy.   600

Even so poor birds, deceiv'd with painted grapes,
Do surfeit by the eye and pine the maw;
Even so she languisheth in her mishaps
As those poor birds that helpless berries saw.
  The warm effects which she in him finds missing
  She seeks to kindle with continual kissing.

But all in vain; good queen, it will not be.
She hath assay'd as much as may be prov'd;
Her pleading hath deserv'd a greater fee;
She 's Love, she loves, and yet she is not lov'd.   610

'Fie, fie,' he says, 'you crush me, let me go;
You have no reason to withhold me so.'

'Thou hadst been gone,' quoth she, 'sweet boy, ere this,
But that thou told'st me thou wouldst hunt the boar.
O, be advis'd! thou know'st not what it is
With javelin's point a churlish swine to gore,
  Whose tushes never sheath'd he whetteth still,
  Like to a mortal butcher bent to kill.

'On his bow-back he hath a battle set
Of bristly pikes, that ever threat his foes;   620
His eyes, like glow-worms, shine when he doth fret;
His snout digs sepulchres where'er he goes;
  Being mov'd, he strikes whate'er is in his way,
  And whom he strikes his crooked tushes slay.

'His brawny sides, with hairy bristles arm'd,
Are better proof than thy spear's point can enter;
His short thick neck cannot be easily harm'd;
Being ireful, on the lion he will venture;
  The thorny brambles and embracing bushes,
  As fearful of him, part, through whom he rushes. 630

'Alas, he nought esteems that face of thine,
To which Love's eyes pay tributary gazes,
Nor thy soft hands, sweet lips, and crystal eyne,
Whose full perfection all the world amazes,
  But having thee at vantage, — wondrous dread! —
  Would root these beauties as he roots the mead.

'O, let him keep his loathsome cabin still;
Beauty hath nought to do with such foul fiends.
Come not within his danger by thy will;
They that thrive well take counsel of their friends.   640
   When thou didst name the boar, not to dissemble,
    I fear'd thy fortune, and my joints did tremble.

'Didst thou not mark my face? was it not white?
Saw'st thou not signs of fear lurk in mine eye?
Grew I not faint? and fell I not downright?
Within my bosom, whereon thou dost lie,
   My boding heart pants, beats, and takes no rest,
    But, like an earthquake, shakes thee on my breast.

'For where Love reigns, disturbing Jealousy
Doth call himself Affection's sentinel,   650
Gives false alarms, suggesteth mutiny,
And in a peaceful hour doth cry "Kill, kill!"
   Distempering gentle Love in his desire,
    As air and water do abate the fire.

'This sour informer, this bate-breeding spy,
This canker that eats up Love's tender spring,
This carry-tale, dissentious Jealousy,
That sometime true news, sometime false doth bring,
   Knocks at my heart and whispers in mine ear
    That if I love thee, I thy death should fear;   660

'And more than so, presenteth to mine eye
The picture of an angry-chafing boar,

Under whose sharp fangs on his back doth lie
An image like thyself, all stain'd with gore,
  Whose blood upon the fresh flowers being shed
  Doth make them droop with grief and hang the head.

' What should I do, seeing thee so indeed,
That tremble at the imagination?
The thought of it doth make my faint heart bleed,
And fear doth teach it divination;   670
  I prophesy thy death, my living sorrow,
  If thou encounter with the boar to-morrow.

' But if thou needs wilt hunt, be rul'd by me;
Uncouple at the timorous flying hare,
Or at the fox, which lives by subtlety,
Or at the roe, which no encounter dare.
  Pursue these fearful creatures o'er the downs,
  And on thy well-breath'd horse keep with thy hounds.

' And when thou hast on foot the purblind hare,
Mark the poor wretch, to overshoot his troubles   680
How he outruns the wind, and with what care
He cranks and crosses with a thousand doubles;
  The many musits through the which he goes
  Are like a labyrinth to amaze his foes.

' Sometime he runs among a flock of sheep,
To make the cunning hounds mistake their smell,
And sometime where earth-delving conies keep,
To stop the loud pursuers in their yell,

And sometime sorteth with a herd of deer;
Danger deviseth shifts, wit waits on fear;   690

'For there his smell with others being mingled,
The hot scent-snuffing hounds are driven to doubt,
Ceasing their clamorous cry till they have singled
With much ado the cold fault cleanly out.
　　Then do they spend their mouths; Echo replies,
　　As if another chase were in the skies.

'By this, poor Wat, far off upon a hill,
Stands on his hinder legs with listening ear,
To hearken if his foes pursue him still;
Anon their loud alarums he doth hear,   700
　　And now his grief may be compared well
　　To one sore sick that hears the passing-bell.

'Then shalt thou see the dew-bedabbled wretch
Turn and return, indenting with the way;
Each envious brier his weary legs doth scratch,
Each shadow makes him stop, each murmur stay;
　　For misery is trodden on by many,
　　And being low never reliev'd by any.

'Lie quietly, and hear a little more;
Nay, do not struggle, for thou shalt not rise.   710
To make thee hate the hunting of the boar,
Unlike myself thou hear'st me moralize,
　　Applying this to that, and so to so;
　　For love can comment upon every woe.

'Where did I leave?'   'No matter where,' quoth he,
'Leave me and then the story aptly ends;
The night is spent.'   'Why, what of that?' quoth she.
'I am,' quoth he, 'expected of my friends;
    And now 't is dark, and going I shall fall.'
    'In night,' quoth she, 'desire sees best of all.   720

'But if thou fall, O, then imagine this,
The earth, in love with thee, thy footing trips,
And all is but to rob thee of a kiss.
Rich preys make true men thieves; so do thy lips
    Make modest Dian cloudy and forlorn,
    Lest she should steal a kiss and die forsworn.

'Now of this dark night I perceive the reason:
Cynthia for shame obscures her silver shine,
Till forging Nature be condemn'd of treason,
For stealing moulds from heaven that were divine,   730
    Wherein she fram'd thee in high heaven's despite,
    To shame the sun by day and her by night.

'And therefore hath she brib'd the Destinies
To cross the curious workmanship of nature,
To mingle beauty with infirmities,
And pure perfection with impure defeature,
    Making it subject to the tyranny
    Of mad mischances and much misery;

'As burning fevers, agues pale and faint,
Life-poisoning pestilence and frenzies wood,   740

The marrow-eating sickness, whose attaint
Disorder breeds by heating of the blood.
  Surfeits, imposthumes, grief, and damn'd despair,
  Swear Nature's death for framing thee so fair.

' And not the least of all these maladies
But in one minute's fight brings beauty under;
Both favour, savour, hue, and qualities,
Whereat the impartial gazer late did wonder,
  Are on the sudden wasted, thaw'd, and done,
  As mountain snow melts with the mid-day sun.   750

' Therefore, despite of fruitless chastity,
Love-lacking vestals and self-loving nuns,
That on the earth would breed a scarcity
And barren dearth of daughters and of sons,
  Be prodigal; the lamp that burns by night
  Dries up his oil to lend the world his light.

' What is thy body but a swallowing grave,
Seeming to bury that posterity
Which by the rights of time thou needs must have,
If thou destroy them not in dark obscurity?   760
  If so, the world will hold thee in disdain,
  Sith in thy pride so fair a hope is slain.

' So in thyself thyself art made away;
A mischief worse than civil home-bred strife,
Or theirs whose desperate hands themselves do slay,
Or butcher-sire that reaves his son of life.

Foul-cankering rust the hidden treasure frets,
But gold that 's put to use more gold begets.'

' Nay, then,' quoth Adon, ' you will fall again
Into your idle over-handled theme.   770
The kiss I gave you is bestow'd in vain,
And all in vain you strive against the stream;
  For, by this black-fac'd night, desire's foul nurse,
  Your treatise makes me like you worse and worse.

' If love have lent you twenty thousand tongues,
And every tongue more moving than your own,
Bewitching like the wanton mermaid's songs,
Yet from mine ear the tempting tune is blown;
  For know, my heart stands armed in mine ear,
  And will not let a false sound enter there,   780

' Lest the deceiving harmony should run
Into the quiet closure of my breast;
And then my little heart were quite undone,
In his bedchamber to be barr'd of rest.
  No, lady, no; my heart longs not to groan,
  But soundly sleeps while now it sleeps alone.

' What have you urg'd that I cannot reprove?
The path is smooth that leadeth on to danger.
I hate not love, but your device in love,
That lends embracements unto every stranger.   790
  You do it for increase; O strange excuse,
  When reason is the bawd to lust's abuse!

' Call it not love, for Love to heaven is fled,
Since sweating Lust on earth usurp'd his name,
Under whose simple semblance he hath fed
Upon fresh beauty, blotting it with blame,
    Which the hot tyrant stains and soon bereaves,
    As caterpillars do the tender leaves.

' Love comforteth like sunshine after rain,
But Lust's effect is tempest after sun ;   800
Love's gentle spring doth always fresh remain,
Lust's winter comes ere summer half be done ;
    Love surfeits not, Lust like a glutton dies ;
    Love is all truth, Lust full of forged lies.

' More I could tell, but more I dare not say ;
The text is old, the orator too green.
Therefore, in sadness, now I will away.
My face is full of shame, my heart of teen ;
    Mine ears, that to your wanton talk attended,
    Do burn themselves for having so offended.'   810

With this, he breaketh from the sweet embrace
Of those fair arms which bound him to her breast,
And homeward through the dark laund runs apace,
Leaves Love upon her back deeply distress'd.
    Look, how a bright star shooteth from the sky,
    So glides he in the night from Venus' eye,

Which after him she darts, as one on shore
Gazing upon a late-embarked friend

Till the wild waves will have him seen no more,
Whose ridges with the meeting clouds contend;   820
  So did the merciless and pitchy night
  Fold in the object that did feed her sight.

Whereat amaz'd, as one that unaware
Hath dropp'd a precious jewel in the flood,
Or 'stonish'd as night-wanderers often are,
Their light blown out in some mistrustful wood,
  Even so confounded in the dark she lay,
  Having lost the fair discovery of her way.

And now she beats her heart, whereat it groans,
That all the neighbour caves, as seeming troubled,   830
Make verbal repetition of her moans.
Passion on passion deeply is redoubled;
  'Ay me!' she cries, and twenty times 'Woe, woe!'
  And twenty echoes twenty times cry so.

She marking them begins a wailing note
And sings extemporally a woeful ditty:
How love makes young men thrall and old men dote;
How love is wise in folly, foolish-witty.
  Her heavy anthem still concludes in woe,
  And still the choir of echoes answer so.   840

Her song was tedious and outwore the night,
For lovers' hours are long, though seeming short;
If pleas'd themselves, others, they think, delight
In such-like circumstance, with such-like sport;

Their copious stories oftentimes begun
End without audience and are never done.

For who hath she to spend the night withal
But idle sounds resembling parasites,
Like shrill-tongu'd tapsters answering every call,
Soothing the humour of fantastic wits ?　　　　850
　　She says ' 'T is so ; ' they answer all ' 'T is so,'
　　And would say after her, if she said ' No.'

Lo, here the gentle lark, weary of rest,
From his moist cabinet mounts up on high,
And wakes the morning, from whose silver breast
The sun ariseth in his majesty,
　　Who doth the world so gloriously behold
　　That cedar-tops and hills seem burnish'd gold.

Venus salutes him with this fair good-morrow :
' O thou clear god, and patron of all light,　　　　860
From whom each lamp and shining star doth borrow
The beauteous influence that makes him bright,
　　There lives a son that suck'd an earthly mother
　　May lend thee light, as thou dost lend to other.'

This said, she hasteth to a myrtle grove,
Musing the morning is so much o'erworn,
And yet she hears no tidings of her love.
She hearkens for his hounds and for his horn ;
　　Anon she hears them chant it lustily,
　　And all in haste she coasteth to the cry.　　　　870

And as she runs, the bushes in the way
Some catch her by the neck, some kiss her face,
Some twine about her thigh to make her stay ;
She wildly breaketh from their strict embrace,
 Like a milch doe, whose swelling dugs do ache,
 Hasting to feed her fawn hid in some brake.

By this, she hears the hounds are at a bay,
Whereat she starts, like one that spies an adder
Wreath'd up in fatal folds just in his way, 879
The fear whereof doth make him shake and shudder ;
 Even so the timorous yelping of the hounds
 Appals her senses and her spirit confounds.

For now she knows it is no gentle chase,
But the blunt boar, rough bear, or lion proud,
Because the cry remaineth in one place,
Where fearfully the dogs exclaim aloud ;
 Finding their enemy to be so curst,
 They all strain courtesy who shall cope him first.

This dismal cry rings sadly in her ear,
Through which it enters to surprise her heart, 890
Who, overcome by doubt and bloodless fear,
With cold-pale weakness numbs each feeling part ;
 Like soldiers, when their captain once doth yield,
 They basely fly and dare not stay the field.

Thus stands she in a trembling ecstasy,
Till, cheering up her senses all dismay'd,

She tells them 't is a causeless fantasy
And childish error, that they are afraid,
　　Bids them leave quaking, bids them fear no more ; —
　　And with that word she spied the hunted boar,　900

Whose frothy mouth, bepainted all with red,
Like milk and blood being mingled both together,
A second fear through all her sinews spread,
Which madly hurries her she knows not whither.
　　This way she runs, and now she will no further,
　　But back retires to rate the boar for murther.

A thousand spleens bear her a thousand ways ;
She treads the path that she untreads again ;
Her more than haste is mated with delays,
Like the proceedings of a drunken brain,　　　910
　　Full of respects, yet nought at all respecting,
　　In hand with all things, nought at all effecting.

Here kennell'd in a brake she finds a hound,
And asks the weary caitiff for his master,
And there another licking of his wound,
'Gainst venom'd sores the only sovereign plaster ;
　　And here she meets another sadly scowling,
　　To whom she speaks, and he replies with howling.

When he hath ceas'd his ill-resounding noise,
Another flap-mouth'd mourner, black and grim,　920
Against the welkin volleys out his voice ;
Another and another answer him,

Clapping their proud tails to the ground below,
Shaking their scratch'd ears, bleeding as they go.

Look, how the world's poor people are amaz'd
At apparitions, signs, and prodigies,
Whereon with fearful eyes they long have gaz'd,
Infusing them with dreadful prophecies ;
    So she at these sad signs draws up her breath,
    And, sighing it again, exclaims on Death.   930

' Hard-favour'd tyrant, ugly, meagre, lean,
Hateful divorce of love,' — thus chides she Death, —
' Grim-grinning ghost, earth's worm, what dost thou
        mean
To stifle beauty and to steal his breath
    Who, when he liv'd, his breath and beauty set
    Gloss on the rose, smell to the violet ?

' If he be dead, — O no, it cannot be,
Seeing his beauty, thou shouldst strike at it ! —
O yes, it may ! thou hast no eyes to see,
But hatefully at random dost thou hit.   940
    Thy mark is feeble age, but thy false dart
    Mistakes that aim and cleaves an infant's heart.

' Hadst thou but bid beware, then he had spoke,
And, hearing him, thy power had lost his power.
The Destinies will curse thee for this stroke ;
They bid thee crop a weed, thou pluck'st a flower.
    Love's golden arrow at him should have fled,
    And not Death's ebon dart to strike him dead.

SHAKESPEARE'S POEMS — 6

'Dost thou drink tears, that thou provok'st such weeping?
What may a heavy groan advantage thee?   950
Why hast thou cast into eternal sleeping
Those eyes that taught all other eyes to see?
   Now Nature cares not for thy mortal vigour,
   Since her best work is ruin'd with thy rigour.'

Here overcome, as one full of despair,
She vail'd her eyelids, who, like sluices, stopt
The crystal tide that from her two cheeks fair
In the sweet channel of her bosom dropt;
   But through the flood-gates breaks the silver rain,
   And with his strong course opens them again.   960

O, how her eyes and tears did lend and borrow!
Her eyes seen in the tears, tears in her eye;
Both crystals, where they view'd each other's sorrow,
Sorrow that friendly sighs sought still to dry;
   But like a stormy day, now wind, now rain,
   Sighs dry her cheeks, tears make them wet again.

Variable passions throng her constant woe,
As striving who should best become her grief;
All entertain'd, each passion labours so
That every present sorrow seemeth chief,   970
   But none is best; then join they all together,
   Like many clouds consulting for foul weather.

By this, far off she hears some huntsman hollo;
A nurse's song ne'er pleas'd her babe so well.

The dire imagination she did follow
This sound of hope doth labour to expel,
  For now reviving joy bids her rejoice,
  And flatters her it is Adonis' voice.

Whereat her tears began to turn their tide,
Being prison'd in her eye like pearls in glass;   980
Yet sometimes falls an orient drop beside,
Which her cheek melts, as scorning it should pass
  To wash the foul face of the sluttish ground,
  Who is but drunken when she seemeth drown'd.

O hard-believing love, how strange it seems
Not to believe, and yet too credulous!
Thy weal and woe are both of them extremes;
Despair and hope makes thee ridiculous:
  The one doth flatter thee in thoughts unlikely,
  In likely thoughts the other kills thee quickly.   990

Now she unweaves the web that she hath wrought;
Adonis lives, and Death is not to blame;
It was not she that call'd him all to naught.
Now she adds honours to his hateful name;
  She clepes him king of graves and grave for kings,
  Imperious supreme of all mortal things.

'No, no,' quoth she, 'sweet Death, I did but jest;
Yet pardon me I felt a kind of fear
Whenas I met the boar, that bloody beast,
Which knows no pity, but is still severe;   1000

Then, gentle shadow, — truth I must confess, —
I rail'd on thee, fearing my love's decease.

' 'T is not my fault; the boar provok'd my tongue.
Be wreak'd on him, invisible commander ;
'T is he, foul creature, that hath done thee wrong;
I did but act, he 's author of thy slander.
    Grief hath two tongues, and never woman yet
    Could rule them both without ten women's wit.'

Thus hoping that Adonis is alive,
Her rash suspect she doth extenuate ;   1010
And that his beauty may the better thrive,
With Death she humbly doth insinuate,
    Tells him of trophies, statues, tombs, and stories
    His victories, his triumphs, and his glories.

' O Jove,' quoth she, ' how much a fool was I
To be of such a weak and silly mind
To wail his death who lives and must not die
Till mutual overthrow of mortal kind !
    For he being dead, with him is beauty slain,
    And, beauty dead, black chaos comes again.   1020

' Fie, fie, fond love, thou art so full of fear
As one with treasure laden hemm'd with thieves ;
Trifles, unwitnessed with eye or ear,
Thy coward heart with false bethinking grieves.'
    Even at this word she hears a merry horn,
    Whereat she leaps that was but late forlorn.

As falcon to the lure, away she flies —
The grass stoops not, she treads on it so light —
And in her haste unfortunately spies
The foul boar's conquest on her fair delight,   1030
   Which seen, her eyes, as murther'd with the view,
   Like stars asham'd of day, themselves withdrew;

Or, as the snail, whose tender horns being hit,
Shrinks backward in his shelly cave with pain,
And there, all smother'd up, in shade doth sit,
Long after fearing to creep forth again;
   So, at his bloody view, her eyes are fled
   Into the deep-dark cabins of her head,

Where they resign their office and their light
To the disposing of her troubled brain,   1040
Who bids them still consort with ugly night,
And never wound the heart with looks again,
   Who, like a king perplexed in his throne,
   By their suggestion gives a deadly groan,

Whereat each tributary subject quakes;
As when the wind, imprison'd in the ground,
Struggling for passage, earth's foundation shakes,
Which with cold terror doth men's minds confound.
   This mutiny each part doth so surprise
   That from their dark beds once more leap her eyes,

And, being open'd, threw unwilling light   1051
Upon the wide wound that the boar had trench'd

In his soft flank, whose wonted lily white
With purple tears that his wound wept was drench'd;
    No flower was nigh, no grass, herb, leaf, or weed,
    But stole his blood and seem'd with him to bleed.

This solemn sympathy poor Venus noteth;
Over one shoulder doth she hang her head;
Dumbly she passions, franticly she doteth;
She thinks he could not die, he is not dead;   1060
    Her voice is stopt, her joints forget to bow;
    Her eyes are mad that they have wept till now.

Upon his hurt she looks so steadfastly
That her sight dazzling makes the wound seem three;
And then she reprehends her mangling eye
That makes more gashes where no breach should be.
    His face seems twain, each several limb is doubled;
    For oft the eye mistakes, the brain being troubled.

'My tongue cannot express my grief for one,
And yet,' quoth she, 'behold two Adons dead!   1070
My sighs are blown away, my salt tears gone,
Mine eyes are turn'd to fire, my heart to lead.
    Heavy heart's lead, melt at mine eyes' red fire!
    So shall I die by drops of hot desire.

'Alas, poor world, what treasure hast thou lost!
What face remains alive that's worth the viewing?
Whose tongue is music now? what canst thou boast
Of things long since, or any thing ensuing?

The flowers are sweet, their colours fresh and trim;
But true-sweet beauty liv'd and died with him.   1080

'Bonnet nor veil henceforth no creature wear!
Nor sun nor wind will ever strive to kiss you.
Having no fair to lose, you need not fear;
The sun doth scorn you and the wind doth hiss you;
    But when Adonis liv'd, sun and sharp air
    Lurk'd like two thieves, to rob him of his fair.

'And therefore would he put his bonnet on,
Under whose brim the gaudy sun would peep;
The wind would blow it off and, being gone,
Play with his locks; then would Adonis weep,   1090
    And straight, in pity of his tender years,
    They both would strive who first should dry his tears.

'To see his face the lion walk'd along
Behind some hedge, because he would not fear him;
To recreate himself when he hath sung,
The tiger would be tame and gently hear him;
    If he had spoke, the wolf would leave his prey,
    And never fright the silly lamb that day.

'When he beheld his shadow in the brook,
The fishes spread on it their golden gills;   1100
When he was by, the birds such pleasure took
That some would sing, some other in their bills
    Would bring him mulberries and ripe-red cherries;
    He fed them with his sight, they him with berries.

' But this foul, grim, and urchin-snouted boar,
Whose downward eye still looketh for a grave,
Ne'er saw the beauteous livery that he wore;
Witness the entertainment that he gave.
    If he did see his face, why then I know
    He thought to kiss him, and hath kill'd him so.   1110

' 'T is true, 't is true; thus was Adonis slain !
He ran upon the boar with his sharp spear,
Who did not whet his teeth at him again,
But by a kiss thought to persuade him there;
    And nuzzling in his flank, the loving swine
    Sheath'd unaware the tusk in his soft groin.

' Had I been tooth'd like him, I must confess,
With kissing him I should have kill'd him first;
But he is dead, and never did he bless
My youth with his — the more am I accurst.'   1120
    With this, she falleth in the place she stood,
    And stains her face with his congealed blood.

She looks upon his lips, and they are pale;
She takes him by the hand, and that is cold;
She whispers in his ears a heavy tale,
As if they heard the woeful words she told;
    She lifts the coffer-lids that close his eyes,
    Where, lo, two lamps burnt out in darkness lies!

Two glasses, where herself herself beheld
A thousand times, and now no more reflect;   1130

Their virtue lost, wherein they late excell'd,
And every beauty robb'd of his effect.
'Wonder of time,' quoth she, 'this is my spite,
That, thou being dead, the day should yet be light.

'Since thou art dead, lo, here I prophesy:
Sorrow on love hereafter shall attend;
It shall be waited on with jealousy,
Find sweet beginning, but unsavoury end;
Ne'er settled equally, but high or low,
That all love's pleasure shall not match his woe.

'It shall be fickle, false, and full of fraud,   1141
Bud and be blasted in a breathing-while;
The bottom poison, and the top o'erstraw'd
With sweets that shall the truest sight beguile;
The strongest body shall it make most weak,
Strike the wise dumb, and teach the fool to speak.

'It shall be sparing and too full of riot,
Teaching decrepit age to tread the measures;
The staring ruffian shall it keep in quiet,
Pluck down the rich, enrich the poor with treasures;
It shall be raging-mad and silly-mild,   1151
Make the young old, the old become a child.

'It shall suspect where is no cause of fear;
It shall not fear where it should most mistrust;
It shall be merciful and too severe,
And most deceiving when it seems most just;

Perverse it shall be where it shows most toward,
Put fear to valour, courage to the coward.

' It shall be cause of war and dire events,
And set dissension 'twixt the son and sire ;   1160
Subject and servile to all discontents,
As dry combustious matter is to fire ;
   Sith in his prime Death doth my love destroy,
   They that love best their loves shall not enjoy.'

By this, the boy that by her side lay kill'd
Was melted like a vapour from her sight,
And in his blood that on the ground lay spill'd
A purple flower sprung up, chequer'd with white,
   Resembling well his pale cheeks and the blood   1169
   Which in round drops upon their whiteness stood.

She bows her head the new-sprung flower to smell,
Comparing it to her Adonis' breath,
And says within her bosom it shall dwell,
Since he himself is reft from her by death ;
   She crops the stalk, and in the breach appears
   Green-dropping sap, which she compares to tears.

' Poor flower,' quoth she, ' this was thy father's guise —
Sweet issue of a more sweet-smelling sire —
For every little grief to wet his eyes.
To grow unto himself was his desire,   1180
   And so 't is thine ; but know, it is as good
   To wither in my breast as in his blood.

' Here was thy father's bed, here in my breast;
Thou art the next of blood, and 't is thy right.
Lo, in this hollow cradle take thy rest,
My throbbing heart shall rock thee day and night;
    There shall not be one minute in an hour
    Wherein I will not kiss my sweet love's flower.'

Thus weary of the world, away she hies
And yokes her silver doves, by whose swift aid   1190
Their mistress mounted through the empty skies
In her light chariot quickly is convey'd ;
    Holding their course to Paphos, where their queen
    Means to immure herself and not be seen.

THE RAPE OF LUCRECE

TO THE

RIGHT HONOURABLE HENRY WRIOTHESLEY,

EARL OF SOUTHAMPTON AND BARON OF TICHFIELD

The love I dedicate to your Lordship is without end, whereof this pamphlet, without beginning, is but a superfluous moiety.   The warrant I have of your honourable disposition, not the worth of my untutored lines, makes it assured of acceptance.   What I have done is yours ; what I have to do is yours ; being part in all I have, devoted yours.   Were my worth greater, my duty would show greater; meantime, as it is, it is bound to your Lordship, to whom I wish long life, still lengthened with all happiness.

Your Lordship's in all duty,

WILLIAM SHAKESPEARE.

ARDEA

THE RAPE OF LUCRECE

THE ARGUMENT

LUCIUS TARQUINIUS, for his excessive pride surnamed Superbus, after he had caused his own father-in-law Servius Tullius to be cruelly murthered, and, contrary to the Roman laws and customs, not requiring or staying for the people's suffrages, had possessed himself of the kingdom, went, accompanied with his sons and other noblemen of Rome, to besiege Ardea. During which siege the principal men of the army meeting one evening at the tent of Sextus Tarquinius, the king's son, in their discourses after supper every one commended the virtues of his own wife; among whom Collatinus extolled the incomparable chastity of his wife Lucretia. In that pleasant humour they all posted to Rome; and intending, by their secret and sudden arrival, to make trial of that which every one had before avouched, only Collatinus finds his wife, though it were late in the night, spinning amongst her maids; the other ladies were all found dancing and revelling, or in several disports. Whereupon the noblemen yielded Collatinus the victory and his wife the fame. At that time Sextus Tarquinius, being inflamed with Lucrece' beauty, yet smothering his passions for the present, departed with the rest back to the camp; from whence he shortly after privily withdrew himself, and was, according to his estate, royally entertained and lodged by Lucrece at Collatium. The same night he treacherously stealeth into her chamber, violently ravished her, and early in the morning speedeth away. Lucrece, in this lamentable plight, hastily dispatcheth messengers, one to Rome for her father, another to the camp for Collatine. They came, the one accompanied with Junius Brutus, the other with Publius Valerius, and finding Lucrece attired in mourning habit, demanded the cause of her sorrow. She, first taking an oath of them for her revenge, revealed the actor and whole manner of his dealing, and withal suddenly stabbed herself. Which done, with one consent they all vowed to root out the whole hated family of the Tarquins; and, bearing the dead body to Rome, Brutus acquainted the people with the doer and manner of the vile deed, with a bitter invective against the tyranny of the king; wherewith the people were so moved that with one consent and a general acclamation the Tarquins were all exiled, and the state government changed from kings to consuls.

———————

From the besieged Ardea all in post,
Borne by the trustless wings of false desire,
Lust-breathed Tarquin leaves the Roman host
And to Collatium bears the lightless fire
Which, in pale embers hid, lurks to aspire
    And girdle with embracing flames the waist
    Of Collatine's fair love, Lucrece the chaste.

Haply that name of 'chaste' unhappily set
This bateless edge on his keen appetite,
When Collatine unwisely did not let   10
To praise the clear unmatched red and white
Which triumph'd in that sky of his delight,
    Where mortal stars, as bright as heaven's beauties,
    With pure aspects did him peculiar duties.

For he the night before, in Tarquin's tent,
Unlock'd the treasure of his happy state,
What priceless wealth the heavens had him lent
In the possession of his beauteous mate ;
Reckoning his fortune at such high-proud rate
    That kings might be espoused to more fame,   20
    But king nor peer to such a peerless dame.

O happiness enjoy'd but of a few !
And, if possess'd, as soon decay'd and done
As is the morning's silver-melting dew
Against the golden splendour of the sun,
An expir'd date, cancell'd ere well begun !
    Honour and beauty, in the owner's arms,
    Are weakly fortress'd from a world of harms.

Beauty itself doth of itself persuade
The eyes of men without an orator ;   30
What needeth then apologies be made,
To set forth that which is so singular ?
Or why is Collatine the publisher

Of that rich jewel he should keep unknown
From thievish ears, because it is his own ?

Perchance his boast of Lucrece' sovereignty
Suggested this proud issue of a king,
For by our ears our hearts oft tainted be ;
Perchance that envy of so rich a thing,
Braving compare, disdainfully did sting   40
   His high-pitch'd thoughts that meaner men should
     vaunt
   That golden hap which their superiors want.

But some untimely thought did instigate
His all-too-timeless speed, if none of those ;
His honour, his affairs, his friends, his state,
Neglected all, with swift intent he goes
To quench the coal which in his liver glows.
   O rash false heat, wrapp'd in repentant cold,
   Thy hasty spring still blasts and ne'er grows old !

When at Collatium this false lord arriv'd,   50
Well was he welcom'd by the Roman dame,
Within whose face beauty and virtue striv'd
Which of them both should underprop her fame.
When virtue bragg'd, beauty would blush for shame ;
   When beauty boasted blushes, in despite
   Virtue would stain that o'er with silver white.

But beauty, in that white intituled,
From Venus' doves doth challenge that fair field ;

Then virtue claims from beauty beauty's red,
Which virtue gave the golden age to gild   60
Their silver cheeks, and call'd it then their shield,
  Teaching them thus to use it in the fight, —
  When shame assail'd, the red should fence the white.

This heraldry in Lucrece' face was seen,
Argued by beauty's red and virtue's white.
Of either's colour was the other queen,
Proving from world's minority their right;
Yet their ambition makes them still to fight,
  The sovereignty of either being so great
  That oft they interchange each other's seat.   70

This silent war of lilies and of roses,
Which Tarquin view'd in her fair face's field,
In their pure ranks his traitor eye encloses;
Where, lest between them both it should be kill'd,
The coward captive vanquished doth yield
  To those two armies that would let him go
  Rather than triumph in so false a foe.

Now thinks he that her husband's shallow tongue —
The niggard prodigal that prais'd her so —
In that high task hath done her beauty wrong,   80
Which far exceeds his barren skill to show;
Therefore that praise which Collatine doth owe
  Enchanted Tarquin answers with surmise,
  In silent wonder of still-gazing eyes.

This earthly saint, adored by this devil,
Little suspecteth the false worshipper,
For unstain'd thoughts do seldom dream on evil,
Birds never lim'd no secret bushes fear;
So guiltless she securely gives good cheer
　　And reverend welcome to her princely guest,　　90
　　Whose inward ill no outward harm express'd.

For that he colour'd with his high estate,
Hiding base sin in plaits of majesty,
That nothing in him seem'd inordinate,
Save sometime too much wonder of his eye,
Which, having all, all could not satisfy,
　　But, poorly rich, so wanteth in his store
　　That, cloy'd with much, he pineth still for more.

But she, that never cop'd with stranger eyes,
Could pick no meaning from their parling looks,　　100
Nor read the subtle-shining secrecies
Writ in the glassy margents of such books.
She touch'd no unknown baits, nor fear'd no hooks;
　　Nor could she moralize his wanton sight,
　　More than his eyes were open'd to the light.

He stories to her ears her husband's fame,
Won in the fields of fruitful Italy,
And decks with praises Collatine's high name,
Made glorious by his manly chivalry
With bruised arms and wreaths of victory;　　110

Her joy with heav'd-up hand she doth express,
And, wordless, so greets heaven for his success.

Far from the purpose of his coming hither,
He makes excuses for his being there;
No cloudy show of stormy blustering weather
Doth yet in his fair welkin once appear
Till sable Night, mother of dread and fear,
  Upon the world dim darkness doth display
  And in her vaulty prison stows the day.

For then is Tarquin brought unto his bed,   120
Intending weariness with heavy spright;
For, after supper, long he questioned
With modest Lucrece and wore out the night.
Now leaden slumber with life's strength doth fight,
  And every one to rest themselves betake,
  Save thieves, and cares, and troubled minds, that
    wake;

As one of which doth Tarquin lie revolving
The sundry dangers of his will's obtaining,
Yet ever to obtain his will resolving,
Though weak-built hopes persuade him to abstain-
    ing.   130
Despair to gain doth traffic oft for gaining,
  And when great treasure is the meed propos'd,
  Though death be adjunct, there's no death sup-
    pos'd.

Those that much covet are with gain so fond,
For what they have not, that which they possess
They scatter and unloose it from their bond,
And so, by hoping more, they have but less;
Or, gaining more, the profit of excess
　　Is but to surfeit, and such griefs sustain
　　That they prove bankrupt in this poor-rich gain.　140

The aim of all is but to nurse the life
With honour, wealth, and ease, in waning age;
And in this aim there is such thwarting strife
That one for all or all for one we gage,
As life for honour in fell battle's rage,
　　Honour for wealth; and oft that wealth doth cost
　　The death of all, and all together lost.

So that in venturing ill we leave to be
The things we are for that which we expect,
And this ambitious foul infirmity,　　　　　　150
In having much, torments us with defect
Of that we have; so then we do neglect
　　The thing we have and, all for want of wit,
　　Make something nothing by augmenting it.

Such hazard now must doting Tarquin make,
Pawning his honour to obtain his lust,
And for himself himself he must forsake;
Then where is truth, if there be no self-trust?
When shall he think to find a stranger just,

When he himself himself confounds, betrays   160
   To slanderous tongues and wretched hateful days ?

Now stole upon the time the dead of night
When heavy sleep had clos'd up mortal eyes.
No comfortable star did lend his light,
No noise but owls' and wolves' death-boding cries ;
Now serves the season that they may surprise
    The silly lambs ; pure thoughts are dead and still,
    While lust and murther wakes to stain and kill.

And now this lustful lord leap'd from his bed,
Throwing his mantle rudely o'er his arm,   170
Is madly toss'd between desire and dread.
The one sweetly flatters, the other feareth harm ;
But honest fear, bewitch'd with lust's foul charm,
    Doth too too oft betake him to retire,
    Beaten away by brain-sick rude desire.

His falchion on a flint he softly smiteth,
That from the cold stone sparks of fire do fly,
Whereat a waxen torch forthwith he lighteth
Which must be lode-star to his lustful eye,
And to the flame thus speaks advisedly :   180
    ' As from this cold flint I enforc'd this fire,
    So Lucrece must I force to my desire.'

Here pale with fear he doth premeditate
The dangers of his loathsome enterprise,

And in his inward mind he doth debate
What following sorrow may on this arise;
Then looking scornfully, he doth despise
 His naked armour of still-slaughter'd lust,
  And justly thus controls his thoughts unjust:

'Fair torch, burn out thy light, and lend it not   190
To darken her whose light excelleth thine;
And die, unhallow'd thoughts, before you blot
With your uncleanness that which is divine.
Offer pure incense to so pure a shrine;
 Let fair humanity abhor the deed
  That spots and stains love's modest snow-white
   weed.

'O shame to knighthood and to shining arms!
O foul dishonour to my household's grave!
O impious act, including all foul harms!
A martial man to be soft fancy's slave!   200
True valour still a true respect should have;
 Then my digression is so vile, so base,
  That it will live engraven in my face.

'Yea, though I die, the scandal will survive,
And be an eye-sore in my golden coat;
Some loathsome dash the herald will contrive,
To cipher me how fondly I did dote;
That my posterity, sham'd with the note,
 Shall curse my bones, and hold it for no sin
  To wish that I their father had not been.   210

' What win I, if I gain the thing I seek?
A dream, a breath, a froth of fleeting joy.
Who buys a minute's mirth to wail a week,
Or sells eternity to get a toy?
For one sweet grape who will the vine destroy?
    Or what fond beggar, but to touch the crown,
    Would with the sceptre straight be strucken down?

' If Collatinus dream of my intent,
Will he not wake, and in a desperate rage
Post hither, this vile purpose to prevent?   220
This siege that hath engirt his marriage,
This blur to youth, this sorrow to the sage,
    This dying virtue, this surviving shame,
    Whose crime will bear an ever-during blame?

' O, what excuse can my invention make
When thou shalt charge me with so black a deed?
Will not my tongue be mute, my frail joints shake,
Mine eyes forego their light, my false heart bleed?
The guilt being great, the fear doth still exceed;
    And extreme fear can neither fight nor fly,   230
    But coward-like with trembling terror die.

' Had Collatinus kill'd my son or sire,
Or lain in ambush to betray my life,
Or were he not my dear friend, this desire
Might have excuse to work upon his wife,
As in revenge or quittal of such strife;

But as he is my kinsman, my dear friend,
The shame and fault finds no excuse nor end.

'Shameful it is; ay, if the fact be known.
Hateful it is; there is no hate in loving.   240
I 'll beg her love; but she is not her own.
The worst is but denial and reproving;
My will is strong, past reason's weak removing.
    Who fears a sentence or an old man's saw
    Shall by a painted cloth be kept in awe.'

Thus, graceless, holds he disputation
'Tween frozen conscience and hot-burning will,
And with good thoughts makes dispensation,
Urging the worser sense for vantage still,
Which in a moment doth confound and kill   250
    All pure effects, and doth so far proceed
    That what is vile shows like a virtuous deed.

Quoth he, 'She took me kindly by the hand,
And gaz'd for tidings in my eager eyes,
Fearing some hard news from the warlike band
Where her beloved Collatinus lies.
O, how her fear did make her colour rise!
    First red as roses that on lawn we lay,
    Then white as lawn, the roses took away.

'And how her hand, in my hand being lock'd,   260
Forc'd it to tremble with her loyal fear!

Which struck her sad, and then it faster rock'd
Until her husband's welfare she did hear;
Whereat she smiled with so sweet a cheer
    That had Narcissus seen her as she stood
    Self-love had never drown'd him in the flood.

'Why hunt I then for colour or excuses?
All orators are dumb when beauty pleadeth;
Poor wretches have remorse in poor abuses;   269
Love thrives not in the heart that shadows dreadeth;
Affection is my captain, and he leadeth;
    And when his gaudy banner is display'd
    The coward fights and will not be dismay'd.

'Then, childish fear avaunt! debating die!
Respect and reason wait on wrinkled age!
My heart shall never countermand mine eye.
Sad pause and deep regard beseems the sage;
My part is youth, and beats these from the stage.
    Desire my pilot is, beauty my prize;   279
    Then who fears sinking where such treasure lies?'

As corn o'ergrown by weeds, so heedful fear
Is almost chok'd by unresisted lust.
Away he steals with open listening ear,
Full of foul hope and full of fond mistrust,
Both which, as servitors to the unjust,
    So cross him with their opposite persuasion
    That now he vows a league, and now invasion.

Within his thought her heavenly image sits,
And in the self-same seat sits Collatine.
That eye which looks on her confounds his wits;   290
That eye which him beholds, as more divine,
Unto a view so false will not incline,
    But with a pure appeal seeks to the heart,
    Which once corrupted takes the worser part,

And therein heartens up his servile powers,
Who, flatter'd by their leader's jocund show,
Stuff up his lust, as minutes fill up hours;
And as their captain, so their pride doth grow,
Paying more slavish tribute than they owe.
    By reprobate desire thus madly led,   300
    The Roman lord marcheth to Lucrece' bed.

The locks between her chamber and his will,
Each one by him enforc'd, retires his ward;
But, as they open, they all rate his ill,
Which drives the creeping thief to some regard.
The threshold grates the door to have him heard;
    Night-wandering weasels shriek to see him there;
    They fright him, yet he still pursues his fear.

As each unwilling portal yields him way,
Through little vents and crannies of the place   310
The wind wars with his torch to make him stay,
And blows the smoke of it into his face,
Extinguishing his conduct in this case;

But his hot heart, which fond desire doth scorch,
   Puffs forth another wind that fires the torch;

And being lighted, by the light he spies
Lucretia's glove, wherein her needle sticks.
He takes it from the rushes where it lies,
And griping it, the needle his finger pricks,
As who should say 'This glove to wanton tricks   320
   Is not inur'd; return again in haste;
   Thou see'st our mistress' ornaments are chaste.'

But all these poor forbiddings could not stay him;
He in the worst sense construes their denial.
The doors, the wind, the glove, that did delay him,
He takes for accidental things of trial;
Or as those bars which stop the hourly dial,
   Who with a lingering stay his course doth let
   Till every minute pays the hour his debt.

' So, so,' quoth he, ' these lets attend the time,   330
Like little frosts that sometime threat the spring,
To add a more rejoicing to the prime
And give the sneaped birds more cause to sing.
Pain pays the income of each precious thing;
   Huge rocks, high winds, strong pirates, shelves and
      sands,
   The merchant fears, ere rich at home he lands.'

Now is he come unto the chamber-door
That shuts him from the heaven of his thought,

Which with a yielding latch, and with no more,
Hath barr'd him from the blessed thing he sought.   340
So from himself impiety hath wrought
    That for his prey to pray he doth begin,
    As if the heavens should countenance his sin.

But in the midst of his unfruitful prayer,
Having solicited the eternal power
That his foul thoughts might compass his fair fair,
And they would stand auspicious to the hour,
Even there he starts.   Quoth he, 'I must deflower;
    The powers to whom I pray abhor this fact,
    How can they then assist me in the act?   350

'Then Love and Fortune be my gods, my guide!
My will is back'd with resolution.
Thoughts are but dreams till their effects be tried;
The blackest sin is clear'd with absolution;
Against love's fire fear's frost hath dissolution.
    The eye of heaven is out, and misty night
    Covers the shame that follows sweet delight.'

This said, his guilty hand pluck'd up the latch,
And with his knee the door he opens wide.
The dove sleeps fast that this night-owl will catch;   360
Thus treason works ere traitors be espied.
Who sees the lurking serpent steps aside;
    But she, sound sleeping, fearing no such thing,
    Lies at the mercy of his mortal sting.

Into the chamber wickedly he stalks,
And gazeth on her yet unstained bed.
The curtains being close, about he walks,
Rolling his greedy eyeballs in his head;
By their high treason is his heart misled,
    Which gives the watchword to his hand full soon
    To draw the cloud that hides the silver moon.   371

Look, as the fair and fiery-pointed sun,
Rushing from forth a cloud, bereaves our sight,
Even so, the curtain drawn, his eyes begun
To wink, being blinded with a greater light;
Whether it is that she reflects so bright
    That dazzleth them, or else some shame suppos'd,
    But blind they are and keep themselves enclos'd.

O, had they in that darksome prison died!
Then had they seen the period of their ill;   380
Then Collatine again, by Lucrece' side,
In his clear bed might have reposed still;
But they must ope, this blessed league to kill,
    And holy-thoughted Lucrece to their sight
    Must sell her joy, her life, her world's delight.

Her lily hand her rosy cheek lies under,
Cozening the pillow of a lawful kiss,
Who, therefore angry, seems to part in sunder,
Swelling on either side to want his bliss;
Between whose hills her head entombed is,   390

Where, like a virtuous monument, she lies,
To be admir'd of lewd unhallow'd eyes.

Without the bed her other fair hand was,
On the green coverlet, whose perfect white
Show'd like an April daisy on the grass,
With pearly sweat, resembling dew of night.
Her eyes, like marigolds, had sheath'd their light,
    And canopied in darkness sweetly lay
    Till they might open to adorn the day.

Her hair, like golden threads, play'd with her breath;
O modest wantons! wanton modesty!   401
Showing life's triumph in the map of death,
And death's dim look in life's mortality;
Each in her sleep themselves so beautify
    As if between them twain there were no strife,
    But that life liv'd in death, and death in life.

Her breasts, like ivory globes circled with blue,
A pair of maiden worlds unconquered,
Save of their lord no bearing yoke they knew,
And him by oath they truly honoured.   410
These worlds in Tarquin new ambition bred,
    Who, like a foul usurper, went about
    From this fair throne to heave the owner out.

What could he see but mightily he noted?
What did he note but strongly he desir'd?

What he beheld, on that he firmly doted,
And in his will his wilful eye he tir'd.
With more than admiration he admir'd
    Her azure veins, her alabaster skin,
    Her coral lips, her snow-white dimpled chin.   420

As the grim lion fawneth o'er his prey,
Sharp hunger by the conquest satisfied,
So o'er this sleeping soul doth Tarquin stay,
His rage of lust by gazing qualified;
Slack'd, not suppress'd, for standing by her side,
    His eye, which late this mutiny restrains,
    Unto a greater uproar tempts his veins.

And they, like straggling slaves for pillage fighting,
Obdurate vassals fell exploits effecting,
In bloody death and ravishment delighting,   430
Nor children's tears nor mothers' groans respecting,
Swell in their pride, the onset still expecting;
    Anon his beating heart, alarum striking,
    Gives the hot charge and bids them do their liking.

His drumming heart cheers up his burning eye,
His eye commends the leading to his hand;
His hand, as proud of such a dignity,
Smoking with pride, march'd on to make his stand
On her bare breast, the heart of all her land,
    Whose ranks of blue veins, as his hand did scale,
    Left their round turrets destitute and pale.   441

They, mustering to the quiet cabinet
Where their dear governess and lady lies,
Do tell her she is dreadfully beset
And fright her with confusion of their cries;
She, much amaz'd, breaks ope her lock'd-up eyes,
   Who, peeping forth this tumult to behold,
    Are by his flaming torch dimm'd and controll'd.

Imagine her as one in dead of night
From forth dull sleep by dreadful fancy waking,   450
That thinks she hath beheld some ghastly sprite
Whose grim aspect sets every joint a-shaking;
What terror 't is! but she, in worser taking,
   From sleep disturbed, heedfully doth view
    The sight which makes supposed terror true.

Wrapp'd and confounded in a thousand fears,
Like to a new-kill'd bird she trembling lies.
She dares not look; yet, winking, there appears
Quick-shifting antics, ugly in her eyes.
Such shadows are the weak brain's forgeries,   460
   Who, angry that the eyes fly from their lights,
    In darkness daunts them with more dreadful sights.

His hand, that yet remains upon her breast, —
Rude ram, to batter such an ivory wall! —
May feel her heart — poor citizen! — distress'd,
Wounding itself to death, rise up and fall,
Beating her bulk, that his hand shakes withal.

This moves in him more rage and lesser pity,
  To make the breach and enter this sweet city.

First, like a trumpet, doth his tongue begin   470
To sound a parley to his heartless foe,
Who o'er the white sheet peers her whiter chin,
The reason of this rash alarm to know,
Which he by dumb demeanour seeks to show;
  But she with vehement prayers urgeth still
  Under what colour he commits this ill.

Thus he replies : ' The colour in thy face,
That even for anger makes the lily pale
And the red rose blush at her own disgrace,
Shall plead for me and tell my loving tale.   480
Under that colour am I come to scale
  Thy never-conquer'd fort ; the fault is thine,
  For those thine eyes betray thee unto mine.

' Thus I forestall thee, if thou mean to chide :
Thy beauty hath ensnar'd thee to this night,
Where thou with patience must my will abide ;
My will that marks thee for my earth's delight,
Which I to conquer sought with all my might,
  But as reproof and reason beat it dead,
  By thy bright beauty was it newly bred.   490

' I see what crosses my attempt will bring ;
I know what thorns the growing rose defends ;

I think the honey guarded with a sting;
All this beforehand counsel comprehends,
But will is deaf and hears no heedful friends;
    Only he hath an eye to gaze on beauty,
    And dotes on what he looks, 'gainst law or duty.

' I have debated, even in my soul,
What wrong, what shame, what sorrow I shall breed;
But nothing can affection's course control,   500
Or stop the headlong fury of his speed.
I know repentant tears ensue the deed,
    Reproach, disdain, and deadly enmity;
    Yet strive I to embrace mine infamy.'

This said, he shakes aloft his Roman blade,
Which, like a falcon towering in the skies,
Coucheth the fowl below with his wings' shade,
Whose crooked beak threats if he mount he dies;
So under his insulting falchion lies
    Harmless Lucretia, marking what he tells   510
    With trembling fear, as fowl hear falcon's bells.

' Lucrece,' quoth he, ' this night I must enjoy thee;
If thou deny, then force must work my way,
For in thy bed I purpose to destroy thee.
That done, some worthless slave of thine I 'll slay,
To kill thine honour with thy life's decay;
    And in thy dead arms do I mean to place him,
    Swearing I slew him, seeing thee embrace him.

' So thy surviving husband shall remain
The scornful mark of every open eye; 520
Thy kinsmen hang their heads at this disdain,
Thy issue blurr'd with nameless bastardy;
And thou, the author of their obloquy,
  Shalt have thy trespass cited up in rhymes
  And sung by children in succeeding times.

' But if thou yield, I rest thy secret friend.
The fault unknown is as a thought unacted;
A little harm done to a great good end
For lawful policy remains enacted.
The poisonous simple sometimes is compacted 530
  In a pure compound; being so applied,
  His venom in effect is purified.

' Then, for thy husband and thy children's sake,
Tender my suit; bequeath not to their lot
The shame that from them no device can take,
The blemish that will never be forgot,
Worse than a slavish wipe or birth-hour's blot,
  For marks descried in men's nativity
  Are nature's faults, not their own infamy.'

Here with a cockatrice' dead-killing eye
He rouseth up himself and makes a pause;
While she, the picture of pure piety,
Like a white hind under the gripe's sharp claws,
Pleads, in a wilderness where are no laws,

To the rough beast that knows no gentle right,
Nor aught obeys but his foul appetite.

But when a black-fac'd cloud the world doth threat,
In his dim mist the aspiring mountains hiding,
From earth's dark womb some gentle gust doth get,
Which blows these pitchy vapours from their biding,
Hindering their present fall by this dividing;   551
    So his unhallow'd haste her words delays,
    And moody Pluto winks while Orpheus plays.

Yet, foul night-working cat, he doth but dally,
While in his hold-fast foot the weak mouse panteth;
Her sad behaviour feeds his vulture folly,
A swallowing gulf that even in plenty wanteth.
His ear her prayers admits, but his heart granteth
    No penetrable entrance to her plaining;
    Tears harden lust, though marble wear with raining.

Her pity-pleading eyes are sadly fix'd   561
In the remorseless wrinkles of his face;
Her modest eloquence with sighs is mix'd,
Which to her oratory adds more grace.
She puts the period often from his place,
    And midst the sentence so her accent breaks
    That twice she doth begin ere once she speaks.

She conjures him by high almighty Jove,
By knighthood, gentry, and sweet friendship's oath,

By her untimely tears, her husband's love, 57c
By holy human law, and common troth,
By heaven and earth, and all the power of both,
   That to his borrow'd bed he make retire,
   And stoop to honour, not to foul desire.

Quoth she, ' Reward not hospitality
With such black payment as thou hast pretended ;
Mud not the fountain that gave drink to thee ;
Mar not the thing that cannot be amended ;
End thy ill aim before thy shoot be ended ;
   He is no woodman that doth bend his bow 58c
   To strike a poor unseasonable doe.

' My husband is thy friend ; for his sake spare me.
Thyself art mighty ; for thine own sake leave me.
Myself a weakling ; do not then ensnare me.
Thou look'st not like deceit ; do not deceive me.
My sighs, like whirlwinds, labour hence to heave thee.
   If ever man were mov'd with woman's moans,
   Be moved with my tears, my sighs, my groans,

' All which together, like a troubled ocean,
Beat at thy rocky and wrack-threatening heart, 590
To soften it with their continual motion,
For stones dissolv'd to water do convert.
O, if no harder than a stone thou art,
   Melt at my tears, and be compassionate !
   Soft pity enters at an iron gate.

'In Tarquin's likeness I did entertain thee;
Hast thou put on his shape to do him shame?
To all the host of heaven I complain me,
Thou wrong'st his honour, wound'st his princely name.
Thou art not what thou seem'st; and if the same,   600
    Thou seem'st not what thou art, a god, a king,
        For kings like gods should govern every thing.

'How will thy shame be seeded in thine age,
When thus thy vices bud before thy spring!
If in thy hope thou dar'st do such outrage,
What dar'st thou not when once thou art a king?
O, be remember'd, no outrageous thing
    From vassal actors can be wip'd away;
        Then kings' misdeeds cannot be hid in clay.

'This deed will make thee only lov'd for fear,   610
But happy monarchs still are fear'd for love;
With foul offenders thou perforce must bear,
When they in thee the like offences prove.
If but for fear of this, thy will remove;
    For princes are the glass, the school, the book,
        Where subjects' eyes do learn, do read, do look.

'And wilt thou be the school where Lust shall learn?
Must he in thee read lectures of such shame?
Wilt thou be glass wherein it shall discern
Authority for sin, warrant for blame,   620
To privilege dishonour in thy name?

Thou back'st reproach against long-living laud,
And mak'st fair reputation but a bawd.

' Hast thou command? by him that gave it thee,
From a pure heart command thy rebel will;
Draw not thy sword to guard iniquity,
For it was lent thee all that brood to kill.
Thy princely office how canst thou fulfil,
     When, pattern'd by thy fault, foul sin may say,
     He learn'd to sin, and thou didst teach the way?

' Think but how vile a spectacle it were   631
To view thy present trespass in another.
Men's faults do seldom to themselves appear;
Their own transgressions partially they smother;
This guilt would seem death-worthy in thy brother.
     O, how are they wrapp'd in with infamies
     That from their own misdeeds askance their eyes!

' To thee, to thee, my heav'd-up hands appeal,
Not to seducing lust, thy rash relier.
I sue for exil'd majesty's repeal;   640
Let him return, and flattering thoughts retire.
His true respect will prison false desire,
     And wipe the dim mist from thy doting eyne,
     That thou shalt see thy state and pity mine.'

' Have done,' quoth he; ' my uncontrolled tide
Turns not, but swells the higher by this let.

Small lights are soon blown out, huge fires abide,
And with the wind in greater fury fret ;
The petty streams that pay a daily debt
   To their salt sovereign, with their fresh falls' haste
   Add to his flow, but alter not his taste.'   651

'Thou art,' quoth she, 'a sea, a sovereign king ;
And lo, there falls into thy boundless flood
Black lust, dishonour, shame, misgoverning,
Who seek to stain the ocean of thy blood.
If all these petty ills shall change thy good,
   Thy sea within a puddle's womb is hears'd,
   And not the puddle in thy sea dispers'd.

'So shall these slaves be king, and thou their slave ;
Thou nobly base, they basely dignified ;   660
Thou their fair life, and they thy fouler grave ;
Thou loathed in their shame, they in thy pride.
The lesser thing should not the greater hide ;
   The cedar stoops not to the base shrub's foot,
   But low shrubs wither at the cedar's root.

'So let thy thoughts, low vassals to thy state —
'No more,' quoth he ; 'by heaven, I will not hear thee.
Yield to my love ; if not, enforced hate,
Instead of love's coy touch, shall rudely tear thee.
That done, despitefully I mean to bear thee   670
   Unto the base bed of some rascal groom,
   To be thy partner in this shameful doom.'

This said, he sets his foot upon the light,
For light and lust are deadly enemies;
Shame folded up in blind concealing night,
When most unseen, then most doth tyrannize.
The wolf hath seiz'd his prey, the poor lamb cries;
    Till with her own white fleece her voice controll'd
    Entombs her outcry in her lips' sweet fold.

For with the nightly linen that she wears   680
He pens her piteous clamours in her head,
Cooling his hot face in the chastest tears
That ever modest eyes with sorrow shed.
O, that prone lust should stain so pure a bed!
    The spots whereof could weeping purify,
    Her tears should drop on them perpetually.

But she hath lost a dearer thing than life,
And he hath won what he would lose again.
This forced league doth force a further strife;
This momentary joy breeds months of pain;   690
This hot desire converts to cold disdain;
    Pure Chastity is rifled of her store,
    And Lust, the thief, far poorer than before.

Look, as the full-fed hound or gorged hawk,
Unapt for tender smell or speedy flight,
Make slow pursuit, or altogether balk
The prey wherein by nature they delight,
So surfeit-taking Tarquin fares this night;

His taste delicious, in digestion souring,
Devours his will that liv'd by foul devouring.   700

O, deeper sin than bottomless conceit
Can comprehend in still imagination!
Drunken Desire must vomit his receipt
Ere he can see his own abomination.
While Lust is in his pride, no exclamation
    Can curb his heat or rein his rash desire
    Till like a jade Self-will himself doth tire.

And then with lank and lean discolour'd cheek,
With heavy eye, knit brow, and strengthless pace,
Feeble Desire, all recreant, poor, and meek,   710
Like to a bankrupt beggar wails his case.
The flesh being proud, Desire doth fight with Grace,
    For there it revels; and when that decays,
    The guilty rebel for remission prays.

So fares it with this faultful lord of Rome
Who this accomplishment so hotly chas'd;
For now against himself he sounds this doom,
That through the length of times he stands disgrac'd.
Besides, his soul's fair temple is defac'd,
    To whose weak ruins muster troops of cares   720
    To ask the spotted princess how she fares.

She says her subjects with foul insurrection
Have batter'd down her consecrated wall,

And by their mortal fault brought in subjection
Her immortality, and made her thrall
To living death and pain perpetual,
    Which in her prescience she controlled still,
    But her foresight could not forestall their will.

Even in this thought through the dark night he stealeth,
A captive victor that hath lost in gain;   730
Bearing away the wound that nothing healeth,
The scar that will, despite of cure, remain;
Leaving his spoil perplex'd in greater pain.
    She bears the load of lust he left behind,
    And he the burthen of a guilty mind.

He like a thievish dog creeps sadly thence;
She like a wearied lamb lies panting there;
He scowls and hates himself for his offence;
She, desperate, with her nails her flesh doth tear;
He faintly flies, sweating with guilty fear;   740
    She stays, exclaiming on the direful night;
    He runs, and chides his vanish'd, loath'd delight.

He thence departs a heavy convertite;
She there remains a hopeless castaway;
He in his speed looks for the morning light;
She prays she never may behold the day,
'For day,' quoth she, 'night's scapes doth open lay,
    And my true eyes have never practis'd how
    To cloak offences with a cunning brow.

' They think not but that every eye can see   750
The same disgrace which they themselves behold,
And therefore would they still in darkness be,
To have their unseen sin remain untold ;
For they their guilt with weeping will unfold,
    And grave, like water that doth eat in steel,
    Upon my cheeks what helpless shame I feel.'

Here she exclaims against repose and rest,
And bids her eyes hereafter still be blind ;
She wakes her heart by beating on her breast,
And bids it leap from thence, where it may find   760
Some purer chest to close so pure a mind.
    Frantic with grief thus breathes she forth her spite
    Against the unseen secrecy of night :

' O comfort-killing Night, image of hell !
Dim register and notary of shame !
Black stage for tragedies and murthers fell !
Vast sin-concealing chaos ! nurse of blame !
Blind muffled bawd ! dark harbour for defame !
    Grim cave of death ! whispering conspirator
    With close-tongu'd treason and the ravisher !   770

' O hateful, vaporous, and foggy Night !
Since thou art guilty of my cureless crime,
Muster thy mists to meet the eastern light,
Make war against proportion'd course of time ;
Or if thou wilt permit the sun to climb

His wonted height, yet ere he go to bed
Knit poisonous clouds about his golden head.

'With rotten damps ravish the morning air;
Let their exhal'd unwholesome breaths make sick
The life of purity, the supreme fair,   780
Ere he arrive his weary noon-tide prick;
And let thy misty vapours march so thick
    That in their smoky ranks his smother'd light
    May set at noon and make perpetual night.

'Were Tarquin Night, as he is but Night's child,
The silver-shining queen he would distain;
Her twinkling handmaids too, by him defil'd,
Through Night's black bosom should not peep again.
So should I have co-partners in my pain,
    And fellowship in woe doth woe assuage,   790
    As palmers' chat makes short their pilgrimage;

'Where now I have no one to blush with me,
To cross their arms and hang their heads with mine,
To mask their brows and hide their infamy,
But I alone alone must sit and pine,
Seasoning the earth with showers of silver brine,
    Mingling my talk with tears, my grief with groans,
    Poor wasting monuments of lasting moans.

'O Night, thou furnace of foul-reeking smoke,
Let not the jealous Day behold that face   800

Which underneath thy black all-hiding cloak
Immodestly lies martyr'd with disgrace!
Keep still possession of thy gloomy place,
    That all the faults which in thy reign are made
    May likewise be sepulchred in thy shade!

'Make me not object to the tell-tale Day!
The light will show, character'd in my brow,
The story of sweet chastity's decay,
The impious breach of holy wedlock vow;
Yea, the illiterate, that know not how   810
    To cipher what is writ in learned books,
    Will quote my loathsome trespass in my looks.

'The nurse, to still her child, will tell my story,
And fright her crying babe with Tarquin's name;
The orator, to deck his oratory,
Will couple my reproach to Tarquin's shame;
Feast-finding minstrels, tuning my defame,
    Will tie the hearers to attend each line,
    How Tarquin wronged me, I Collatine.

'Let my good name, that senseless reputation,   820
For Collatine's dear love be kept unspotted;
If that be made a theme for disputation,
The branches of another root are rotted,
And undeserv'd reproach to him allotted
    That is as clear from this attaint of mine
    As I, ere this, was pure to Collatine.

'O unseen shame! invisible disgrace!
O unfelt sore! crest-wounding, private scar!
Reproach is stamp'd in Collatinus' face,
And Tarquin's eye may read the mot afar,   830
How he in peace is wounded, not in war.
  Alas, how many bear such shameful blows,
    Which not themselves, but he that gives them knows!

'If, Collatine, thine honour lay in me,
From me by strong assault it is bereft.
My honey lost, and I, a drone-like bee,
Have no perfection of my summer left,
But robb'd and ransack'd by injurious theft;
  In thy weak hive a wandering wasp hath crept,
    And suck'd the honey which thy chaste bee kept.

'Yet am I guilty of thy honour's wrack;   841
Yet for thy honour did I entertain him;
Coming from thee, I could not put him back,
For it had been dishonour to disdain him.
Besides, of weariness he did complain him,
  And talk'd of virtue; O unlook'd-for evil,
    When virtue is profan'd in such a devil!

'Why should the worm intrude the maiden bud?
Or hateful cuckoos hatch in sparrows' nests?
Or toads infect fair founts with venom mud?   850
Or tyrant folly lurk in gentle breasts?
Or kings be breakers of their own behests?

But no perfection is so absolute
That some impurity doth not pollute.

'The aged man that coffers up his gold
Is plagued with cramps and gouts and painful fits,
And scarce hath eyes his treasure to behold;
But like still-pining Tantalus he sits,
And useless barns the harvest of his wits,
 Having no other pleasure of his gain   860
 But torment that it cannot cure his pain.

'So then he hath it when he cannot use it,
And leaves it to be master'd by his young,
Who in their pride do presently abuse it;
Their father was too weak, and they too strong,
To hold their cursed-blessed fortune long.
 The sweets we wish for turn to loathed sours
 Even in the moment that we call them ours.

'Unruly blasts wait on the tender spring;
Unwholesome weeds take root with precious flowers;
The adder hisses where the sweet birds sing; 871
What virtue breeds iniquity devours.
We have no good that we can say is ours
 But ill-annexed Opportunity
 Or kills his life or else his quality.

'O Opportunity, thy guilt is great!
'T is thou that execut'st the traitor's treason;

Thou set'st the wolf where he the lamb may get;
Whoever plots the sin, thou point'st the season;
'T is thou that spurn'st at right, at law, at reason;   880
    And in thy shady cell, where none may spy him,
    Sits Sin, to seize the souls that wander by him.

' Thou mak'st the vestal violate her oath;
Thou blow'st the fire when temperance is thaw'd;
Thou smother'st honesty, thou murther'st troth;
Thou foul abettor! thou notorious bawd!
Thou plantest scandal and displacest laud;
    Thou ravisher, thou traitor, thou false thief,
    Thy honey turns to gall, thy joy to grief!

' Thy secret pleasure turns to open shame,   890
Thy private feasting to a public fast,
Thy smoothing titles to a ragged name,
Thy sugar'd tongue to bitter wormwood taste;
Thy violent vanities can never last.
    How comes it then, vile Opportunity,
    Being so bad, such numbers seek for thee?

' When wilt thou be the humble suppliant's friend,
And bring him where his suit may be obtain'd?
When wilt thou sort an hour great strifes to end?
Or free that soul which wretchedness hath chain'd?
Give physic to the sick, ease to the pain'd?   901
    The poor, lame, blind, halt, creep, cry out for thee,
    But they ne'er meet with Opportunity.

' The patient dies while the physician sleeps ;
The orphan pines while the oppressor feeds ;
Justice is feasting while the widow weeps ;
Advice is sporting while infection breeds.
Thou grant'st no time for charitable deeds ;
    Wrath, envy, treason, rape, and murther's rages,
    Thy heinous hours wait on them as their pages.   910

' When Truth and Virtue have to do with thee,
A thousand crosses keep them from thy aid.
They buy thy help ; but Sin ne'er gives a fee,
He gratis comes ; and thou art well appaid
As well to hear as grant what he hath said.
    My Collatine would else have come to me
    When Tarquin did, but he was stay'd by thee.

' Guilty thou art of murther and of theft,
Guilty of perjury and subornation,
Guilty of treason, forgery, and shift,   920
Guilty of incest, that abomination ;
An accessary by thine inclination
    To all sins past and all that are to come,
    From the creation to the general doom.

' Misshapen Time, copesmate of ugly Night,
Swift subtle post, carrier of grisly care,
Eater of youth, false slave to false delight,
Base watch of woes, sin's pack-horse, virtue's snare,
Thou nursest all and murther'st all that are ;

O, hear me then, injurious, shifting Time !   930
Be guilty of my death, since of my crime.

' Why hath thy servant, Opportunity,
Betray'd the hours thou gav'st me to repose,
Cancell'd my fortunes, and enchained me
To endless date of never-ending woes ?
Time's office is to fine the hate of foes,
     To eat up errors by opinion bred,
     Not spend the dowry of a lawful bed.

' Time's glory is to calm contending kings,
To unmask falsehood and bring truth to light,   940
To stamp the seal of time in aged things,
To wake the morn and sentinel the night,
To wrong the wronger till he render right,
     To ruinate proud buildings with thy hours,
     And smear with dust their glittering golden towers ;

' To fill with worm-holes stately monuments,
To feed oblivion with decay of things,
To blot old books and alter their contents,
To pluck the quills from ancient ravens' wings,
To dry the old oak's sap and cherish springs,   950
     To spoil antiquities of hammer'd steel,
     And turn the giddy round of Fortune's wheel ;

' To show the beldam daughters of her daughter,
To make the child a man, the man a child,

To slay the tiger that doth live by slaughter,
To tame the unicorn and lion wild,
To mock the subtle in themselves beguil'd,
  To cheer the ploughman with increaseful crops,
  And waste huge stones with little water-drops.

' Why work'st thou mischief in thy pilgrimage,   960
Unless thou couldst return to make amends?
One poor retiring minute in an age
Would purchase thee a thousand thousand friends,
Lending him wit that to bad debtors lends;
  O, this dread night, wouldst thou one hour come
    back,
  I could prevent this storm and shun thy wrack!

' Thou ceaseless lackey to eternity,
With some mischance cross Tarquin in his flight;
Devise extremes beyond extremity,
To make him curse this cursed crimeful night;   970
Let ghastly shadows his lewd eyes affright,
  And the dire thought of his committed evil
  Shape every bush a hideous shapeless devil.

' Disturb his hours of rest with restless trances,
Afflict him in his bed with bedrid groans;
Let there bechance him pitiful mischances,
To make him moan, but pity not his moans;
Stone him with harden'd hearts, harder than stones;
  And let mild women to him lose their mildness,
  Wilder to him than tigers in their wildness.   980

' Let him have time to tear his curled hair,
Let him have time against himself to rave,
Let him have time of Time's help to despair,
Let him have time to live a loathed slave,
Let him have time a beggar's orts to crave,
   And time to see one that by alms doth live
   Disdain to him disdained scraps to give.

' Let him have time to see his friends his foes,
And merry fools to mock at him resort;
Let him have time to mark how slow time goes   990
In time of sorrow, and how swift and short
His time of folly and his time of sport;
   And ever let his unrecalling crime
   Have time to wail the abusing of his time.

' O Time, thou tutor both to good and bad,
Teach me to curse him that thou taught'st this ill!
At his own shadow let the thief run mad,
Himself himself seek every hour to kill!
Such wretched hands such wretched blood should spill;
   For who so base would such an office have   1000
   As slanderous deathsman to so base a slave?

' The baser is he, coming from a king,
To shame his hope with deeds degenerate;
The mightier man, the mightier is the thing
That makes him honour'd or begets him hate,
For greatest scandal waits on greatest state.

The moon being clouded presently is miss'd,
But little stars may hide them when they list.

'The crow may bathe his coal-black wings in mire
And unperceiv'd fly with the filth away,   1010
But if the like the snow-white swan desire,
The stain upon his silver down will stay.
Poor grooms are sightless night, kings glorious day;
    Gnats are unnoted wheresoe'er they fly,
    But eagles gaz'd upon with every eye.

'Out, idle words, servants to shallow fools!
Unprofitable sounds, weak arbitrators!
Busy yourselves in skill-contending schools,
Debate where leisure serves with dull debaters;
To trembling clients be you mediators.   1020
    For me, I force not argument a straw,
    Since that my case is past the help of law.

'In vain I rail at Opportunity,
At Time, at Tarquin, and uncheerful Night;
In vain I cavil with mine infamy,
In vain I spurn at my confirm'd despite;
This helpless smoke of words doth me no right.
    The remedy indeed to do me good
    Is to let forth my foul-defiled blood.

'Poor hand, why quiver'st thou at this decree?   1030
Honour thyself to rid me of this shame;

For if I die, my honour lives in thee,
But if I live, thou liv'st in my defame.
Since thou couldst not defend thy loyal dame
   And wast afeard to scratch her wicked foe,
    Kill both thyself and her for yielding so.'

This said, from her betumbled couch she starteth,
To find some desperate instrument of death;
But this no slaughter-house no tool imparteth
To make more vent for passage of her breath,   1040
Which, thronging through her lips, so vanisheth
   As smoke from Ætna, that in air consumes,
    Or that which from discharged cannon fumes.

'In vain,' quoth she, 'I live, and seek in vain
Some happy mean to end a hapless life.
I fear'd by Tarquin's falchion to be slain,
Yet for the selfsame purpose seek a knife.
But when I fear'd I was a loyal wife;
   So am I now — O no, that cannot be!
    Of that true type hath Tarquin rifled me.   1050

'O, that is gone for which I sought to live,
And therefore now I need not fear to die!
To clear this spot by death, at least I give
A badge of fame to slander's livery,
A dying life to living infamy;
   Poor helpless help, the treasure stolen away,
    To burn the guiltless casket where it lay!

'Well, well, dear Collatine, thou shalt not know
The stained taste of violated troth;
I will not wrong thy true affection so,   1060
To flatter thee with an infringed oath;
This bastard graff shall never come to growth.
    He shall not boast who did thy stock pollute
    That thou art doting father of his fruit.

'Nor shall he smile at thee in secret thought,
Nor laugh with his companions at thy state;
But thou shalt know thy interest was not bought
Basely with gold, but stolen from forth thy gate.
For me, I am the mistress of my fate,
    And with my trespass never will dispense   1070
    Till life to death acquit my forc'd offence.

'I will not poison thee with my attaint,
Nor fold my fault in cleanly-coin'd excuses;
My sable ground of sin I will not paint,
To hide the truth of this false night's abuses.
My tongue shall utter all; mine eyes, like sluices,
    As from a mountain-spring that feeds a dale,
    Shall gush pure streams to purge my impure tale.'

By this, lamenting Philomel had ended
The well-tun'd warble of her nightly sorrow,   1080
And solemn night with slow sad gait descended
To ugly hell; when, lo, the blushing morrow
Lends light to all fair eyes that light will borrow,

But cloudy Lucrece shames herself to see
And therefore still in night would cloister'd be.

Revealing day through every cranny spies
And seems to point her out where she sits weeping,
To whom she sobbing speaks: 'O eye of eyes,
Why pry'st thou through my window? leave thy peep-
     ing;   1089
Mock with thy tickling beams eyes that are sleeping;
  Brand not my forehead with thy piercing light,
  For day hath nought to do what's done by night.'

Thus cavils she with every thing she sees.
True grief is fond and testy as a child,
Who wayward once, his mood with nought agrees;
Old woes, not infant sorrows, bear them mild.
Continuance tames the one; the other wild,
  Like an unpractis'd swimmer plunging still,
  With too much labour drowns for want of skill.

So she, deep-drenched in a sea of care,   1100
Holds disputation with each thing she views,
And to herself all sorrow doth compare;
No object but her passion's strength renews,
And as one shifts another straight ensues;
  Sometime her grief is dumb and hath no words,
  Sometime 't is mad and too much talk affords.

The little birds that tune their morning's joy
Make her moans mad with their sweet melody.

For mirth doth search the bottom of annoy;
Sad souls are slain in merry company;   1110
Grief best is pleas'd with grief's society;
    True sorrow then is feelingly suffic'd
    When with like semblance it is sympathiz'd.

'T is double death to drown in ken of shore;
He ten times pines that pines beholding food;
To see the salve doth make the wound ache more;
Great grief grieves most at that would do it good;
Deep woes roll forward like a gentle flood,
    Who, being stopp'd, the bounding banks o'erflows;
    Grief dallied with nor law nor limit knows.   1120

' You mocking birds,' quoth she, ' your tunes entomb
Within your hollow-swelling feather'd breasts,
And in my hearing be you mute and dumb;
My restless discord loves no stops nor rests;
A woeful hostess brooks not merry guests.
    Relish your nimble notes to pleasing ears;
    Distress likes dumps when time is kept with tears.

' Come, Philomel, that sing'st of ravishment,
Make thy sad grove in my dishevell'd hair.
As the dank earth weeps at thy languishment,   1130
So I at each sad strain will strain a tear,
And with deep groans the diapason bear;
    For burden-wise I 'll hum on Tarquin still,
    While thou on Tereus descant'st better skill.

'And whiles against a thorn thou bear'st thy part,
To keep thy sharp woes waking, wretched I,
To imitate thee well, against my heart
Will fix a sharp knife to affright mine eye,
Who, if it wink, shall thereon fall and die.
    These means, as frets upon an instrument,   1140
    Shall tune our heart-strings to true languishment.

' And for, poor bird, thou sing'st not in the day,
As shaming any eye should thee behold,
Some dark deep desert, seated from the way,
That knows not parching heat nor freezing cold,
Will we find out, and there we will unfold
    To creatures stern sad tunes, to change their kinds ;
    Since men prove beasts, let beasts bear gentle minds.'

As the poor frighted deer, that stands at gaze,
Wildly determining which way to fly,   1150
Or one encompass'd with a winding maze,
That cannot tread the way out readily,
So with herself is she in mutiny,
    To live or die which of the twain were better,
    When life is sham'd, and death reproach's debtor.

' To kill myself,' quoth she, ' alack, what were it
But with my body my poor soul's pollution ?
They that lose half with greater patience bear it
Than they whose whole is swallow'd in confusion.
That mother tries a merciless conclusion   1160

Who, having two sweet babes, when death takes one,
　Will slay the other and be nurse to none.

' My body or my soul, which was the dearer,
When the one pure the other made divine?
Whose love of either to myself was nearer
When both were kept for heaven and Collatine?
Ay me! the bark peel'd from the lofty pine,
　His leaves will wither and his sap decay;
　So must my soul, her bark being peel'd away.

' Her house is sack'd, her quiet interrupted,   1170
Her mansion batter'd by the enemy;
Her sacred temple spotted, spoil'd, corrupted,
Grossly engirt with daring infamy.
Then let it not be call'd impiety,
　If in this blemish'd fort I make some hole
　Through which I may convey this troubled soul.

' Yet die I will not till my Collatine
Have heard the cause of my untimely death,
That he may vow, in that sad hour of mine,
Revenge on him that made me stop my breath.   1180
My stained blood to Tarquin I 'll bequeath,
　Which by him tainted shall for him be spent
　And as his due writ in my testament.

' My honour I 'll bequeath unto the knife
That wounds my body so dishonoured.

'T is honour to deprive dishonour'd life ;
The one will live, the other being dead.
So of shame's ashes shall my fame be bred,
   For in my death I murther shameful scorn ;
   My shame so dead, mine honour is new-born.   1190

' Dear lord of that dear jewel I have lost,
What legacy shall I bequeath to thee ?
My resolution, love, shall be thy boast,
By whose example thou reveng'd mayst be.
How Tarquin must be us'd, read it in me ;
   Myself, thy friend, will kill myself, thy foe,
   And for my sake serve thou false Tarquin so.

' This brief abridgement of my will I make :
My soul and body to the skies and ground ;
My resolution, husband, do thou take ;   1200
Mine honour be the knife's that makes my wound ,
My shame be his that did my fame confound ;
   And all my fame that lives disbursed be
   To those that live and think no shame of me.

' Thou, Collatine, shalt oversee this will ;
How was I overseen that thou shalt see it !
My blood shall wash the slander of mine ill ;
My life's foul deed, my life's fair end shall free it.
Faint not, faint heart, but stoutly say " So be it."   1209
   Yield to my hand ; my hand shall conquer thee.
   Thou dead, both die, and both shall victors be.'

This plot of death when sadly she had laid,
And wip'd the brinish pearl from her bright eyes,
With untun'd tongue she hoarsely calls her maid,
Whose swift obedience to her mistress hies ;
For fleet-wing'd duty with thought's feathers flies.
　　Poor Lucrece' cheeks unto her maid seem so
　　As winter meads when sun doth melt their snow.

Her mistress she doth give demure good-morrow,
With soft-slow tongue, true mark of modesty,　　1220
And sorts a sad look to her lady's sorrow ;
For why, her face wore sorrow's livery,
But durst not ask of her audaciously
　　Why her two suns were cloud-eclipsed so,
　　Nor why her fair cheeks over-wash'd with woe.

But as the earth doth weep, the sun being set,
Each flower moisten'd like a melting eye,
Even so the maid with swelling drops gan wet
Her circled eyne, enforc'd by sympathy
Of those fair suns set in her mistress' sky,　　1230
　　Who in a salt-wav'd ocean quench their light,
　　Which makes the maid weep like the dewy night.

A pretty while these pretty creatures stand,
Like ivory conduits coral cisterns filling.
One justly weeps ; the other takes in hand
No cause, but company, of her drops spilling.
　　Their gentle sex to weep are often willing,

Grieving themselves to guess at others' smarts,
And then they drown their eyes or break their hearts.

For men have marble, women waxen minds,   1240
And therefore are they form'd as marble will;
The weak oppress'd, the impression of strange kinds
Is form'd in them by force, by fraud, or skill.
Then call them not the authors of their ill,
  No more than wax shall be accounted evil
  Wherein is stamp'd the semblance of a devil.

Their smoothness, like a goodly champaign plain,
Lays open all the little worms that creep;
In men, as in a rough-grown grove, remain
Cave-keeping evils that obscurely sleep.   1250
Through crystal walls each little mote will peep;
  Though men can cover crimes with bold stern looks,
  Poor women's faces are their own faults' books.

No man inveigh against the wither'd flower,
But chide rough winter that the flower hath kill'd;
Not that devour'd, but that which doth devour,
Is worthy blame.   O, let it not be hild
Poor women's faults that they are so fulfill'd
  With men's abuses! those proud lords, to blame,
  Make weak-made women tenants to their shame.

The precedent whereof in Lucrece view,   1261
Assail'd by night with circumstances strong

Of present death, and shame that might ensue
By that her death to do her husband wrong.
Such danger to resistance did belong
  That dying fear through all her body spread;
  And who cannot abuse a body dead?

By this, mild patience bid fair Lucrece speak
To the poor counterfeit of her complaining.
' My girl,' quoth she, ' on what occasion break   1270
Those tears from thee that down thy cheeks are rain-
      ing?
If thou dost weep for grief of my sustaining,
  Know, gentle wench, it small avails my mood;
  If tears could help, mine own would do me good.

' But tell me, girl, when went ' — and there she stay'd
Till after a deep groan — ' Tarquin from hence?'
' Madam, ere I was up,' replied the maid,
' The more to blame my sluggard negligence;
Yet with the fault I thus far can dispense,—
  Myself was stirring ere the break of day,   1280
  And ere I rose was Tarquin gone away.

' But, lady, if your maid may be so bold,
She would request to know your heaviness.'
' O, peace!' quoth Lucrece: ' if it should be told,
The repetition cannot make it less,
For more it is than I can well express;
  And that deep torture may be call'd a hell
  When more is felt than one hath power to tell.

'Go, get me hither paper, ink, and pen —
Yet save that labour, for I have them here.   1290
What should I say?   One of my husband's men
Bid thou be ready, by and by, to bear
A letter to my lord, my love, my dear.
   Bid him with speed prepare to carry it;
   The cause craves haste, and it will soon be writ.'

Her maid is gone, and she prepares to write,
First hovering o'er the paper with her quill.
Conceit and grief an eager combat fight;
What wit sets down is blotted straight with will;
This is too curious-good, this blunt and ill;   1300
   Much like a press of people at a door,
   Throng her inventions, which shall go before.

At last she thus begins: 'Thou worthy lord
Of that unworthy wife that greeteth thee,
Health to thy person! next vouchsafe t' afford —
If ever, love, thy Lucrece thou wilt see —
Some present speed to come and visit me.
   So, I commend me from our house in grief;
   My woes are tedious, though my words are brief.'

Here folds she up the tenor of her woe,   1310
Her certain sorrow writ uncertainly.
By this short schedule Collatine may know
Her grief, but not her grief's true quality;
She dares not thereof make discovery,

Lest he should hold it her own gross abuse,
Ere she with blood had stain'd her stain'd excuse.

Besides, the life and feeling of her passion
She hoards, to spend when he is by to hear her;
When sighs and groans and tears may grace the fashion
Of her disgrace, the better so to clear her   1320
From that suspicion which the world might bear her.
  To shun this blot, she would not blot the letter
  With words till action might become them better.

To see sad sights moves more than hear them told;
For then the eye interprets to the ear
The heavy motion that it doth behold,
When every part a part of woe doth bear.
'T is but a part of sorrow that we hear;
  Deep sounds make lesser noise than shallow fords,
  And sorrow ebbs, being blown with wind of words.

Her letter now is seal'd, and on it writ   1331
'At Ardea to my lord with more than haste.'
The post attends, and she delivers it,
Charging the sour-fac'd groom to hie as fast
As lagging fowls before the northern blast.
  Speed more than speed but dull and slow she deems;
  Extremity still urgeth such extremes.

The homely villain curtsies to her low,
And, blushing on her, with a steadfast eye

Receives the scroll without or yea or no   1340
And forth with bashful innocence doth hie.
But they whose guilt within their bosoms lie
    Imagine every eye beholds their blame ;
    For Lucrece thought he blush'd to see her shame,

When, silly groom ! God wot, it was defect
Of spirit, life, and bold audacity.
Such harmless creatures have a true respect
To talk in deeds, while others saucily
Promise more speed, but do it leisurely ;
    Even so this pattern of the worn-out age   1350
    Pawn'd honest looks, but laid no words to gage.

His kindled duty kindled her mistrust,
That two red fires in both their faces blaz'd ;
She thought he blush'd, as knowing Tarquin's lust,
And, blushing with him, wistly on him gaz'd.
Her earnest eye did make him more amaz'd ;
    The more she saw the blood his cheeks replenish,
    The more she thought he spied in her some blemish.

But long she thinks till he return again,
And yet the duteous vassal scarce is gone.   1360
The weary time she cannot entertain,
For now 't is stale to sigh, to weep, and groan ;
So woe hath wearied woe, moan tired moan,
    That she her plaints a little while doth stay,
    Pausing for means to mourn some newer way.

At last she calls to mind where hangs a piece
Of skilful painting, made for Priam's Troy,
Before the which is drawn the power of Greece,
For Helen's rape the city to destroy,
Threatening cloud-kissing Ilion with annoy,   1370
 Which the conceited painter drew so proud
 As heaven, it seem'd, to kiss the turrets bow'd.

A thousand lamentable objects there,
In scorn of nature, art gave lifeless life.
Many a dry drop seem'd a weeping tear,
Shed for the slaughter'd husband by the wife;
The red blood reek'd, to show the painter's strife,
 And dying eyes gleam'd forth their ashy lights,
 Like dying coals burnt out in tedious nights.

There might you see the labouring pioneer   1380
Begrim'd with sweat and smeared all with dust;
And from the towers of Troy there would appear
The very eyes of men through loop-holes thrust,
Gazing upon the Greeks with little lust.
 Such sweet observance in this work was had
 That one might see those far-off eyes look sad.

In great commanders grace and majesty
You might behold, triumphing in their faces;
In youth, quick bearing and dexterity ;
And here and there the painter interlaces   1390
Pale cowards, marching on with trembling paces,

Which heartless peasants did so well resemble
That one would swear he saw them quake and tremble.

In Ajax and Ulysses, O, what art
Of physiognomy might one behold !
The face of either cipher'd either's heart,
Their face their manners most expressly told ;
In Ajax' eyes blunt rage and rigour roll'd,
　　But the mild glance that sly Ulysses lent
　　Show'd deep regard and smiling government.　　1400

There pleading might you see grave Nestor stand,
As 't were encouraging the Greeks to fight,
Making such sober action with his hand
That it beguil'd attention, charm'd the sight ;
In speech, it seem'd, his beard, all silver white,
　　Wagg'd up and down, and from his lips did fly
　　Thin winding breath which purl'd up to the sky.

About him were a press of gaping faces,
Which seem'd to swallow up his sound advice ;
All jointly listening, but with several graces,　　1410
As if some mermaid did their ears entice,
Some high, some low, the painter was so nice ;
　　The scalps of many, almost hid behind,
　　To jump up higher seem'd, to mock the mind.

Here one man's hand lean'd on another's head,
His nose being shadow'd by his neighbour's ear ;

Here one being throng'd bears back, all bollen and red;
Another smother'd seems to pelt and swear;
And in their rage such signs of rage they bear
    As, but for loss of Nestor's golden words,   1420
    It seem'd they would debate with angry swords.

For much imaginary work was there,
Conceit deceitful, so compact, so kind,
That for Achilles' image stood his spear,
Gripp'd in an armed hand; himself, behind,
Was left unseen, save to the eye of mind;
    A hand, a foot, a face, a leg, a head,
    Stood for the whole to be imagined.

And from the walls of strong-besieged Troy
When their brave hope, bold Hector, march'd to field,
Stood many Trojan mothers, sharing joy   1431
To see their youthful sons bright weapons wield;
And to their hope they such odd action yield
    That through their light joy seemed to appear,
    Like bright things stain'd, a kind of heavy fear.

And from the strand of Dardan where they fought
To Simois' reedy banks the red blood ran,
Whose waves to imitate the battle sought
With swelling ridges; and their ranks began
To break upon the galled shore, and than   1440
    Retire again, till, meeting greater ranks,
    They join and shoot their foam at Simois' banks.

To this well-painted piece is Lucrece come,
To find a face where all distress is stell'd.
Many she sees where cares have carved some,
But none where all distress and dolour dwell'd
Till she despairing Hecuba beheld,
   Staring on Priam's wounds with her old eyes,
   Which bleeding under Pyrrhus' proud foot lies.

In her the painter had anatomiz'd   1450
Time's ruin, beauty's wrack, and grim care's reign.
Her cheeks with chaps and wrinkles were disguis'd ;
Of what she was no semblance did remain.
Her blue blood, chang'd to black in every vein,
   Wanting the spring that those shrunk pipes had fed,
   Show'd life imprison'd in a body dead.

On this sad shadow Lucrece spends her eyes
And shapes her sorrow to the beldam's woes,
Who nothing wants to answer her but cries,
And bitter words to ban her cruel foes.   1460
The painter was no god to lend her those ;
   And therefore Lucrece swears he did her wrong,
   To give her so much grief and not a tongue.

' Poor instrument,' quoth she, ' without a sound,
I 'll tune thy woes with my lamenting tongue,
And drop sweet balm in Priam's painted wound,
And rail on Pyrrhus that hath done him wrong,
And with my tears quench Troy that burns so long,

And with my knife scratch out the angry eyes
Of all the Greeks that are thine enemies.   1470

'Show me the strumpet that began this stir,
That with my nails her beauty I may tear.
Thy heat of lust, fond Paris, did incur
This load of wrath that burning Troy doth bear;
Thy eye kindled the fire that burneth here;
　　And here in Troy, for trespass of thine eye,
　　The sire, the son, the dame, and daughter die.

'Why should the private pleasure of some one
Become the public plague of many moe?
Let sin, alone committed, light alone   1480
Upon his head that hath transgressed so;
Let guiltless souls be freed from guilty woe.
　　For one's offence why should so many fall,
　　To plague a private sin in general?

'Lo, here weeps Hecuba, here Priam dies,
Here manly Hector faints, here Troilus swounds,
Here friend by friend in bloody channel lies,
And friend to friend gives unadvised wounds,
And one man's lust these many lives confounds;
　　Had doting Priam check'd his son's desire,   1490
　　Troy had been bright with fame and not with fire.'

Here feelingly she weeps Troy's painted woes,
For sorrow, like a heavy-hanging bell,

Once set on ringing, with his own weight goes;
Then little strength rings out the doleful knell.
So Lucrece, set a-work, sad tales doth tell
 To pencill'd pensiveness and colour'd sorrow;
 She lends them words, and she their looks doth
  borrow.

She throws her eyes about the painting round,
And who she finds forlorn she doth lament.   1500
At last she sees a wretched image bound
That piteous looks to Phrygian shepherds lent.
His face, though full of cares, yet show'd content;
 Onward to Troy with the blunt swains he goes,
 So mild that Patience seem'd to scorn his woes.

In him the painter labour'd with his skill
To hide deceit, and give the harmless show
An humble gait, calm looks, eyes wailing still,
A brow unbent that seem'd to welcome woe;
Cheeks neither red nor pale, but mingled so   1510
 That blushing red no guilty instance gave,
 Nor ashy pale the fear that false hearts have.

But, like a constant and confirmed devil,
He entertain'd a show so seeming just,
And therein so ensconc'd his secret evil,
That jealousy itself could not mistrust
False-creeping craft and perjury should thrust
 Into so bright a day such black-fac'd storms,
 Or blot with hell-born sin such saint-like forms.

The well-skill'd workman this mild image drew   1520
For perjur'd Sinon, whose enchanting story
The credulous old Priam after slew;
Whose words like wildfire burnt the shining glory
Of rich-built Ilion, that the skies were sorry,
    And little stars shot from their fixed places
    When their glass fell wherein they view'd their faces.

This picture she advisedly perus'd,
And chid the painter for his wondrous skill,
Saying some shape in Sinon's was abus'd;
So fair a form lodg'd not a mind so ill.   1530
And still on him she gaz'd; and gazing still
    Such signs of truth in his plain face she spied
    That she concludes the picture was belied.

'It cannot be,' quoth she, 'that so much guile'—
She would have said 'can lurk in such a look;'
But Tarquin's shape came in her mind the while,
And from her tongue 'can lurk' from 'cannot' took.
'It cannot be,' she in that sense forsook,
    And turn'd it thus: 'It cannot be, I find,
    But such a face should bear a wicked mind;   1540

'For even as subtle Sinon here is painted,
So sober-sad, so weary, and so mild,
As if with grief or travail he had fainted
To me came Tarquin armed, so beguil'd
With outward honesty, but yet defil'd

With inward vice. As Priam him did cherish,
So did I Tarquin; so my Troy did perish.

' Look, look, how listening Priam wets his eyes
To see those borrow'd tears that Sinon sheds !—
Priam, why art thou old and yet not wise?   1550
For every tear he falls a Trojan bleeds.
His eye drops fire, no water thence proceeds;
   Those round clear pearls of his that move thy pity
   Are balls of quenchless fire to burn thy city.

' Such devils steal effects from lightless hell;
For Sinon in his fire doth quake with cold,
And in that cold hot-burning fire doth dwell.
These contraries such unity do hold
Only to flatter fools and make them bold;
   So Priam's trust false Sinon's tears doth flatter   1560
   That he finds means to burn his Troy with water.'

Here, all enrag'd, such passion her assails
That patience is quite beaten from her breast.
She tears the senseless Sinon with her nails,
Comparing him to that unhappy guest
Whose deed hath made herself herself detest.
   At last she smilingly with this gives o'er:
   ' Fool, fool!' quoth she, ' his wounds will not be sore.'

Thus ebbs and flows the current of her sorrow,
And time doth weary time with her complaining.   1570

She looks for night, and then she longs for morrow,
And both she thinks too long with her remaining.
Short time seems long in sorrow's sharp sustaining;
 Though woe be heavy, yet it seldom sleeps,
 And they that watch see time how slow it creeps.

Which all this time hath overslipp'd her thought
That she with painted images hath spent;
Being from the feeling of her own grief brought
By deep surmise of others' detriment,
Losing her woes in shows of discontent.   1580
 It easeth some, though none it ever cur'd,
 To think their dolour others have endur'd.

But now the mindful messenger, come back,
Brings home his lord and other company,
Who finds his Lucrece clad in mourning black;
And round about her tear-distained eye
Blue circles stream'd, like rainbows in the sky.
 These water-galls in her dim element
 Foretell new storms to those already spent.

Which when her sad-beholding husband saw, 1590
Amazedly in her sad face he stares;
Her eyes, though sod in tears, look'd red and raw,
Her lively colour kill'd with deadly cares.
He hath no power to ask her how she fares;
 Both stood, like old acquaintance in a trance,
 Met far from home, wondering each other's chance.

At last he takes her by the bloodless hand,
And thus begins : ' What uncouth ill event
Hath thee befallen, that thou dost trembling stand ?
Sweet love, what spite hath thy fair colour spent? 1600
Why art thou thus attir'd in discontent ?
   Unmask, dear dear, this moody heaviness
   And tell thy grief, that we may give redress.'

Three times with sighs she gives her sorrow fire
Ere once she can discharge one word of woe ;
At length address'd to answer his desire,
She modestly prepares to let them know
Her honour is ta'en prisoner by the foe,
   While Collatine and his consorted lords
   With sad attention long to hear her words. 1610

And now this pale swan in her watery nest
Begins the sad dirge of her certain ending.
' Few words,' quoth she, ' shall fit the trespass best
Where no excuse can give the fault amending ;
In me moe woes than words are now depending,
   And my laments would be drawn out too long
   To tell them all with one poor tired tongue.

' Then be this all the task it hath to say :
Dear husband, in the interest of thy bed
A stranger came, and on that pillow lay 1620
Where thou wast wont to rest thy weary head ;
And what wrong else may be imagined

By foul enforcement might be done to me,
From that, alas, thy Lucrece is not free.

' For in the dreadful dead of dark midnight,
With shining falchion in my chamber came
A creeping creature, with a flaming light,
And softly cried " Awake, thou Roman dame,
And entertain my love ; else lasting shame
  On thee and thine this night I will inflict   1630
  If thou my love's desire do contradict.

' " For some hard-favour'd groom of thine," quoth he,
" Unless thou yoke thy liking to my will,
I 'll murther straight, and then I 'll slaughter thee
And swear I found you where you did fulfil
The loathsome act of lust, and so did kill
  The lechers in their deed ; this act will be
  My fame and thy perpetual infamy."

' With this, I did begin to start and cry;
And then against my heart he sets his sword,   1640
Swearing, unless I took all patiently,
I should not live to speak another word ;
So should my shame still rest upon record,
  And never be forgot in mighty Rome
  The adulterate death of Lucrece and her groom.

' Mine enemy was strong, my poor self weak,
And far the weaker with so strong a fear.

My bloody judge forbade my tongue to speak;
No rightful plea might plead for justice there.
His scarlet lust came evidence to swear   1650
  That my poor beauty had purloin'd his eyes;
  And when the judge is robb'd the prisoner dies.

' O, teach me how to make mine own excuse !
Or at the least this refuge let me find:
Though my gross blood be stain'd with this abuse,
Immaculate and spotless is my mind;
That was not forc'd, that never was inclin'd
  To accessary yieldings, but still pure
  Doth in her poison'd closet yet endure.'

Lo, here, the hopeless merchant of this loss,   1660
With head declin'd, and voice damm'd up with woe,
With sad-set eyes, and wretched arms across,
From lips new-waxen pale begins to blow
The grief away that stops his answer so,
  But, wretched as he is, he strives in vain;
  What he breaths out his breath drinks up again.

As through an arch the violent roaring tide
Outruns the eye that doth behold his haste,
Yet in the eddy boundeth in his pride
Back to the strait that forc'd him on so fast,   1670
In rage sent out, recall'd in rage, being past;
  Even so his sighs, his sorrows, make a saw,
  To push grief on, and back the same grief draw.

Which speechless woe of his poor she attendeth
And his untimely frenzy thus awaketh:
' Dear lord, thy sorrow to my sorrow lendeth
Another power; no flood by raining slaketh.
My woe too sensible thy passion maketh
   More feeling-painful; let it then suffice
     To drown one woe, one pair of weeping eyes.   1680

' And for my sake, when I might charm thee so,
For she that was thy Lucrece, now attend me:
Be suddenly revenged on my foe,
Thine, mine, his own; suppose thou dost defend me
From what is past. The help that thou shalt lend me
   Comes all too late, yet let the traitor die,
     For sparing justice feeds iniquity.

' But ere I name him, you fair lords,' quoth she,
Speaking to those that came with Collatine,
' Shall plight your honourable faiths to me,   1690
With swift pursuit to venge this wrong of mine;
For 't is a meritorious fair design
   To chase injustice with revengeful arms.
     Knights, by their oaths, should right poor ladies'
       harms.'

At this request, with noble disposition
Each present lord began to promise aid,
As bound in knighthood to her imposition,
Longing to hear the hateful foe bewray'd.
But she, that yet her sad task hath not said,

The protestation stops. 'O, speak,' quoth she,   1709
'How may this forced stain be wip'd from me?

'What is the quality of mine offence,
Being constrain'd with dreadful circumstance?
May my pure mind with the foul act dispense,
My low-declined honour to advance?
May any terms acquit me from this chance?
   The poison'd fountain clears itself again;
   And why not I from this compelled stain?'

With this, they all at once began to say
Her body's stain her mind untainted clears;   1710
While with a joyless smile she turns away
The face, that map which deep impression bears
Of hard misfortune, carv'd in it with tears.
   'No, no,' quoth she, 'no dame, hereafter living,
   By my excuse shall claim excuse's giving.'

Here with a sigh, as if her heart would break,
She throws forth Tarquin's name: 'He, he,' she says,
But more than 'he' her poor tongue could not speak;
Till after many accents and delays,
Untimely breathings, sick and short assays,   1720
   She utters this: 'He, he, fair lords, 't is he
   That guides this hand to give this wound to me.'

Even here she sheathed in her harmless breast
A harmful knife that thence her soul unsheath'd.

That blow did bail it from the deep unrest
Of that polluted prison where it breath'd;
Her contrite sighs unto the clouds bequeath'd
   Her winged sprite, and through her wounds doth fly
   Life's lasting date from cancell'd destiny.

Stone-still, astonish'd with this deadly deed,   1730
Stood Collatine and all his lordly crew,
Till Lucrece' father, that beholds her bleed,
Himself on her self-slaughter'd body threw,
And from the purple fountain Brutus drew
   The murtherous knife, and, as it left the place,
   Her blood, in poor revenge, held it in chase;

And bubbling from her breast it doth divide
In two slow rivers, that the crimson blood
Circles her body in on every side,
Who, like a late-sack'd island, vastly stood   1740
Bare and unpeopled in this fearful flood.
   Some of her blood still pure and red remain'd,
   And some look'd black and that false Tarquin stain'd.

About the mourning and congealed face
Of that black blood a watery rigol goes,
Which seems to weep upon the tainted place;
And ever since, as pitying Lucrece' woes,
Corrupted blood some watery token shows,
   And blood untainted still doth red abide,
   Blushing at that which is so putrefied.   1750

'Daughter, dear daughter,' old Lucretius cries,
'That life was mine which thou hast here depriv'd.
If in the child the father's image lies,
Where shall I live now Lucrece is unliv'd?
Thou wast not to this end from me deriv'd.
    If children pre-decease progenitors,
    We are their offspring, and they none of ours.

'Poor broken glass, I often did behold
In thy sweet semblance my old age new born;
But now that fair fresh mirror, dim and old,   1760
Shows me a bare-bon'd death by time outworn.
O, from thy cheeks my image thou hast torn
    And shiver'd all the beauty of my glass,
    That I no more can see what once I was!

'O time, cease thou thy course and last no longer,
If they surcease to be that should survive.
Shall rotten death make conquest of the stronger
And leave the faltering feeble souls alive?
The old bees die, the young possess their hive;
    Then live, sweet Lucrece, live again and see   1770
    Thy father die, and not thy father thee!'

By this, starts Collatine as from a dream
And bids Lucretius give his sorrow place;
And then in key-cold Lucrece' bleeding stream
He falls, and bathes the pale fear in his face,
And counterfeits to die with her a space,

Till manly shame bids him possess his breath
And live to be revenged on her death.

The deep vexation of his inward soul
Hath serv'd a dumb arrest upon his tongue,   1780
Who, mad that sorrow should his use control
Or keep him from heart-easing words so long,
Begins to talk; but through his lips do throng
   Weak words, so thick come in his poor heart's aid
   That no man could distinguish what he said.

Yet sometime 'Tarquin' was pronounced plain,
But through his teeth, as if the name he tore.
This windy tempest, till it blow up rain,
Held back his sorrow's tide to make it more;
At last it rains, and busy winds give o'er.   1790
   Then son and father weep with equal strife
   Who should weep most, for daughter or for wife.

The one doth call her his, the other his,
Yet neither may possess the claim they lay.
The father says 'She's mine.' 'O, mine she is,'
Replies her husband; 'do not take away
My sorrow's interest, let no mourner say
   He weeps for her, for she was only mine
   And only must be wail'd by Collatine.'

'O,' quoth Lucretius, 'I did give that life   1800
Which she too early and too late hath spill'd.'

'Woe, woe,' quoth Collatine, 'she was my wife,
I owed her, and 't is mine that she hath kill'd.'
'My daughter' and 'my wife' with clamours fill'd
    The dispers'd air, who, holding Lucrece' life,
    Answer'd their cries, 'my daughter' and 'my wife.'

Brutus, who pluck'd the knife from Lucrece' side,
Seeing such emulation in their woe,
Began to clothe his wit in state and pride,
Burying in Lucrece' wound his folly's show.   1810
He with the Romans was esteemed so
    As silly-jeering idiots are with kings,
    For sportive words and uttering foolish things ;

But now he throws that shallow habit by
Wherein deep policy did him disguise,
And arm'd his long-hid wits advisedly,
To check the tears in Collatinus' eyes.
'Thou wronged lord of Rome,' quoth he, 'arise ;
    Let my unsounded self, suppos'd a fool,
    Now set thy long-experienc'd wit to school.   1820

'Why, Collatine, is woe the cure for woe?
Do wounds help wounds, or grief help grievous deeds ?
Is it revenge to give thyself a blow
For his foul act by whom thy fair wife bleeds ?
Such childish humour from weak minds proceeds ;
    Thy wretched wife mistook the matter so,
    To slay herself that should have slain her foe.

'Courageous Roman, do not steep thy heart
In such relenting dew of lamentations;
But kneel with me and help to bear thy part   1830
To rouse our Roman gods with invocations
That they will suffer these abominations,
    Since Rome herself in them doth stand disgrac'd,
    By our strong arms from forth her fair streets chas'd.

'Now, by the Capitol that we adore,
And by this chaste blood so unjustly stain'd,
By heaven's fair sun that breeds the fat earth's store,
By all our country rights in Rome maintain'd,
And by chaste Lucrece' soul that late complain'd
    Her wrongs to us, and by this bloody knife,   1840
    We will revenge the death of this true wife.'

This said, he struck his hand upon his breast,
And kiss'd the fatal knife, to end his vow;
And to his protestation urg'd the rest,
Who, wondering at him, did his words allow.
Then jointly to the ground their knees they bow;
    And that deep vow which Brutus made before
    He doth again repeat, and that they swore.

When they had sworn to this advised doom,
They did conclude to bear dead Lucrece thence,   1850
To show her bleeding body thorough Rome,
And so to publish Tarquin's foul offence;
Which being done with speedy diligence,
    The Romans plausibly did give consent
    To Tarquin's everlasting banishment.

A LOVER'S COMPLAINT,
THE PASSIONATE PILGRIM, Etc.

A LOVER'S COMPLAINT

From off a hill whose concave womb re-worded
A plaintful story from a sistering vale,
My spirits to attend this double voice accorded,
And down I laid to list the sad-tun'd tale;
Ere long espied a fickle maid full pale,
Tearing of papers, breaking rings a-twain,
Storming her world with sorrow's wind and rain.

Upon her head a platted hive of straw,
Which fortified her visage from the sun,
Whereon the thought might think sometime it saw   10
The carcass of a beauty spent and done;
Time had not scythed all that youth begun,

Nor youth all quit, but, spite of heaven's fell rage,
Some beauty peep'd through lattice of sear'd age.

Oft did she heave her napkin to her eyne,
Which on it had conceited characters,
Laundering the silken figures in the brine
That season'd woe had pelleted in tears,
And often reading what contents it bears;
As often shrieking undistinguish'd woe,   20
In clamours of all size, both high and low.

Sometimes her levell'd eyes their carriage ride,
As they did battery to the spheres intend;
Sometime diverted their poor balls are tied
To the orbed earth; sometimes they do extend
Their view right on; anon their gazes lend
To every place at once, and, nowhere fix'd,
The mind and sight distractedly commix'd.

Her hair, nor loose nor tied in formal plat,
Proclaim'd in her a careless hand of pride,   30
For some, untuck'd, descended her sheav'd hat,
Hanging her pale and pined cheek beside;
Some in her threaden fillet still did bide,
And true to bondage would not break from thence,
Though slackly braided in loose negligence.

A thousand favours from a maund she drew
Of amber, crystal, and of beaded jet,

Which one by one she in a river threw
Upon whose weeping margent she was set;
Like usury, applying wet to wet,   40
Or monarch's hands that let not bounty fall
Where want cries some, but where excess begs all.

Of folded schedules had she many a one,
Which she perus'd, sigh'd, tore, and gave the flood;
Crack'd many a ring of posied gold and bone,
Bidding them find their sepulchres in mud;
Found yet moe letters sadly penn'd in blood,
With sleided silk feat and affectedly
Enswath'd, and seal'd to curious secrecy.

These often bath'd she in her fluxive eyes,   50
And often kiss'd, and often gan to tear:
Cried ' O false blood, thou register of lies,
What unapproved witness dost thou bear!
Ink would have seem'd more black and damned here!'
This said, in top of rage the lines she rents,
Big discontent so breaking their contents.

A reverend man that graz'd his cattle nigh —
Sometime a blusterer, that the ruffle knew
Of court, of city, and had let go by
The swiftest hours, observed as they flew —   60
Towards this afflicted fancy fastly drew,
And, privileg'd by age, desires to know
In brief the grounds and motives of her woe.

So slides he down upon his grained bat,
And comely-distant sits he by her side,
When he again desires her, being sat,
Her grievance with his hearing to divide;
If that from him there may be aught applied
Which may her suffering ecstasy assuage,
'T is promis'd in the charity of age.   70

'Father,' she says, 'though in me you behold
The injury of many a blasting hour,
Let it not tell your judgment I am old;
Not age, but sorrow, over me hath power.
I might as yet have been a spreading flower,
Fresh to myself, if I had self-applied
Love to myself and to no love beside.

'But, woe is me! too early I attended
A youthful suit — it was to gain my grace —
Of one by nature's outwards so commended   80
That maidens' eyes stuck over all his face;
Love lack'd a dwelling and made him her place,
And when in his fair parts she did abide
She was new lodg'd and newly deified.

'His browny locks did hang in crooked curls,
And every light occasion of the wind
Upon his lips their silken parcels hurls.
What's sweet to do, to do will aptly find;
Each eye that saw him did enchant the mind,

For on his visage was in little drawn　90
What largeness thinks in Paradise was sawn.

' Small show of man was yet upon his chin ;
His phœnix down began but to appear
Like unshorn velvet on that termless skin
Whose bare out-bragg'd the web it seem'd to wear.
Yet show'd his visage by that cost more dear,
And nice affections wavering stood in doubt
If best were as it was, or best without.

' His qualities were beauteous as his form,
For maiden-tongued he was, and thereof free ;　100
Yet, if men mov'd him, was he such a storm
As oft 'twixt May and April is to see,
When winds breathe sweet, unruly though they be.
His rudeness so with his authoriz'd youth
Did livery falseness in a pride of truth.

' Well could he ride, and often men would say
" That horse his mettle from his rider takes ;
Proud of subjection, noble by the sway,
What rounds, what bounds, what course, what stop he
　　makes ! "
And controversy hence a question takes,　110
Whether the horse by him became his deed,
Or he his manage by the well-doing steed.

' But quickly on this side the verdict went :
His real habitude gave life and grace

To appertainings and to ornament,
Accomplish'd in himself, not in his case.
All aids, themselves made fairer by their place,
Came for additions ; yet their purpos'd trim
Piec'd not his grace, but were all grac'd by him.

' So on the tip of his subduing tongue   120
All kind of arguments and question deep,
All replication prompt and reason strong,
For his advantage still did wake and sleep.
To make the weeper laugh, the laugher weep,
He had the dialect and different skill,
Catching all passions in his craft of will ;

' That he did in the general bosom reign
Of young, of old, and sexes both enchanted,
To dwell with him in thoughts, or to remain
In personal duty, following where he haunted.   130
Consents bewitch'd, ere he desire, have granted,
And dialogu'd for him what he would say,
Ask'd their own wills, and made their wills obey.

' Many there were that did his picture get,
To serve their eyes, and in it put their mind ;
Like fools that in the imagination set
The goodly objects which abroad they find
Of lands and mansions, theirs in thought assign'd,
And labouring in moe pleasures to bestow them   139
Than the true gouty landlord which doth owe them.

' So many have that never touch'd his hand
Sweetly suppos'd them mistress of his heart.
My woeful self, that did in freedom stand
And was my own fee-simple, not in part,
What with his art in youth and youth in art,
Threw my affections in his charmed power,
Reserv'd the stalk and gave him all my flower.

' Yet did I not, as some my equals did,
Demand of him, nor being desired yielded;
Finding myself in honour so forbid,   150
With safest distance I mine honour shielded.
Experience for me many bulwarks builded
Of proofs new-bleeding, which remain'd the foil
Of this false jewel, and his amorous spoil.

' But, ah, who ever shunn'd by precedent
The destin'd ill she must herself assay?
Or forc'd examples, 'gainst her own content,
To put the by-past perils in her way?
Counsel may stop awhile what will not stay;
For when we rage, advice is often seen   160
By blunting us to make our wits more keen.

' Nor gives it satisfaction to our blood
That we must curb it upon others' proof;
To be forbod the sweets that seem so good,
For fear of harms that preach in our behoof.
O appetite, from judgment stand aloof!

The one a palate hath that needs will taste,
Though Reason weep, and cry " It is thy last."

' For further I could say " This man 's untrue,"
And knew the patterns of his foul beguiling,   170
Heard where his plants in others' orchards grew,
Saw how deceits were gilded in his smiling,
Knew vows were ever brokers to defiling,
Thought characters and words merely but art
And bastards of his foul adulterate heart.

' And long upon these terms I held my city,
Till thus he gan besiege me : " Gentle maid,
Have of my suffering youth some feeling pity,
And be not of my holy vows afraid.
That 's to ye sworn to none was ever said ;   180
For feasts of love I have been call'd unto,
Till now did ne'er invite, nor never woo.

' " All my offences that abroad you see
Are errors of the blood, none of the mind.
Love made them not ; with acture they may be,
Where neither party is nor true nor kind.
They sought their shame that so their shame did find ;
And so much less of shame in me remains,
By how much of me their reproach contains.

' " Among the many that mine eyes have seen,   190
Not one whose flame my heart so much as warm'd,

Or my affection put to the smallest teen,
Or any of my leisures ever charm'd ;
Harm have I done to them, but ne'er was harm'd,
Kept hearts in liveries, but mine own was free,
And reign'd, commanding in his monarchy.

' " Look here, what tributes wounded fancies sent me,
Of paled pearls and rubies red as blood ;
Figuring that they their passions likewise lent me
Of grief and blushes, aptly understood   200
In bloodless white and the encrimson'd mood ;
Effects of terror and dear modesty,
Encamp'd in hearts, but fighting outwardly.

' " And, lo, behold these talents of their hair,
With twisted metal amorously impleach'd,
I have receiv'd from many a several fair;
Their kind acceptance weepingly beseech'd,
With the annexions of fair gems enrich'd,
And deep-brain'd sonnets that did amplify
Each stone's dear nature, worth, and quality.   210

' " The diamond, — why, 't was beautiful and hard,
Whereto his invis'd properties did tend ;
The deep-green emerald, in whose fresh regard
Weak sights their sickly radiance do amend ;
The heaven-hued sapphire and the opal blend
With objects manifold ; each several stone,
With wit well blazon'd, smil'd or made some moan.

' " Lo, all these trophies of affections hot,
Of pensiv'd and subdued desires the tender,
Nature hath charg'd me that I hoard them not,   220
But yield them up where I myself must render,
That is, to you, my origin and ender ;
For these, of force, must your oblations be,
Since, I their altar, you enpatron me.

' " O, then, advance of yours that phraseless hand,
Whose white weighs down the airy scale of praise ;
Take all these similes to your own command,
Hallow'd with sighs that burning lungs did raise.
What me your minister, for you obeys,
Works under you ; and to your audit comes   230
Their distract parcels in combined sums.

' " Lo, this device was sent me from a nun,
A sister sanctified, of holiest note,
Which late her noble suit in court did shun,
Whose rarest havings made the blossoms dote ;
For she was sought by spirits of richest coat,
But kept cold distance, and did thence remove,
To spend her living in eternal love.

' " But, O my sweet, what labour is 't to leave
The thing we have not, mastering what not strives,
Paling the place which did no form receive,   241
Playing patient sports in unconstrained gyves ?
She that her fame so to herself contrives

The scars of battle scapeth by the flight,
And makes her absence valiant, not her might.

'"O, pardon me, in that my boast is true;
The accident which brought me to her eye
Upon the moment did her force subdue,
And now she would the caged cloister fly.
Religious love put out Religion's eye;   250
Not to be tempted, would she be immur'd,
And now, to tempt, all liberty procur'd.

'"How mighty then you are, O, hear me tell!
The broken bosoms that to me belong
Have emptied all their fountains in my well,
And mine I pour your ocean all among;
I strong o'er them, and you o'er me being strong,
Must for your victory us all congest,
As compound love to physic your cold breast.

'"My parts had power to charm a sacred nun,   260
Who, disciplin'd, ay, dieted in grace,
Believ'd her eyes when they to assail begun,
All vows and consecrations giving place;
O most potential love! vow, bond, nor space,
In thee hath neither sting, knot, nor confine,
For thou art all, and all things else are thine.

'"When thou impressest, what are precepts worth
Of stale example?   When thou wilt inflame,

How coldly those impediments stand forth
Of wealth, of filial fear, law, kindred, fame !   270
Love's arms are proof 'gainst rule, 'gainst sense, 'gainst
    shame,
And sweetens, in the suffering pangs it bears,
The aloes of all forces, shocks, and fears.

' " Now all these hearts that do on mine depend,
Feeling it break, with bleeding groans they pine;
And supplicant their sighs to you extend,
To leave the battery that you make 'gainst mine,
Lending soft audience to my sweet design,
And credent soul to that strong-bonded oath
That shall prefer and undertake my troth."   280

' This said, his watery eyes he did dismount,
Whose sights till then were levell'd on my face;
Each cheek a river running from a fount
With brinish current downward flow'd apace.
O, how the channel to the stream gave grace !
Who glaz'd with crystal gate the glowing roses
That flame through water which their hue encloses.

' O father, what a hell of witchcraft lies
In the small orb of one particular tear !
But with the inundation of the eyes   290
What rocky heart to water will not wear ?
What breast so cold that is not warmed here ?
O cleft effect ! cold modesty, hot wrath,
Both fire from hence and chill extincture hath.

' For, lo, his passion, but an art of craft,
Even there resolv'd my reason into tears;
There my white stole of chastity I daff'd,
Shook off my sober guards and civil fears,
Appear to him, as he to me appears,
All melting; though our drops this difference bore,   300
His poison'd me, and mine did him restore.

' In him a plenitude of subtle matter,
Applied to cautels, all strange forms receives,
Of burning blushes, or of weeping water,
Or swooning paleness; and he takes and leaves,
In either's aptness, as it best deceives, —
To blush at speeches rank, to weep at woes,
Or to turn white and swoon at tragic shows;

' That not a heart which in his level came
Could scape the hail of his all-hurting aim,   310
Showing fair nature is both kind and tame,
And, veil'd in them, did win whom he would maim.
Against the thing he sought he would exclaim;
When he most burn'd in heart-wish'd luxury
He preach'd pure maid and prais'd cold chastity.

' Thus merely with the garment of a Grace
The naked and concealed fiend he cover'd,
That the unexperient gave the tempter place,
Which like a cherubin above them hover'd.
Who, young and simple, would not be so lover'd?   320

Ay me! I fell, and yet do question make
What I should do again for such a sake.

'O, that infected moisture of his eye,
O, that false fire which in his cheek so glow'd,
O, that forc'd thunder from his heart did fly,
O, that sad breath his spongy lungs bestow'd,
O, all that borrow'd motion seeming owed,
Would yet again betray the fore-betray'd
And new pervert a reconciled maid!'

THE PASSIONATE PILGRIM

I

Sweet Cytherea, sitting by a brook
With young Adonis, lovely, fresh, and green,
Did court the lad with many a lovely look,
Such looks as none could look but beauty's queen.
She told him stories to delight his ear;
She show'd him favours to allure his eye;
To win his heart, she touch'd him here and there,—
Touches so soft still conquer chastity.
But whether unripe years did want conceit,
Or he refus'd to take her figur'd proffer,
The tender nibbler would not touch the bait,
But smile and jest at every gentle offer.
    Then fell she on her back, fair queen, and toward;
    He rose and ran away—ah, fool too froward!

II

Scarce had the sun dried up the dewy morn,
And scarce the herd gone to the hedge for shade,
When Cytherea, all in love forlorn,
A longing tarriance for Adonis made
Under an osier growing by a brook,
A brook where Adon us'd to cool his spleen.
Hot was the day; she hotter that did look
For his approach that often there had been.
Anon he comes, and throws his mantle by,
And stood stark naked on the brook's green brim;
The sun look'd on the world with glorious eye,
Yet not so wistly as this queen on him.
  He, spying her, bounc'd in, whereas he stood;
  'O Jove,' quoth she, 'why was not I a flood!'

III

Fair was the morn when the fair queen of love,
  *   *   *   *   *   *
Paler for sorrow than her milk-white dove,
For Adon's sake, a youngster proud and wild.
Her stand she takes upon a steep-up hill.
Anon Adonis comes with horn and hounds;
She, silly queen, with more than love's good will,
Forbade the boy he should not pass those grounds.
'Once,' quoth she, 'did I see a fair sweet youth
Here in these brakes deep-wounded with a boar,

Deep in the thigh, a spectacle of ruth!
See, in my thigh,' quoth she, ' here was the sore.'
   She showed hers; he saw more wounds than one,
   And blushing fled and left her all alone.

IV

Fair is my love, but not so fair as fickle;
Mild as a dove, but neither true nor trusty;
Brighter than glass, and yet, as glass is, brittle;
Softer than wax, and yet, as iron, rusty:
   A lily pale, with damask dye to grace her,
   None fairer, nor none falser to deface her.

Her lips to mine how often hath she joined,
Between each kiss her oaths of true love swearing!
How many tales to please me hath she coined,
Dreading my love, the loss thereof still fearing!
   Yet in the midst of all her pure protestings,
   Her faith, her oaths, her tears, and all were jestings.

She burn'd with love, as straw with fire flameth;
She burn'd out love, as soon as straw out-burneth;
She fram'd the love, and yet she foil'd the framing;
She bade love last, and yet she fell a-turning.
   Was this a lover, or a lecher whether?
   Bad in the best, though excellent in neither.

V

Sweet rose, fair flower, untimely pluck'd, soon vaded,
Pluck'd in the bud, and vaded in the spring!

Bright orient pearl, alack, too timely shaded!
Fair creature, kill'd too soon by death's sharp sting!
  Like a green plum that hangs upon a tree,
  And falls, through wind, before the fall should be.

I weep for thee, and yet no cause I have;
For why, thou left'st me nothing in thy will.
And yet thou left'st me more than I did crave;
For why, I craved nothing of thee still.
  O yes, dear friend, I pardon crave of thee,
  Thy discontent thou didst bequeath to me.

VI

Crabbed age and youth cannot live together.
Youth is full of pleasance, age is full of care;
Youth like summer morn, age like winter weather;
Youth like summer brave, age like winter bare.
Youth is full of sport, age's breath is short;
  Youth is nimble, age is lame;
Youth is hot and bold, age is weak and cold;
  Youth is wild, and age is tame.
Age, I do abhor thee; youth, I do adore thee;
  O, my love, my love is young!
Age, I do defy thee; O, sweet shepherd, hie thee,
  For methinks thou stay'st too long.

VII

Beauty is but a vain and doubtful good;
A shining gloss that vadeth suddenly;

A flower that dies when first it gins to bud;
A brittle glass that's broken presently:
  A doubtful good, a gloss, a glass, a flower,
  Lost, vaded, broken, dead within an hour.

And as goods lost are seld or never found,
As vaded gloss no rubbing will refresh,
As flowers dead lie wither'd on the ground,
As broken glass no cement can redress,
  So beauty blemish'd once 's for ever lost,
  In spite of physic, painting, pain, and cost.

VIII

Good night, good rest. Ah, neither be my share!
She bade good night that kept my rest away,
And daff'd me to a cabin hang'd with care,
To descant on the doubts of my decay.
  'Farewell,' quoth she, 'and come again to-morrow;'
  Fare well I could not, for I supp'd with sorrow.

Yet at my parting sweetly did she smile,
In scorn or friendship, nill I construe whether;
'T may be, she joy'd to jest at my exile,
'T may be, again to make me wander thither,—   10
  'Wander,' a word for shadows like myself,
  As take the pain, but cannot pluck the pelf.

Lord, how mine eyes throw gazes to the east!
My heart doth charge the watch; the morning rise

Doth cite each moving sense from idle rest.
Not daring trust the office of mine eyes,
  While Philomela sits and sings, I sit and mark,
  And wish her lays were tuned like the lark;

For she doth welcome daylight with her ditty,
And drives away dark dismal-dreaming night.   20
The night so pack'd, I post unto my pretty;
Heart hath his hope, and eyes their wished sight;
  Sorrow chang'd to solace, solace mix'd with sorrow;
  For why, she sigh'd and bade me come to-morrow.

Were I with her, the night would post too soon;
But now are minutes added to the hours;
To spite me now, each minute seems a moon;
Yet not for me shine sun to succour flowers!   28
  Pack night, peep day; good day, of night now borrow;
  Short, night, to-night, and length thyself to-morrow.

IX

Whenas thine eye hath chose the dame,
And stall'd the deer that thou shouldst strike,
Let reason rule things worthy blame,
As well as partial fancy like;
  Take counsel of some wiser head,
  Neither too young nor yet unwed.

And when thou com'st thy tale to tell,
Smooth not thy tongue with filed talk,

Lest she some subtle practice smell, —
A cripple soon can find a halt ; —   10
   But plainly say thou lov'st her well,
   And set her person forth to sell.

What though her frowning brows be bent,
Her cloudy looks will clear ere night ;
And then too late she will repent
That thus dissembled her delight,
   And twice desire, ere it be day,
   That which with scorn she put away.

What though she strive to try her strength,
And ban and brawl, and say thee nay,   20
Her feeble force will yield at length,
When craft hath taught her thus to say,
   ' Had women been so strong as men,
   In faith, you had not had it then.'

And to her will frame all thy ways ;
Spare not to spend, and chiefly there
Where thy desert may merit praise,
By ringing in thy lady's ear.
   The strongest castle, tower, and town,
   The golden bullet beats it down.   30

Serve always with assured trust,
And in thy suit be humble-true ;
Unless thy lady prove unjust,
Press never thou to choose anew.

When time shall serve, be thou not slack
To proffer, though she put thee back.

The wiles and guiles that women work,
Dissembled with an outward show,
The tricks and toys that in them lurk,
The cock that treads them shall not know.   40
    Have you not heard it said full oft,
    A woman's nay doth stand for nought?

Think women still to strive with men,
To sin and never for to saint.
Here is no heaven; be holy then,
When time with age shall thee attaint.
    Were kisses all the joys in bed,
    One woman would another wed.

But, soft! enough — too much, I fear —
Lest that my mistress hear my song;   50
She will not stick to round me i' the ear,
To teach my tongue to be so long;
    Yet will she blush, here be it said,
    To hear her secrets so bewray'd.

THE PHŒNIX AND THE TURTLE

LET the bird of loudest lay,
On the sole Arabian tree,
Herald sad and trumpet be,
To whose sound chaste wings obey.

But thou shrieking harbinger,
Foul precurrer of the fiend,
Augur of the fever's end,
To this troop come thou not near!

From this session interdict
Every fowl of tyrant wing,
Save the eagle, feather'd king;
Keep the obsequy so strict.

Let the priest in surplice white,
That defunctive music can,
Be the death-divining swan,
Lest the requiem lack his right.

And thou treble-dated crow,
That thy sable gender mak'st
With the breath thou giv'st and tak'st,
'Mongst our mourners shalt thou go.   20

Here the anthem doth commence:
Love and constancy is dead;
Phœnix and the turtle fled
In a mutual flame from hence.

So they lov'd as love in twain
Had the essence but in one,
Two distincts, division none;
Number there in love was slain.

Hearts remote, yet not asunder;
Distance, and no space was seen   30
'Twixt the turtle and his queen;
But in them it were a wonder.

So between them love did shine
That the turtle saw his right
Flaming in the phœnix' sight;
Either was the other's mine.

Property was thus appall'd,
That the self was not the same;
Single nature's double name
Neither two nor one was call'd.   40

Reason, in itself confounded,
Saw division grow together,
To themselves yet either neither,
Simple were so well compounded

That it cried, How true a twain
Seemeth this concordant one!
Love hath reason, reason none,
If what parts can so remain.

Whereupon it made this threne
To the phœnix and the dove,   50
Co-supremes and stars of love,
As chorus to their tragic scene.

THRENOS

Beauty, truth, and rarity,
Grace in all simplicity,
Here enclos'd in cinders lie.

Death is now the phœnix' nest,
And the turtle's loyal breast
To eternity doth rest,

Leaving no posterity ;
'T was not their infirmity,   60
It was married chastity.

Truth may seem, but cannot be ;
Beauty brag, but 't is not she ;
Truth and beauty buried be.

To this urn let those repair
That are either true or fair ;
For these dead birds sigh a prayer.

NOTES

FLIGHT OF TARQUIN

NOTES

VENUS AND ADONIS

THE EARLY EDITIONS. — Richard Field, the printer of the first ed. (see p. 9 above), was a native of Stratford, and the son of the Henry Field whose goods John Shakespeare was employed to value in 1592. He adopted the device of an anchor, with the motto "Anchora spei," because they had been used by his father-in-law, Thomas Vautrollier, a celebrated and learned printer, who resided in Blackfriars, and to whose business, at his death in 1589, Field succeeded.

The poem was licensed by the Archbishop of Canterbury (John Whitgift), and entered in the Stationers' Register, April 18, 1593.

The second edition, likewise printed and published by Field, must have been brought out early in 1594, as the transfer of the copyright from Field to Harrison is recorded as having taken place on the 25th of June in that year.

The third edition was printed by Field, though published by Harrison, and must have appeared before June, 1596, when Harrison transferred the copyright to Leake.

It is probable that there were editions between this of 1596 and that of 1599. The poem had evidently been very popular, and it would be strange if Leake did not issue an edition until three years after he had secured the copyright. When we consider that of several early eds. only single copies have come down to our day, and of others only two or three copies, it is not unreasonable to suppose that of some editions not a single copy has survived. It is also probable that there were editions between 1602 and 1627, when the poem was reprinted in Edinburgh. The edition published in 1599 (see p. 10 above) was not known until 1867; and the edition of 1630 (see p. 11) was discovered more recently.

It has been suggested that the book may have fallen under the ban of the Privy Council. A decree of the Star Chamber, dated June 23, 1585, gave unlimited power to the ecclesiastical authorities to seize and destroy whatever books they thought proper. A notable instance of this interference with books already printed occurred in 1599, at Stationers' Hall, when a number of objectionable works were burned, and special admonitions given then and there to the printers, some of the most eminent of the time, and among them our friend Richard Field (Edmonds).

THE METRE OF THE POEM. — The verse is the iambic measure, already familiar to the student of Shakespeare in the plays : the ten-syllable line, subject to the usual variations. The stanza is the "staffe of sixe verses" (*ab ab cc*) described by Puttenham in *The Arte of English Poesie*, 1589, as "not only most usual, but also very pleasant to th' eare." There is no reason to suppose, as some have done, that S. borrowed it from Lodge, though the latter used it in his *Scylla's Metamorphosis*, 1589, in which there is a slight allusion to the death of Adonis.

Verity notes "the extraordinary verbal beauty of the verse," which links it with the early plays, like *R. and J.* and *M. N. D.* "We have the same elaborate harmonies, the 'linked sweetness long drawn out,' the cadences, the 'dying falls,' the lyric charm and rapture of Shakespeare's earliest, most purely poetic style."

Coleridge has observed that, "in the *Venus and Adonis*, the first and most obvious excellence is the perfect sweetness of the versification ; its adaptation to the subject ; and the power displayed in varying the march of the words without passing into a loftier and more majestic rhythm than was demanded by the thoughts, or permitted by the propriety of preserving a sense of melody predominant." Knight, quoting this, adds : "This self-controlling power of 'varying the march of the words without passing into a loftier and more majestic rhythm' is perhaps one of the most signal instances of Shakspere's consummate mastery of his art, even as a very young man. He who, at the proper season, knew how to strike the grandest music within the compass of our own powerful and sonorous language, in his early productions breathes out his thoughts
>   'to the Dorian mood
> Of flutes and soft recorders.'

The sustained sweetness of the versification is never cloying ; and yet there are no violent contrasts, no sudden elevations : all is equable in its infinite variety. The early comedies are full of the same rare beauty. In *Love's Labour 's Lost*, *The Comedy of Errors*, and *A Midsummer-Night's Dream*, we have verses of alternate rhymes formed upon the same model as those of the *Venus and Adonis*, and producing the same feeling of placid delight by their exquisite harmony. The same principles on which he built the versification of the *Venus and Adonis* exhibited to him the grace which these elegiac harmonies would impart to the scenes of repose in the progress of a dramatic action."

THE DEDICATION. — For the *Earl of Southampton*, see p. 20 above. For a much fuller account, with the many poetical tributes paid him, see the *Variorum* of 1821, vol. xx. pp. 427–468.

6. *Invention.* Imagination; as often. Cf. *Sonn.* 38. 8, 76. 6, 103. 7, 105. 11, etc.

7. *Ear.* Plough, till. Cf. *Rich. II.* iii. 2. 212, *A. and C.* i. 2. 115, i. 4. 49, etc.

9. *Your Honour.* Your lordship; as often.

VENUS AND ADONIS. — The *motto* of the poem is from Ovid's *Amores* (i. 15), which at that time had not been translated into English. Marlowe's version appeared in or about 1598. This particular elegy in it was evidently by Ben Jonson. See *The Poetaster,* i. 1, where the couplet reads : —

> " Kneel hinds to trash : me let bright Phœbus swell
> With cups full flowing from the Muses' well."

In Marlowe the reading is : —

> " Let base-conceited wits admire vild things;
> Fair Phœbus lead me to the Muses' springs."

3. *Rose-cheek'd Adonis.* Marlowe applies the same epithet to the youth in his *Hero and Leander :* —

> " The men of wealthy Sestos every year,
> For his sake whom their goddess held so dear,
> Rose-cheek'd Adonis, kept a solemn feast."

Cf. *T. of A.* iv. 3. 86.

6. *Gins.* Some eds. print " 'gins; " but see any of the large dictionaries. Richardson says : " *Gin,* and the pret. *gan,* are in common use with our old writers without the prefix *be;* " and one of his examples (Hakluyt's *Voyages,* vol. i. p. 187 : " Therefore I ginne to wryte now of the see ") proves that the word had not ceased to be used, even *in prose,* in the time of S. The editors often confound obsolete simple words (like *fore, gree, scape,* etc.) with contractions of their compounds now in use. See on 53 below.

9. *Stain to all nymphs.* That is, by eclipsing them. Cf. *Cor.* i. 10. 18, *Sonn.* 109. 8, etc.

10. *Doves or roses.* Farmer conjectures "and" for *or;* but the latter is doubtless what S. wrote.

11. *With herself at strife.* Cf. 291 below.

16. *Honey.* For the adjective use, cf. 452 and 538 below.

19. *Satiety.* The first four eds. and the 10th have "sacietie."

20. *Famish them,* etc. Cf. *A. and C.* ii. 2. 241 : —

> "Other women cloy
> The appetites they feed ; but she makes hungry
> Where most she satisfies."

25. *His sweating palm.* Cf. *A. and C.* i. 2. 53 : "Nay, if an oily palm be not a fruitful prognostication," etc. See also 143 below, and *Oth.* iii. 4. 36 fol.

26. *Pith.* Vigour. Cf. *Hen. V.* iii. chor. 21 : "pith and puissance," etc. *Precedent =* indication.

29. *Enrag'd.* Mad with love and desire ; as in 317 below. Cf. *Much Ado,* ii. 3. 105 : "that she loves him with an enraged affection," etc.

32. *Her other.* The 5th and later eds. have "the other."

40. *Prove.* Try; as in 608 below.

50. *Maiden.* For the masculine use, cf. *K. John,* iv. 2. 52, I *Hen. IV.* v. 4. 134, etc.

51. *Hairs.* For the rhyme, see on 192 below.

53. *Miss.* Misbehaviour. Malone and others print "'miss," but it is not a contraction of *amiss.*

54. *Murthers.* The 1st, 2d, 3d, and 4th eds. have "murthers," the others "smothers."

55. *Empty eagle.* We have the same expression in 2 *Hen. VI.* iii. 1. 248 and 3 *Hen. VI.* i. 1. 268.

56. *Tires.* Tears and feeds ravenously upon. Cf. *Cymb.* iii. 4. 97, etc.

61. *Forc'd to content.* "Forced to content himself in a situation from which he had no means of escaping" (Steevens).

62. *Breatheth.* The reading of the first three eds. ; "breathing" in the 4th and the rest.

66. *Such distilling.* Walker would read "such-distilling."

71. *Rank.* Exuberant, high. Cf. the use of the noun in *K. John*, v. 4. 54 : —

> " And, like a bated and retired flood,
>   Leaving our rankness and irregular course,
>   Stoop low within those bounds we have o'erlook'd."

76. *Ashy-pale.* Malone at first made this refer to Adonis, but subsequently saw that it goes with *anger*.

78. *More.* Cf. *R. of L.* 332 : " A more rejoicing," etc.

82. *Take truce.* Make peace. Cf. *K. John*, iii. 1. 17 : " With my vex'd spirits I cannot take a truce," etc.

86. *Divedapper.* The didapper or dabchick (*Podiceps minor*); mentioned by S. only here.

90. *Winks.* Shuts his eyes; as in 121 below.

91. *Passenger.* Wayfarer; the only sense in S. Cf. *T. G. of V.* iv. 1, 72, v. 4. 15, etc.

94. *Yet her.* The reading of the first four eds.; the rest have " Yet in."

96. *Coy?* Contemptuous. Cf. 112 below. See also *T. G. of V.* i. 1. 30, etc.

97. *I have been woo'd*, etc. For other allusions to the loves of Mars and Venus, see *Temp.* iv. 1. 98, *A. and C.* i. 5. 18, etc.

100. *Jar.* Conflict.

104. *Crest.* Helmet ; as often.

106. *To toy.* All the early eds., except the 1st and 2d, have " To coy."

107. *Churlish drum.* Repeated in *K. John*, ii. 1. 79. and iii. 1. 303.

109. *He that overrul'd.* S. often confounds the inflections of personal pronouns.

118. *In the ground?* That is, on it. Cf. *M. N. D.* ii. 1. 85, etc.

119. *There.* Changed to " where " in the 4th and later eds.

123. *There are.* The reading of the 1st ed.; "there be" in the rest, except the 10th, which has "they be."

126. *Nor know not.* The 5th and later eds. read "nor know they."

133. *Hard-favour'd.* Hard-featured, ill-looking; as in 931 below. The hyphen in *wrinkled-old* is due to Malone.

134. *Ill-nurtur'd.* Ill-bred; used again in *2 Hen. VI.* i. 2. 42 : "Presumptuous dame, ill-nurtur'd Eleanor," etc.

135. *O'erworn.* Cf. *Rich. III.* i. 1. 81 : "The jealous, o'erworn widow," etc. In 866 below, the word is used of time = spent.

140. *Gray.* Explained by Malone, Hudson, and others as = blue (and so in sundry other passages), but I think it has its usual meaning.

142. *Plump.* The 4th ed. has "plumbe;" all the later ones (according to the Cambridge ed.) have "plum."

143. *Moist hand.* See on 25 above.

148. *No footing seen.* Malone quotes *Temp.* v. 1. 34 : —

> "And ye that on the sands with printless feet
> Do chase the ebbing Neptune," etc.

149. *Compact of fire.* Cf. *M. N. D.* v. 1. 8 : "of imagination all compact;" *A. Y. L.* ii. 7. 5 : "compact of jars," etc.

150. *Not gross to sink*, etc. Cf. *C. of E.* iii. 2. 52 : "Let Love, being light, be drowned if she sink."

153. *Doves.* Cf. *Temp.* iv. 1. 94, where Venus is referred to as "dove-drawn." See also 1190 below, and *R. and J.* ii. 5. 7.

156. *Heavy.* Burdensome; in antithesis to *light.*

160. *Complain on.* The 3d and subsequent eds. have "complain of." Cf. 544 below.

161. *Narcissus.* Cf. *R. of L.* 265 and *A. and C.* ii. 5. 96.

163. *Torches are made to light.* Cf. *M. for M.* i. 1. 33 : —

> "Heaven doth with us as we with torches do,
> Not light them for themselves."

166. *To themselves.* For themselves alone, "without producing

fruit or benefiting mankind" (Malone). Cf. 1180 below. See also *Sonn.* 13. 14.

177. *Titan.* The sun; as in *T. and C.* v. 10. 25, *R. and J.* ii. 3. 4, *Cymb.* iii. 4. 166, etc.

Tired is explained by Boswell as = attired; and Schmidt and Wyndham favour that explanation. Cf. *L. L. L.* iv. 2. 131 : "the tired horse." The word is here a dissyllable.

181. *Spright.* Spirit; as in *R. of L.* 121.

192. *Tears.* The rhyme was not so bad in the time of S. as now, *ea* in many words being pronounced like long *a*. *Hairs* is spelled *heares* in the early eds. Cf. 51 above.

193. *Shines but warm.* "Affords only a natural and genial heat; it warms but it does not burn" (Malone).

199. *Obdurate.* Accented on the second syllable, as elsewhere in S. Cf. *R. of L.* 429, *M. of V.* iv. 1. 8, etc.

203. *Hard.* The reading of the 1st ed.; "bad" in all the rest.

204. *Unkind!* Leaving none of her *kind*, or race ; childless. Malone explains it as "unnatural," but the antithesis favours the other explanation.

205. *Contemn me this.* "Contemptuously refuse this favour" (Malone). The 10th ed. has "thus" for *this*, and Steevens was inclined to that reading. "*Thus* and *kiss*," he says, "correspond in sound as well as *unlikely* and *quickly*, *adder* and *shudder*, which we meet with afterwards."

211. *Lifeless.* The early eds. have "liuelesse," except the 4th, which has "liueles."

222. *Intendments.* Intentions. Cf. *A. Y. L.* i. 1. 140, etc. S. uses the word four times, *intention* only twice.

229. *Fondling.* Darling (Schmidt and the Cambridge ed.); used by S. only here. Wyndham takes it to be descriptive of the action of Venus, and he may be right.

230. *Pale.* Enclosure ; as in *C. of E.* ii. 1. 100, etc.

236. *Bottom-grass.* Rich valley grass. Cf. *A. Y. L.* iv. 3. 79 and 1 *Hen. IV.* iii. 1. 105.

240. *Rouse.* A hunter's term. Guillim, in his *Display of Her-
aldrie*, which has an " Addition " of *Termes of Hawking and Hunting*, 1632 (quoted by Wyndham), says : —

	Dislodge			Bucke
	Start			Hare
" You shall say	un-Kennell	} the {		Foxe
	Rowse			Hart
	Bowlt			Conie."

242. *That.* So that. Cf. 599, 830, and 1140 below.

257. *Remorse !* Pity, tenderness ; as very often. We still use
remorseless = pitiless.

260. *Jennet.* A small Spanish horse. Cf. *Oth.* i. 1. 113.

272. *Compass'd.* Curved, arched. In *T. and C.* i. 2. 120, " com-
passed window " = bow-window, and in *T. of S.* iv. 3. 140, " com-
passed cape " = round cape.

Stand is the reading of the first four eds. ; changed in the later
ones to "stands." *Mane,* " as composed of many hairs " (Malone),
is here used as a plural.

275. *Scornfully glisters.* Some editors follow Sewell in trans-
posing these words. S. has *glister* nine times, *glisten* not at all.

277. *Told.* Counted ; as in 520 below.

279. *Leaps.* Malone infers from the rhyme that the word was
pronounced *leps,* as it still is in Ireland ; but it is hardly safe to
draw an inference from a single rhyme. In *Sonn.* 128. 5, we have
leap rhymed with *reap. Curvet* (= prance) was a technical term
in horsemanship.

281. *This I do.* The 4th and later eds. have "thus I do."

296. *Eye.* Changed to " eyes " in the 5th and following eds.

301. *Sometime.* The later eds. have " Sometimes." The words
were used by S. interchangeably.

303. *To bid the wind a base.* To challenge the wind to a race.
See *Cymb.* v. 3. 19 and *T. G. of V.* i. 2. 97. It alludes to the game
of prisoner's base, or prison-base.

304. *And whether.* The early eds. have "And where." Malone prints "And whe'r." *Whether* is often monosyllabic, even when spelled in full. In *Sonn.* 59. 11 the quarto has *whether* and *where* in the same line, both monosyllabic.

306. *Who.* The 10th ed. "corrects" this to "which"; but *who* for *which* (like *which* for *who*) was common in Elizabethan English.

312. *Embracements.* Cf. 790 below. S. uses the word oftener than *embrace* (noun), though in this poem the latter is found three times (539, 811, 874), or as many times as in all his other works.

313. *Malcontent.* The 4th ed. has "male content."

314. *Vails.* Lowers; as in 956 below. Cf. *M. of V.* i. 1. 28, *Ham.* i. 2. 70, etc. This obsolete *vail* is often confounded, even by editors, with *veil*, a word of wholly different origin.

315. *Buttock.* Changed to the plural in the 4th and following eds.

319. *Goeth about.* Attempts. Cf. *Much Ado*, i. 3. 11 : "I wonder that thou goest about . . . to apply a moral medicine to a mortifying mischief." See also *R. of L.* 412, *M. for M.* iii. 2. 215, *Hen. V.* iv. 1. 212, etc.

325. *Chafing.* Often used of sweating or the effects of heat. Cf. *T. of S.* i. 2. 203: "chafed with sweat," etc. See also 662 below. The later eds. have "chasing."

326. *Banning.* Cursing. Cf. *2 Hen. VI.* iii. 2. 319 : "to curse and ban," etc.

334. *Fire.* A dissyllable ; as not unfrequently. The first three eds. print it "fier ; " as they do in 402 below, where it is a monosyllable.

335. *The heart's attorney.* That is, the tongue. Steevens aptly quotes *Rich. III.* iv. 4. 127 : —

> "*Duchess.* Why should calamity be full of words ?
> *Queen Elizabeth.* Windy attorneys to their client woes," etc.

343. *Wistly.* Wistfully ; modifying *came stealing*, not *view*. Cf. *R. of L.* 1355 : "wistly on him gaz'd," etc. Schmidt makes it = "attentively, observingly, with scrutiny," in both passages.

Venus and Adonis

209

346. *How white and red,* etc. Steevens compares *T. of S.* iv. 5. 30 : "Such war of white and red within her cheeks ! "

350. *Lowly.* The 4th ed. has " slowly."

352. *Cheek.* Made plural in the 5th and later eds. In the next line the 4th and the rest read " cheeks (or " cheekes ") reuiues " or " cheekes receiue ; " and all eds. except the 1st have " tender " for *tenderer.*

359. *His.* Its ; as often before *its* came into general use. The allusion is to the *chorus,* or interpreter, in a *dumb-show,* or panto-mime. Cf. *T. G. of V.* ii. 1. 101, *T. of A.* i. 1. 34, etc.

363. *Alabaster.* Spelled " allablaster " or " alablaster " in the early eds., as elsewhere in S. and his contemporaries.

365. *And unwilling.* The 4th ed. has " and willing."

367. *The engine of her thoughts.* That is, her tongue. Cf. *T. A.* iii. 1. 82, where the expression is similarly used.

370. *Thy heart my wound.* " Thy heart wounded as mine is " (Malone).

376. *Grave.* Engrave, impress. Schmidt makes it = " cut a little, wound slightly, graze."

388. *Suffer'd.* That is, allowed to burn. Cf. *3 Hen. VI.* iv. 8. 8 : —

> " A little fire is quickly trodden out,
> Which, being suffer'd, rivers cannot quench."

397. *Sees.* The 2d, 3d, and 4th eds. have " seekes." *In her naked bed,* as some take the trouble to inform us, means " naked in her bed." This rhetorical transference of an epithet is familiar to every schoolboy ; but the expression (as it occurred in *Jeronimo*) was ridiculed by Jonson and others. Cf. " idle bed " (*J. C.* ii. 1. 117), " lazy bed " (*T. and C.* i. 3. 147), " tired bed " (*Lear,* i. 2. 13), etc. So *sick bed,* etc.

398. *A whiter hue than white.* Cf. *Cymb.* ii. 2. 14 : —

> " How bravely thou becom'st thy bed, fresh lily,
> And whiter than the sheets ! "

SHAKESPEARE'S POEMS — 14

and *R. of L.* 472 : " Who o'er the white sheet peers her whiter chin."

411. *Owe.* Own, possess ; as very often. Cf. *R. of L.* 1803, etc.

424. *Alarms.* Alarums, attacks. The 5th and later eds. have " alarme." The 4th has " alarum."

429. *Mermaid.* Siren ; the usual meaning in S. Cf. 777 below.

432. *Ear's.* Misprinted " Earths " in the 4th and later eds.

434. *Invisible.* Steevens conjectures " invincible ; " but, as Malone remarks, " an opposition is clearly intended between *external* beauty, of which the eye is the judge, and a melody of voice (which the poet calls *inward* beauty) striking not the sight, but the ear."

436. *Sensible.* Endowed with sensibility, sensitive. Cf. *L. L. L.* iv. 2. 28, iv. 3. 337, etc.

443. *Stillitory.* Alembic, still ; used by S. only here.

448. *And bid Suspicion*, etc. Malone thinks that " a bolder or happier personification than this " is hardly to be found in Shakespeare's works !

453. *Like a red morn*, etc. A common bit of folk-lore. Cf. the familiar proverb (often varied in form) : —

> " A red sky at night is a shepherd's delight ;
> A red sky at morning is a shepherd's warning."

See also *Matthew*, xvi. 2.

454. *Wrack.* The regular form of the word in S. Cf. the rhymes in 558 below, *R. of L.* 841, 965, etc.

456. *Flaws.* Sudden gusts, or "squalls." Cf. *Cor.* v. 3. 74, *Ham.* v. 1. 239, etc.

462. *Struck.* Spelt " strucke," " stroake," " stroke," and " strooke " in the early eds. Elsewhere we find " strucken," " stricken," " stroken," etc.

466. *Bankrupt.* " Bankrout," " banckrout," or " banquerout " in the old eds., as often in other passages. Hudson adopts Walker's plausible conjecture of " loss " for *love*.

469. *All amaz'd.* The 4th and later eds. have "in a maze."

472. *Fair fall*, etc. May good luck befall, etc.

481. *Night of sorrow.* Cf. *Sonn.* 120. 9 : "night of woe."

482. *Blue windows.* That is, eyelids, on account of their "blue veins" (*R. of L.* 440). Cf. *Cymb.* ii. 2. 21 : —

> "would under-peep her lids,
> To see the enclosed lights, now canopied
> Under these windows, white and azure lac'd
> With blue of heaven's own tinct."

Malone cites both this last passage and *V. and A.* 482 as referring to blue eyes ; but the "azure *lac'd*" ought to settle the question in regard to the former, and "windows" evidently has the same meaning in both. If the "blue windows" *were* blue eyes, Malone would make out his case, for in *V. and A.* 140 the goddess says "Mine eyes are grey and bright." But why should the poet call them *blue* in the one place and *grey* in the other, when the former word would suit the verse equally well in both ? In my opinion, when he says *blue* he means blue, and when he says *grey* he means grey. See note on 140.

484. *Earth.* All the early eds. except the 1st have "world."

488. *Shine.* For the noun, cf. 728 below.

490. *Repine.* The only instance of the noun in S. The verb occurs only three times.

492. *Shone like the moon*, etc. Malone compares *L. L. L.* iv. 3. 30 fol.

497. *Annoy.* For the noun, cf. 599 below, *R. of L.* 1109, etc.

500. *Shrewd.* Evil ; the original sense, occurring often in S.

506. *Their crimson liveries.* Referring, of course, to the lips. The transition to *verdure* in the next line is curious, and the whole passage is a good example of the quaint "conceits" of the time. The allusion, as Malone remarks, is to the practice of strewing rooms with rue and other strong-smelling herbs as a means of preventing infection. The astrological allusion is also to be noted.

Writ on death = predicted death by their horoscopes. The 4th ed. has "neither" for *never*.

508–510. *To drive infection*, etc. Clearly an allusion to the plague in London in 1592, when the play was either written or revised for publication. See p. 22 above.

509. *The star-gazers*, etc. Cf. *Sonn.* 107. 5 fol.

511. *Sweet seals.* Cf. *M. for M.* iv. 1. 6, etc.

515. *Slips.* A play on the word as applied to counterfeit coin. For a similar quibble, see *R. and J.* ii. 4. 51.

519. *Touches.* "Kisses" in the 5th and following eds.

520. *Told.* Counted; as in 277 above.

521. *Say, for non-payment*, etc. "The poet was thinking of a conditional bond's becoming forfeited for non-payment; in which case the entire penalty (usually the double of the principal sum lent by the obligee) was formerly recoverable at law" (Malone).

524. *Strangeness.* Bashfulness, reserve. Cf. 310 above.

526. *Fry.* Or "small fry," as we still say. Cf. *A. W.* iv. 3. 250, *Macb.* iv. 2. 84, etc.

529. *The world's comforter.* Cf. 799 below.

538. *Honey fee.* For the adjective, cf. 16 above and *Sonn.* 65. 5 : "honey breath," etc. *Honey* occurs much oftener than *sugar* in S., both literally and figuratively, but it was then the more familiar sweet.

540. *Incorporate.* Cf. *M. N. D.* iii. 2. 208 : —

> "As if our hands, our sides, voices, and minds,
>   Had been incorporate. So we grew together," etc.

544. *Complain on.* Cf. 160 above.

550. *The insulter.* The exulting victor; the only instance of the noun in S. For *insult* = exult, cf. *Sonn.* 107. 12, 3 *Hen. VI.* i. 3. 14, etc.

565. *With tempering.* Cf. 2 *Hen. IV.* iv. 3. 140 : "I have him already tempering between my finger and my thumb, and shortly will I seal with him."

565, 567. *Tempering . . . venturing.* An imperfect rhyme, but see on 192 above, and 628 below. That in 566, 568 is also noticeable.

568. *Leave.* License. Cf. the play on the word in 3 *Hen. VI.* iii. 2. 34 : —

> "Ay, good leave have you; for you will have leave
> Till youth take leave, and leave you to the crutch."

Commission = warrant ; as often.

570. *Wooes.* The 4th ed. has "woes."

571. *Had she then gave.* Elsewhere S. has the participle *given* (usually monosyllabic). It is a wonder that all the editors have let *gave* alone here.

574. *Prickles.* The 5th and later eds. have "pricks," and "is it" for *'t is*.

589. *Pale.* For the noun, cf. *R. of L.* 1512 and *W. T.* iv. 3. 4.

590. *Like lawn*, etc. Cf. *R. of L.* 258.

591. *Cheek.* Made plural in the 4th ed. *et al.* See on 352 above.

593. *Hanging by.* The 4th and later eds. have "hanging on."

595. *Lists of love.* Steevens quotes Dryden, *Don Sebastian:* —

> "The sprightly bridegroom on his wedding night
> More gladly enters not the lists of love."

597. *Prove.* Experience. Cf. 608 below, and *A. and C.* i. 2. 33 : "You have seen and prov'd a fairer former fortune," etc.

598. *Manage.* For the noun as applied to the training of a horse, cf. *A. Y. L.* i. 1. 13, *Rich. II.* iii. 3. 179, etc. This is the only instance in S. of the verb similarly used.

599. *That.* So that. See on 242 above. For the allusion to *Tantalus*, cf. *R. of L.* 858.

600. *Clip.* Embrace. Cf. *Oth.* iii. 3. 464, *Cymb.* ii. 3. 139, etc.

601. *Even so poor birds*, etc. The original reading, generally changed to "Even as," etc. ; but, as Wyndham notes, this change and the comma for the colon (or semicolon) in 602 make the construction awkward in 604.

602. *Pine.* Starve. For the transitive use, cf. *Rich. II.* v. 1. 77; the only other instance in S.

604. *Helpless.* Affording no help, or sustenance. Cf. *R. of L.* 1027 and 1056.

The allusion is to the celebrated picture of Zeuxis, mentioned by Pliny, in which some grapes were so well represented that birds came to peck them. Cf. Sir John Davies, *Nosce Teipsum,* 1599: "And birds of grapes the cunning shadow peck."

612. *Withhold.* Detain, restrain; as in *Rich. III.* iii. 1. 30, etc.

615. *Be advis'd!* Take heed; as often.

616. *Churlish boar.* Cf. *T. and C.* i. 2. 21: "Churlish as the bear," etc.

617. *Tushes.* Tusks. Cf. 1116 below. S. uses the word only ᴉn this poem.

618. *Mortal.* Death-dealing; as in 953 below. See also *R. of L.* 364, 724, etc. Schmidt takes it to be here = human.

619. *Battle.* Battalion, host. Cf. *Hen. V.* iv. chor. 9, iv. 2. 54, etc.

624. *Crooked.* The *Variorum* of 1821 has "cruel;" apparently accidental, as it is given without comment.

626. *Proof.* Defensive armour. Cf. *Macb.* i. 2. 54: "lapp'd in proof," etc.

628. *Venture.* Commonly pronounced *venter* in the time of S. See on 565, 567 above.

632. *Eyes pay.* The early eds. have "eyes (or "eies") paies" (or "payes") or "eie (or "eye") paies" (or "payes"); corrected by Malone.

633. *Eyne.* The old plural, used for the sake of the rhyme, as in *R. of L.* 643, *M. N. D.* i. 1. 244, ii. 2. 99, iii. 2. 138, v. 1. 178, etc. In *R. of L.* 1229 it is not a rhyming word.

639. *Within his danger.* Cf. *M. of V.* iv. 1. 180: "You stand within his danger, do you not?" *T. N.* v. 1. 87: —

Venus and Adonis 215

> " for his sake
> Did I expose myself, pure for his love,
> Into the danger of this adverse town," etc.

652. *Kill, kill!* The old English battle-cry in charging the enemy. Cf. *Lear*, iv. 6. 191, etc.

655. *Bate-breeding.* Causing quarrel or contention. Cf. 2 *Hen. IV.* ii. 4. 271: " breeds no bate with telling of discreet stories." The 4th ed. has " bare-breeding."

656. *Canker.* Canker-worm. Cf. *M. N. D.* ii. 2. 3, *Temp.* i. 2. 415, etc. *Love's tender spring* = " the tender bud of growing love " (Malone). Cf. *C. of E.* iii. 2. 3: " Even in the spring of love thy love-springs rot."

657. *Carry-tale.* Used again in *L. L. L.* v. 2. 463: " Some carry-tale," etc.

662. *Angry-chafing.* Fretting with rage. The hyphen was inserted by Malone. See on 325 above.

668. *Imagination.* Metrically six syllables. For *tremble*, the 3d and later eds. have " trembling."

674. *Uncouple.* Set loose the hounds; as in *M. N. D.* iv. 1. 112, etc.

677. *Fearful.* Full of fear, timorous. Cf. 927 below.

679-702. *And when thou hast . . . reliev'd by any.* Knight remarks: " In Coleridge's *Literary Remains* the *Venus and Adonis* is cited as furnishing a signal example of 'that affectionate love of nature and natural objects, without which no man could have observed so steadily, or painted so truly and passionately, the very minutest beauties of the external world.' The description of the hare-hunt is there given at length as a specimen of this power. A remarkable proof of the completeness as well as accuracy of Shakspere's description lately presented itself to our mind, in running through a little volume, full of talent, published in 1825 — *Essays and Sketches of Character*, by the late Richard Ayton, Esq. There is a paper on hunting, and especially on hare-hunting. He says: ' I am not one of the perfect fox-hunters of these realms; but having been in the way of late of seeing a good deal of various modes of hunting, I would, for the benefit of the uninitiated, set down the results of my observations.' In this matter he writes with a perfect unconsciousness that he is describing what any one has described before; but as accurate an observer *had* been before him:—

"'She (the hare) generally returns to the seat from which she was put up, running, as all the world knows, in a circle, or something sometimes like it, we had better say, that we may keep on good terms with the mathematical. At starting, she tears away at her utmost speed for a mile or more, and distances the dogs halfway: she then returns, diverging a little to the right or left, that she may not run into the mouths of her enemies—a necessity which accounts for what we call the circularity of her course. Her flight from home is direct and precipitate; but on her way back when she has gained a little time for consideration and stratagem, she describes a curious labyrinth of short turnings and windings, as if to perplex the dogs by the intricacy of her track.'

"Compare this with Shakspere [lines 679–684: 'And when thou hast on foot the purblind hare,' etc.].

"Mr. Ayton thus goes on: 'The hounds, whom we left in full cry, continue their music without remission as long as they are faithful to the scent; as a summons, it should seem, like the seaman's cry, to pull together, or keep together, and it is a certain proof to themselves and their followers that they are in the right way. On the instant that they are "at fault," or lose the scent, they are silent. . . . The weather, in its impression on the scent, is the great father of "faults;" but they may arise from other accidents, even when the day is in every respect favourable. The intervention of ploughed land, on which the scent soon cools or evaporates, is at least perilous; but sheep-stains, recently left by a flock, are fatal: they cut off the scent irrecoverably—making a gap, as it were, in the clue, in which the dogs have not even a hint for their guidance.'

"Compare Shakspere again [lines 685–696: 'Sometime he runs among a flock of sheep,' etc.].

"One more extract from Mr. Ayton: 'Suppose then, after the usual rounds, that you see the hare at last (a sorry mark for so many foes) sorely beleaguered — looking dark and draggled — and limping heavily along; then stopping to listen — again tottering on a little — and again stopping; and at every step, and every pause, hearing the death-cry grow nearer and louder.'

"One more comparison, and we have exhausted Shakspere's description [lines 697–702: 'By this, poor Wat, far off upon a hill,' etc.].

"Here, then, be it observed, are not only the same objects, the same accidents, the same movement, in each description, but the very words employed to convey the scene to the mind are often the same in each. It would be easy to say that Mr. Ayton copied Shakspere. We believe he did not. There is a sturdy ingenuousness about his writings which would have led him to notice the *Venus and Adonis* if he had had it in his mind. Shakspere and he had each looked minutely and practically upon the same scene; and the wonder is, not that Shakspere was an accurate describer, but that in him the accurate is so thoroughly fused with the poetical that it is one and the same life."

680. *Overshoot.* The early eds. have "ouer-shut" or "ouershut;" corrected by Dyce (the conjecture of Steevens). Wyndham retains the old reading as = shut up, conclude.

682. *Cranks.* Turns, winds. Cf. 1 *Hen. IV.* iii. 1. 98: "See how this river comes me cranking in."

683. *Musits.* Holes for creeping through; used by S. only here. Cf. *Two Noble Kinsmen*, iii. 1. 97, where it is = hiding-place.

684. *Amaze.* Bewilder. Cf. *K. John*, iv. 3. 140.

694. *Cold fault.* Cold scent, loss of scent. Cf. *T. of S.* ind. I. 20: —

> "Saw'st thou not, boy, how Silver made it good
> At the hedge-corner, in the coldest fault?
> I would not lose the dog for twenty pound."

695. *Spend their mouths.* That is, bark; a sportsman's expression. Cf. *Hen. V.* ii. 4. 70: —

> "for coward dogs
> Most spend their mouths when what they seem to threaten
> Runs far before them."

697. *Wat.* "A familiar term among sportsmen for a hare; why, does not appear. Perhaps for no better reason than *Philip* for a sparrow [cf. *K. John,* i. 1. 231], *Tom* for a cat, and the like" (Nares).

700. *Their.* The 4th ed. has "with."

703. *Wretch.* On the use of the word as a term of pity or tenderness, cf. *Oth.* iii. 3. 90: "Excellent wretch!" "It expresses the utmost degree of amiableness, joined with an idea which perhaps all tenderness includes, of feebleness, softness, and want of protection" (Johnson). See also *R. and J.* i. 3. 44: "The pretty wretch left crying," etc.

704. *Indenting.* The 4th ed. has "intending."

705. *Envious.* Malicious; as often. So *envy* is often = malice.

712. *Myself.* The 4th and following eds. have "thy selfe."

724. *True men thieves.* The 1st and 2d eds. have "true-men theeves," the 3d "rich-men theeve," the rest "rich men theeves." The use of *true men* in opposition to *thieves* is common in S. and other writers of the time.

726. *Forsworn.* "That is, having broken her vow of virginity" (Steevens).

734. *Curious.* Careful, elaborate. Cf. *A. W.* i. 2. 20: —

> "Frank Nature, rather curious than in haste,
> Hath well compos'd thee."

736. *Defeature.* Deformity; as in *C. of E.* ii. 1. 98 and v. 1. 299.

738. *Mad.* "Sad" in the 5th and later eds.

740. *Wood.* Mad, frantic. Cf. the play on the word in *M. N. D.* ii. 1. 192: "And here am I, and wood [or "wode"] within this wood."

743. *Imposthumes.* Abscesses. Cf. *Ham.* iv. 4. 27 and *T. and C.* v. 1. 24.

746. *Fight.* The 5th and following eds. have "sight;" and in **748** the 4th and the rest have "imperiall" for *impartial.*

751. *Fruitless.* Barren. Cf. *M. N. D.* i. 1. 73: "the cold fruitless moon," etc.

754. *Dearth.* The 4th ed. has "death."

755. *The lamp*, etc. "Ye nuns and vestals, says Venus, imitate the example of the lamp, that profiteth mankind at the expense of its own oil" (Malone).

760. *Dark.* The 4th and later eds. have "their."

762. *Sith.* Since. Cf. 1163 below.

766. *Reaves.* Bereaves. For the participle, still used in poetry, see 1174 below.

767. *Frets.* Corrodes, wears away. Cf. *A. and C.* iv. 12. 8, etc.

768. *Use.* Interest. Cf. *Much Ado*, ii. 1. 288, etc.

774. *Treatise.* Discourse, talk, tale. Cf. *Much Ado*, i. 1. 317 and *Macb.* v. 5. 12, the only other instances of the word in S.

777. *Mermaid's.* Siren's. Cf. 429 above.

782. *Closure.* Enclosure; as in *Sonn.* 48. 11 and *Rich. III.* iii. 3. 11. In *T. A.* v. 3. 134 it is = close, conclusion.

787. *Reprove?* Disprove, confute; as in *Much Ado*, ii. 3. 241: "'t is so; I cannot reprove it," etc.

795. *Simple.* Artless, guileless.

797. *Bereaves.* Impairs, spoils; as in *R. of L.* 373, etc.

807. *In sadness.* In earnest. Cf. *R. and J.* i. 1. 191. In *A. W.* iv. 3. 230, we have "in good sadness."

808. *Teen.* Sorrow. Cf. *Temp.* i. 2. 64: "the teen I have turn'd you to;" *L. L. L.* iv. 3. 164: "of sorrow and of teen," etc.

813. *Laund.* Lawn (in the old sense of glade). The 4th and later eds. have "lawnes." Cf. *3 Hen. VI.* iii. 1. 2.

826. *Mistrustful.* Causing mistrust; here used actively. In *3 Hen. VI.* iv. 2. 8 (the only instance of the word in the plays) it has its ordinary meaning (wanting confidence, or suspicious).

830. *That.* So that. See on 242 above.

833. *Ay me !* Changed by Hudson to " Ah me ! " which occurs in the early eds. of S. only in *R. and J.* v. 1. 10, where it is probably a misprint. *Ay me !* is used often by S., as by Milton.

837. *Thrall.* Enslaved. Cf. *R. of L.* 725.

840. *Answer.* The plural may be explained either by the implied plural in the collective *choir* or by " confusion of proximity."

848. *Idle sounds resembling parasites.* That is, servilely echoing what she says, as the context shows. Staunton reads " idle, sounds-resembling parasites."

849. *Shrill-tongued tapsters,* etc. Cf. 1 *Hen. IV.* ii. 4, where Prince Henry amuses himself with the tapster Francis.

850. *Wits?* Theobald conjectured " wights," for the sake of the rhyme; but *parasites* is spelled " parasits " in the first three eds., and may have been intended to be so pronounced. See on 1001, 1002 below. But the rhyme of *parasites* and *wits* is no worse than many in the poem. Cf., for instance, 449, 450, and 635, 636 above. See also on 51, 192, etc.

854. *Cabinet.* Poetically for nest, as *cabin* in 637 above for lair or den.

858. *Seem burnish'd gold.* Malone compares the opening lines of *Sonn.* 33.

865. *Myrtle grove.* It will be recollected that the myrtle was sacred to Venus.

866. *Musing.* Wondering. Cf. *K. John,* iii. 1. 317, *Macb.* iii. 4. 85, etc.

868. *For his hounds.* The 4th ed. omits *his.*

870. *Coasteth.* Schmidt well explains the word: " to steer, to sail not by the direct way but in sight of the coast, and as it were gropingly." Cf. *Hen. VIII.* iii. 2. 38 : —

> " The king in this perceives him, how he coasts
>   And hedges his own way."

871. *And as she runs,* etc. Wyndham omits the comma after

runs, which he takes to be transitive, as in "the fox ran the meadows," etc.

873. *Twine.* The 1st and 2d eds. have "twin'd," the 3d "twind," and the 4th "twinde;" corrected in the 5th. Wyndham has "twined."

877. *At a bay.* The state of a chase when the game is driven to extremity and turns against its pursuers. Cf. *T. of S.* v. 2. 56, etc.

882. *Spirit.* A monosyllable, as often. Cf. *L. C.* 3, etc.

884. *Blunt.* Rough, savage.

887. *Curst.* Snappish, fierce. Cf. *W. T.* iii. 3. 135: "they [bears] are never curst but when they are hungry;" *Much Ado,* ii. 1. 22: "a curst cow," etc. The word is often used in the sense of shrewish in *T. of S.*; as in i. 1. 185, i. 2. 70, 128, ii. 1. 187, 294, 307, etc. We have the comparative *curster* in *T. of S.* iii. 2. 156 and the superlative in ii. 1. 315.

888. *Cope him.* Cope with him, encounter him. Cf. *T. and C.* i. 2. 34, ii. 3. 275, etc.

891. *Who.* Often used "to personify irrational antecedents." Cf. 956 and 1041 below.

892. *Cold-pale.* The hyphen is in the early eds.

895. *Ecstasy.* Excitement. In S. it means "any state of being beside one's self" (Schmidt). It is often equivalent to insanity; as in *Ham.* ii. 1. 102, iii. 1. 168, iii. 4. 74, etc.

896. *All dismay'd.* The reading of the 1st and 2d eds.; "Sore dismay'd" in the rest.

899. For the second *bids* the 6th and some later eds. have "will's."

901. *Bepainted.* Cf. *R. and J.* ii. 2. 86; the only other instance in S.

907. *Spleens.* Passionate impulses. Cf. 1 *Hen. IV.* v. 2. 19, *J. C.* iv. 3. 47, etc.

908. *Untreads.* Retraces; as in *K. John,* v. 4. 52 and *M. of V.* ii. 6. 10.

909. *Mated.* Bewildered, paralyzed. Cf. *C. of E.* iii. 2. 54, v. 1. 281, etc.

911. *Respects.* Considerations, thoughts; as in *L. L. L.* v. 2. 792, etc.

912. *In hand with.* Taking in hand, undertaking.

930. *Exclaims on.* Cries out against. Cf. *R. of L.* 741, *M. of V.* iii. 2. 176, etc.

933. *Worm.* Serpent; as often.

947. *Love's golden arrow*, etc. Malone remarks that S. had probably in mind the old fable of Love and Death exchanging their arrows by mistake; and he quotes Massinger, *Virgin Martyr* : —

> "Strange affection!
> Cupid once more hath chang'd his darts with Death,
> And kills instead of giving life."

949. *Drink tears.* Cf. *T. A.* ii. 2. 37: "no other drink but tears."

956. *Vail'd.* Let fall. See on 314 above.

963. *Both crystals*, etc. "Magic crystals, as Dr. Dee's, in which one in sympathy with another could see the scene of his distress" (Wyndham).

981. *Orient.* Pearly, or lustrous like pearl. Cf. *M. N. D.* iv. 1. 59, etc.

988. *Makes.* The 5th and later eds. have "make." Herford says the singular is right, the true subject being "the rapid interchange of despair and hope."

990. *In likely.* The reading of the 1st and 2d eds. The 3d and 4th have "The likely," and the rest "With likely."

993. *All to naught.* Good for nothing. Some print "all-to naught," and others "all to-naught."

995. *Clepes.* Calls. Cf. *Ham.* i. 4. 19 : "They clepe us drunkards," etc.

996. *Imperious.* "Imperial" (the reading of the 5th and later eds.). Cf. *T. and C.* iv. 5. 272 : "most imperious Agamemnon," etc.

998. *Pardon me I felt.* That is, *that* I felt. Some make *pardon me* parenthetical.

999. *Whenas.* When; as not unfrequently.

1002. *Decease.* The early eds. have "decesse," "deceass," or "deceasse." See on 850 above.

1004. *Wreak'd.* Revenged. Cf. *R. and J.* iii. 5. 102 and *T. A.* iv. 3. 51. See also the noun in *Cor.* iv. 5. 91, *T. A.* iv. 3. 33, etc. The 4th ed. prints "Bewreakt."

1010. *Suspect.* For the noun, cf. *Sonn.* 70. 3, *Rich. III.* i. 3. 89, etc.

1012. *Insinuate With.* Try to ingratiate herself with. Cf. *A. Y. L.* epil. 9; the only other instance of the phrase in S.

1013. *Stories.* For the verb, cf. *R. of L.* 106 and *Cymb.* i. 4. 34.

1020. *Chaos comes again.* Cf. *Oth.* iii. 3. 92 : "Chaos is come again."

1021. *Fond.* Foolish; the usual meaning in S. Cf. *R. of L.* 216, 1094, etc.

1027. *Falcon.* The reading of the 5th ed., and to be preferred on the whole to the plural of the earlier eds.

1028. *The grass stoops not,* etc. A hyperbole found in Virgil (*Æneid,* viii. 808), Milton (*Comus*), Pope (*Essay on Criticism*), Tennyson (*The Talking Oak*), and elsewhere.

1038. *Deep-dark.* Hyphened in the first three eds.

1041. *Who.* See on 891 above.

1046. *As when the wind,* etc. The vulgar explanation of the earthquake. Cf. 1 *Hen. IV.* iii. 1. 32. See also Marlowe, *Tamburlaine,* Part I. i. 2. 51 : —

> " Even as when windy exhalations,
> Fighting for passage, tilt within the earth."

1048. *Which with cold terror,* etc. There was an earthquake in England in 1580, when S. was sixteen years old (Malone).

1051. *Light.* The reading of the 1st and 2d eds. The 3d and 4th have "night," and the rest "sight."

1052. *Trench'd.* Gashed. Cf. *Macb.* iii. 4. 27: "trenched gashes," etc. The 3d and 4th eds. have "drencht."

1059. *Passions.* Grieves. Cf. *T. G. of V.* iv. 4. 172: "Ariadne passioning," etc.

1062. *That they have wept till now.* That is, that they have wasted their tears on inferior "hints of woe."

1073. *Eyes' red fire!* The 1st and 2d eds. have "eyes red fire," the 3d has "eyes red as fire," the 4th "eies as red as fire," and the rest have "eyes, as fire."

1083. *Fair.* Beauty; as in *C. of E.* ii. 1. 98, *A. Y. L.* iii. 2. 99, etc. There is a play on *fair* and *fear*, which were pronounced nearly alike. See on 51 and 192 above.

1094. *Fear.* Frighten. See *M. of V.* ii. 1. 9, *T. of S.* i. 2. 211, etc.

1098. *Silly.* Innocent, helpless. Cf. *R. of L.* 167: "the silly lambs;" 3 *Hen. VI.* ii. 5. 43: "silly sheep," etc.

1105. *Urchin-snouted.* With snout like that of a hedgehog. For *urchin*, cf. *Temp.* i. 2. 326, ii. 2. 5, etc.

1108. *Entertainment.* Treatment. The word is used by S. in both a good and a bad sense.

1110. *He thought to kiss him*, etc. This conceit, as Malone notes, is found in the 30th Idyl of Theocritus, and in a Latin poem by Antonius Sebastianus Minturnus entitled *De Adoni ab Apro Inter empto :* —

> "iterum atque juro iterum,
> Formosum hunc juvenem tuum haud volui
> Meis diripere his cupidinibus;
> Verum dum specimen nitens video
> (Aestus impatiens tenella dabat
> Nuda femina mollibus zephyris),
> Ingens me miserum libido capit
> Mille suavia dulcia hinc capere,
> Atque me impulit ingens indomitus."

Cf. Milton, *Death of a Fair Infant :* —

"O fairest flower, no sooner blown but blasted!
Soft silken primrose fading timelessly,
Summer's chief honour, if thou hadst outlasted
Bleak Winter's force that made thy blossom dry;
For he, being amorous on that lovely dye
That did thy cheek envermeil, thought to kiss,
But kill'd, alas! and then bewail'd his fatal bliss."

1113. *Did not.* All the eds. except the 1st have "would not."

1115. *Nuzzling.* Thrusting his nose in; the only instance of the word in S. It is spelled "nousling" in all the early eds.

1128. *Lies!* For the singular, cf. *Ham.* iii. 2. 214: "The great man down, you mark his favourites flies." See also *L. L. L.* v. 2. 750 and many similar instances. Abbott (*Grammar*, 333) calls it the "third person plural in -*s*," and among his examples includes sundry instances of *is*, like "What manners is in this?" (*R. and J.* v. 3. 214.) On the present passage, cf. *R. of L.* 1378.

1143. *O'erstraw'd.* Overstrewn; used of course for the rhyme. S. has neither form elsewhere.

1144. *Truest.* The reading of the first three eds.; "sharpest" in the rest.

1148. *Measures.* Grave and formal dances. Cf. *Much Ado,* ii. 1. 80: "as a measure, full of state and ancientry," etc.

1149. *Staring.* Schmidt gives the word the ordinary meaning, as in 301 above. Wyndham says: "perhaps = bristly and unkempt, as in the 'staring coat' of an ungroomed horse." In *J. C.* iv. 3. 280: "makest . . . my hair to stare," it means to stand on end.

1151. *Raging-mad and silly-mild.* The hyphens were first inserted by Malone.

1157. *Toward.* Forward, eager. Cf. *P. P.* 13, *T. of S.* v. 2. 182, etc.

1162. *Combustious.* Combustible; used by S. nowhere else.

1163. *Sith.* See on 762 above.

1168. *A purple flower.* The anemone. The 4th ed. has "pur-pul'd." According to Bion, the anemone sprang from his tears, the rose from his blood.

1174. *Reft.* See on 766 above.

1183. *Here in.* The reading of the 1st and 2d eds.; "here is" in the rest.

1190. *Doves.* See on 153 above.

1193. *Paphos.* A town in Cyprus, the chief seat of the worship of Venus. Cf. *Temp.* iv. 1. 93 and *Per.* iv. prol. 32.

1194. *Immure.* Seclude. Cf. *L. C.* 251, *L. L. L.* iii. 1. 126, etc.

THE RAPE OF LUCRECE

THE METRE OF THE POEM. — The measure is the ten-syllable iambic, as in *V. and A.*, but the seven-lined stanza (*ab abb cc*) was borrowed by Chaucer from Guillaume de Machault, a French poet. Chaucer used it in his *Complaint unto Pité* and his *Troilus and Criseyde*. Puttenham (1589) had noted it as "heroicall, very grave and stately," and "most usuall with our auncient makers" (poets). Daniel had used it for his *Rosamond*, four years before *Lucrece*, and Spenser for his *Hymnes*, published the year after.

THE DEDICATION. — 2. *Moiety.* Often used by S. of a portion other than an exact half.

6. *Would.* The reading of the first three eds.; "should" in the rest.

THE ARGUMENT. — "This appears to have been written by Shakespeare, being prefixed to the original edition of 1594; and is a curiosity, this and the two dedications to the Earl of Southampton being the only prose compositions of our great poet (not in a dramatic form) now remaining" (Malone).

3. *Requiring.* Asking. Cf. *Hen. VIII.* ii. 4. 144: "In humblest manner I require your highness," etc.

16. *Disports.* For the noun, cf. *Oth.* i. 3. **272**, the only other instance in S.

THE RAPE OF LUCRECE. — For the title, see p. **11** above. The Cambridge editors give "The Rape of Lucrece" throughout.

1. *Ardea.* As Dyce notes, S. accents the word on the first syllable, as it should be. The *Variorum* of 1821 and some other eds. have "besieg'd," which requires "Ardēa."

In post. Cf. *C. of E.* i. 2. 63 : "I from my mistress come to you in post," etc. We find "in all post" in *Rich. III.* iii. 5. 73.

3. *Lust-breathed.* Animated by lust.

8. *Unhappily.* The early eds. have "vnhap'ly" or "vnhaply," except the 7th, which misprints "unhappy."

9. *Bateless.* Not to be blunted. Cf. *unbated* in *Ham.* iv. 7, **139** and v. 2. 328. See also the verb *bate* in *L. L. L.* i. 1. 6.

10. *Let.* Forbear. Cf. 328 below, where it is = hinder.

13. *Heaven's beauties.* The stars.

14. *Aspects.* Accented on the last syllable, as regularly in S. Cf. **452** below.

19. *Such high-proud.* Hyphened by Malone. The later eds. have "so high a."

21. *Peer.* The reading of the 1st ed. ; "prince" in all the rest.

23. *Done.* Brought to an end, ruined. Cf. *V. and A.* **197, 749**, *A. W.* iv. 2. 65, etc.

26. *Expir'd.* Accented on the first syllable because preceding a noun so accented. Cf. *unstain'd* in 87, *extreme* in 230, *supreme* in 780, *unfelt* in 828, *dispers'd* in 1805, etc. The later eds. have "A date expir'd : and canceld ere begun."

37. *Suggested.* Incited, tempted; as often. Cf. *Rich. II.* iii. 4. 75, etc.

40. *Braving compare.* Challenging comparison. For the noun, cf. *V. and A.* 8, *Sonn.* 21. 5, etc.

44. *All-too-timeless.* Too unseasonable ; first hyphened by Malone.

47. *Liver*. For the liver as the seat of sensual passion, cf. *Temp.* iv. 1. 56, *M. W.* ii. 1. 121, etc.

49. *Blasts*. For the intransitive use, cf. *T. G. of V.* i. 1. 48: "blasting in the bud."

56. *O'er*. "Ore" or "or'e" in the early eds. Malone was inclined to take it as the noun *ore* "in the sense of *or* or *gold*;" and Wyndham considers that this view is favoured by the terms of heraldry that follow.

57. *In that white intituled*. Consisting in that whiteness, or taking its *title* from it (Steevens). Wyndham takes *intituled* in the heraldic sense of "formally blazoned (in white, which is virtue's colour) by derivation *from Venus' doves*."

58. *Venus' doves*. Cf. *V. and A.* 153 and 1190.

63. *Fence*. Defend, guard; as in 3 *Hen. VI.* ii. 6. 75, iii. 3. 98, etc.

71. *War of lilies and of roses*. Steevens compares *Cor.* ii. 1. 232 and *V. and A.* 345; and Malone adds *T. of S.* iv. 5. 30.

72. *Field*. There is a kind of play upon the word in its heraldic sense and that of a field of battle.

82. *That praise which Collatine doth owe*. Malone and Hudson make *praise* = object of praise, and *owe* = possess. This interpretation seems forced and inconsistent with the next line, which they do not explain. I prefer to take both *praise* and *owe* in the ordinary sense. For *owe* = possess, cf. 1803 below.

87. *Unstain'd thoughts*. The words are transposed in the 5th and later eds.

88. *Lim'd*. Ensnared by bird-lime. Cf. *Ham.* iii. 3. 68, *Much Ado*, iii. 1. 104, etc.

89. *Securely*. Unsuspiciously. Cf. *M. W.* ii. 2. 252, *K. John*, ii. 1. 374, etc.

92. *For that he colour'd*. For that *inward ill* he covered or disguised.

93. *Plaits*. That is, plaited robes. The old eds. spell it "pleats," which is a common New England pronunciation of the word. Boswell quotes *Lear*, i. 1. 183 : "Time shall unfold what plaited cunning hides." These are the only instances of the word in S.

94. *That.* So that. See on *V. and A.* 242. For *inordinate*, cf. 1 *Hen. IV.* iii. 2. 12 and *Oth.* ii. 3. 311.

100. *Parling.* Speaking, significant. The verb occurs again in *L. L. L.* v. 2. 122.

102. *Margents.* Margins. For other allusions to the practice of writing explanations and comments in the margin of books, cf. *Ham.* v. 2. 162, *R. and J.* i. 3. 86, etc.

104. *Moralize.* Interpret. Cf. *T. of S.* iv. 4. 81 : —

> "*Biondello.* Faith, nothing; but has left me here behind, to expound the meaning or moral of his signs and tokens.
> *Lucentio.* I pray thee, moralize them."

106. *Stories.* For the verb, cf. *V. and A.* 1013.

117. *Mother.* The 5th and later eds. change this to "sad source ; " and *stows* in 119 to "shuts." For *stows*, cf. *Oth.* i. 2. 62: "where hast thou stow'd my daughter ?"

121. *Intending.* Pretending. Cf. *Rich. III.* iii. 5. 8, iii. 7. 45, etc. For *spright*, see on *V. and A.* 181.

122. *Questioned.* Talked, conversed. Cf. *M. of V.* iv. 1. 70, etc.

125. *Themselves betake.* The Bodleian copy of 1st ed. (see p. 11 above) has "himselfe betakes," and "wakes" in the next line ; and these are the readings in the *Variorum* of 1821.

133. *Though death be adjunct.* Cf. *K. John,* iii. 3. 57: "Though that my death were adjunct to my act." These are the only instances of *adjunct* in S. except *Sonn.* 91. 5.

135. *For what,* etc. The first four eds. have "That what," etc., and the rest "That oft," etc. The earliest reading may be explained after a fashion, as by Malone (and Wyndham) : "Poetically speaking, they may be said to scatter *what they have not,* that is, what they cannot be *truly* said to have ; what they do not *enjoy,* though

possessed of it." Malone compares Daniel, *Rosamond:* " As wedded widows, wanting what we have ; " and the same author's *Cleopatra :* " For what thou hast, thou still dost lacke." " Tam avaro deest quod habet, quam quod non habet " is one of the sayings of Publius Syrus. But I have little hesitation in adopting Staunton's conjecture of *For what,* etc., as do the Cambridge editors (in the " Globe " ed.) and Hudson. It is supported by the context : they *scatter* or spend what they have in trying to get what they have not, *and so by hoping more they have but less. Bond* must here be = ownership, or that which a *bond* claims or secures. The reading of the 5th ed. seems to be a clumsy attempt to mend the corruption of the 1st.

140. *Bankrupt.* Spelled " băckrout," " banckrout," or " bankrout " in the early eds. See on *V. and A.* 466.

144. *Gage.* Stake, risk ; as in *Ham.* i. i. 91.

150. *Ambitious foul.* Walker would read " ambitious-foul."

160. *Confounds.* Ruins, destroys ; as in 250, 1202, and 1489 below. Cf. *confusion* = ruin, in 1159 below.

164. *Comfortable.* Comforting ; the " active " use of the adjective, and the most frequent in S. Cf. *R. and J.* v. 3. 148: " O comfortable friar ! " etc.

167. *Silly.* See on *V. and A.* 1098.

168. *Wakes.* Malone and some others have " wake."

169. *Leap'd.* Herford puts a comma before this, and makes it = " having leaped ; " but he puts a semicolon after *arm,* which seems inconsistent pointing.

174. *Too too.* Dyce and Hudson print "too-too." For *retire* as a noun, cf. 573 below.

177. *That.* So that. See on 94 above. The 5th and following eds. have " doth " for *do.*

179. *Lode-star.* The preferable spelling, being the etymological one. S. uses the word again in *M. N. D.* i. 1. 183.

180. *Advisedly.* Deliberately ; as in 1527 and 1816 below.

188. *Naked.* As Schmidt notes, there is a kind of play upon the

word. *Still-slaughtered* (first hyphened by Malone) = ever killed but never dying.

196. *Weed.* Robe, garment ; as often in both numbers.

200. *Fancy's.* Love's ; as often.

202. *Digression.* Transgression, as in *L. L. L.* i. 2. 121. In the only other instance in S. (*2 Hen. IV.* iv. 1. 140) it is = deviation.

205. *Golden coat.* That is, coat-of-arms ; an anachronism here.

206. *Some loathsome dash*, etc. "In the books of heraldry a particular mark of disgrace is mentioned by which the escutcheons of those persons were anciently distinguished who ' discourteously used a widow, maid, or wife, against her will.' " (Malone).

207. *Fondly.* Foolishly. Cf. the adjective in 216, 284, and 1094 below ; and see on *V. and A.* 1021.

208. *That.* So that ; as in 94 and 177 above. *Note* = brand, stigma. Cf. *Rich. II.* i. 1. 43, *L. L. L.* iv. 3. 125 and v. 2. 75.

217. *Strucken.* The early eds. have "stroke," "stroken," or "strucken." See on *V. and A.* 462.

221. *Marriage.* A trisyllable ; as in 1 *Hen. VI.* v. 5. 55, etc.

230. *Extreme.* For the accent, see on 26 above.

236. *Quittal.* Requital ; used by S. only here. Cf. *quittance* in *2 Hen. IV.* i. 1. 108, *Hen. V.* ii. 2. 34, etc.

239. *Ay, if.* The first four eds. have "I, if" (*ay* is regularly printed *I* in the early eds.) ; the rest have "if once."

244. *Saw.* Moral saying, maxim. Cf. *A. Y. L.* ii. 7. 156, etc. For the practice of putting these *saws* on the *painted cloth* or hangings of the poet's time, cf. *A. Y. L.* iii. 2. 291 : "I answer you right painted cloth."

246. *Disputation.* Metrically five syllables. Cf. 352 below.

258. *Roses that on lawn*, etc. Cf. *V. and A.* 590.

264. *Cheer.* Face, look. Cf. *M. N. D.* iii. 2. 96: "pale of cheer," etc.

265. *Narcissus.* Cf. *V. and A.* 161.

268. *Pleadeth.* The 5th and following eds. have "pleads," with "dreads" and "leades" in the rhyming lines.

274. *Then, childish fear avaunt!* etc. In this line and the next I follow the pointing of the early eds. Most of the editors, with Malone, make *fear*, *debating*, etc., vocatives.

275. *Respect.* "Cautious prudence" (Malone), consideration of consequences. Cf. *T. and C.* ii. 2. 49, etc.

277. *Beseems.* Becomes. For the number, cf. 168 above. *Sad* = serious, sober. Cf. the noun in *V. and A.* 807.

278. *My part.* A metaphor taken from the stage. Malone sees a special reference to the conflicts between the Devil and the Vice in the old moralities. Cf. *T. N.* iv. 2. 134 fol.

284. *Fond.* Foolish, weak. See on 207 above.

293. *Seeks to.* Applies to. Cf. Burton, *Anat. of Melan.:* "why should we then seek to any other but to him ?" See also *Deuteronomy*, xii. 5, 1 *Kings*, x. 24, *Isaiah*, viii. 19, xix. 3, etc.

301. *Marcheth.* The 5th and later eds. have "doth march;" and in 303 "recites" for *retires*.

303. *Retires his ward.* Draws back its bolt. For the transitive verb, cf. *Rich. II.* ii. 2. 46 : "might have retir'd his power ; " and for *ward*, see *T. of A.* iii. 3. 38: "Doors that were ne'er acquainted with their wards."

304. *Rate his ill.* That is, *chide* it by the noise they make.

308. *His fear.* That is, the object of his fear. Cf. *M. N. D.* v. 1. 21 : —

> "Or in the night, imagining some fear,
> How often is a bush suppos'd a bear !"

313. *His conduct.* That which *conducts* or guides him. Cf. *R. and J.* iii. 1. 129 : "And fire-eyed fury be my conduct now !" and *Id.* v. 3. 116 : "Come, bitter conduct, come, unsavoury guide," etc.

319. *Needle.* Monosyllabic ; as in *M. N. D.* iii. 2, 204, *K. John*, v. 2. 157, etc. Some print it "neeld."

328. *Let.* Hinder. Cf. the noun just below ; and see *Ham.* i. 4. 85, *T. N.* v. 1. 256, etc.

332. *Prime.* Spring ; as in *Sonn.* 97. 7, etc.

333. *Sneaped.* Nipped, frost-bitten. Cf. *L. L. L.* i. 1. 100 : —

> "an envious sneaping frost
> That bites the first-born infants of the spring."

347. *And they.* Steevens conjectured "And he ; " but *power* is treated as a plural — perhaps on account of the preceding *heavens.* Cf. the plural use of *heaven,* for which see *Rich. II.* i. 1. 23, iii. 3. 17, etc.

349. *Fact.* Deed. Some explain it as "crime ; " the only meaning of the word recognized by Schmidt.

352. *Resolution.* Metrically five syllables. See on 246 above. In 354 the 5th and following eds. have "Blacke" for *The blackest.* The former, it will be seen, will satisfy the measure if *absolution* is made five syllables like *resolution.*

372. *Fiery-pointed.* "Throwing darts with points of fire" (Schmidt). Steevens wanted to read "fire-ypointed ; " and the meaning of *fiery-pointed* may possibly be *pointed* (= appointed, equipped) with fire.

377. *Or else some shame suppos'd.* Or else some shame is imagined by them. Hudson has the following curious note : "An odd use of *supposed,* but strictly classical. So in Chapman's *Byron's Conspiracy,* 1608 : 'Foolish statuaries, that under little saints *suppose* great bases, make less, to sense, the saints.'" How the etymological sense of *supposed* (placed under) can suit the present passage it is not easy to see.

386. *Cheek.* The reading of 1st, 2d, and 4th eds. ; plural in the rest.

388. *Who.* See on *V. and A.* 891. Cf. 447 and 461 below.

389. *To want.* At wanting or missing ; the "indefinite use" of the infinitive.

402. *Map.* Picture, image. Cf. 1712 below.

408. *Maiden worlds.* White calls the epithet "unhappy" and a "heedless misuse of language ; " but the context explains and justifies it. Furnivall remarks that S. uses *maiden* here as we do of a castle, which admits its own lord but not a foe.

419. *Alabaster.* The early eds. have "alablaster." See on *V. and A.* 363.

424. *Qualified.* Abated, diminished ; that is, for the moment. Cf. *M. of V.* iv. 1. 7, *W. T.* iv. 4. 543, etc.

428–443. *And they, like straggling slaves,* etc. "A sustained conceit taken from the assault of a fortress. It is resumed in 464–483" (Wyndham).

429. *Obdurate.* For the accent, see on *V. and A.* 199.

436. *Commends.* Commits ; as often. Cf. *C. of E.* i. 2. 32, *L. L. L.* i. 1. 234, iii. 1. 169, etc.

439. *Breast.* Made plural in the 5th and following eds.

448. *Controll'd.* Restrained. Cf. 500, 678, and 1781 below.

453. *Taking.* Now used only colloquially in this sense. Cf. *M. W.* iii. 3. 491 : "What a taking was he in when your husband asked who was in the basket !"

456. *Wrapp'd.* Involved, overwhelmed. Hudson reads "rapt." Cf. 636 below.

458. *Winking.* Shutting her eyes. See on *V. and A.* 90.

459. *Antics.* Fantastic appearances. The early eds. have "antiques." The words are used interchangeably in the early eds., the accent being always on the first syllable. *Leading* = direction ; as in *Cor.* iv. 5. 143.

467. *Bulk.* Chest. Cf. *Rich. III.* i. 4. 40 and *Ham.* ii. 1. 95. *That* = so that ; as in 94, 177, and 208 above.

471. *Heartless.* Without *heart*, or courage ; as in 1392 below. See also *R. and J.* i. 1. 73 : "heartless hinds." These are the only instances of the word in S.

472. *Peers.* Lets appear, shows. Elsewhere in S. *peer* is intransitive.

476. *Colour.* Pretext. For the play on the word in the reply, cf. *2 Hen. IV.* v. 5. 91 : —

"*Falstaff.* Sir, I will be as good as my word ; this that you heard was but a colour.

Shallow. A colour [= *collar*] that I fear you will die in, Sir John.'

491. *Crosses.* Mischances, vexations. Cf. 912 below.

493. *I think*, etc. " I am aware that the honey is guarded with a sting " (Malone).

496. *Only.* The transposition of the adverb is common in S.

497. *On what he looks.* That is, on what he looks *on ;* as prepositions are often omitted in relative sentences when expressed in what precedes.

500. *Affection's.* Passion's, lust's. Cf. *W. T.* i. 2. 138, etc.

502. *Ensue.* Follow ; as in *Rich. II.* ii. 1. 197 : " Let not to-morrow, then, ensue to-day." See also 1 *Peter*, iii. 11.

506. *Towering.* A technical term in falconry. Cf. *Macb.* ii. 4. 12, etc. *Like* may possibly be = *as*, or there may be a " confusion of construction." Hudson adopts the former explanation, and gives the impression that *like* is " repeatedly " so used by S. The fact is that there is not a single clear instance of it in all his works. The two examples in *Pericles* are not in his part of the play ; and in *M. N. D.* iv. 1. 178 (the only other possible case of the kind) the reading is doubtful, and with either reading the passage may be pointed so as to avoid this awkward use of *like*. If S. had been willing to employ it, he would probably have done so " repeatedly ; " but it seems to have been no part of his English.

507. *Coucheth.* Causes to couch or cower. Cf. the intransitive use in *A. W.* iv. 1. 24, etc.

511. *Falcon's bells.* For the *bells* attached to the necks of tame falcons, cf. *A. Y. L.* iii. 3. 81 and 3 *Hen. VI.* i. 1. 47.

522. *Nameless.* " Because an illegitimate child has no name by inheritance, being considered by the law as *nullius filius* " (Malone). Cf. *T. G. of V.* iii. 1. 321 : " bastard virtues, that indeed know not their fathers, and therefore have no names."

530. *Simple.* Cf. *A. Y. L.* iv. 1. 16 : " compounded of many simples," etc. From this meaning of " an ingredient in a compound " the word came to be applied to medicinal herbs (mainly used in compounds) ; as in *M. W.* i. 4. 65, iii. 3. 79, *R. and J.* v. 1. 40, etc.

531. *A pure compound.* The 5th and later eds. have "purest compounds." In the next line, *his* = its. *Purified* = rendered harmless.

534. *Tender.* Favour. It is often similarly used (= regard or treat kindly) ; as in *T. G. of V.* iv. 4. 145, *C. of E.* v. 1. 132, etc.

537. *Wipe.* Brand ; the only instance of the noun in S. For *birth-hour's blot,* cf. *M. N. D.* v. 1. 416 : —

> "And the blots of Nature's hand
> Shall not in their issue stand ;
> Never mole, hare-lip, nor scar,
> Nor mark prodigious, such as are
> Despised in nativity,
> Shall upon their children be."

540. *Cockatrice' dead-killing eye.* For the fabled cockatrice, or basilisk, which was supposed to kill with a glance of its eye, cf. *W. T.* i. 2. 388, *Hen. V.* v. 2. 17, *Rich. III.* i. 2. 151, etc.

543. *Gripe's.* Griffin's (Steevens). The word is often = vulture ; as in Sidney's *Astrophel :* —

> "Upon whose breast a fiercer gripe doth tire,
> Than did on him who first stole down the fire ; "

Ferrex and Porrex : "Or cruel gripe to gnaw my growing harte," etc. For allusions to the griffin, see *M. N. D.* ii. 1. 232 and 1 *Hen. IV.* iii. 1. 152.

547. *But.* The reading of all the early eds. Changed by Sewell to "As," and by Malone to "Look." Boswell explains the text thus : "He knows no gentle right, *but* still her words delay him, as a gentle gust blows away a black-faced cloud."

550. *Blows.* The early eds. have "blow ; " corrected by Malone.

553. *Winks.* Shuts his eyes, sleeps. See on 458 above. For *Orpheus,* cf. *T. G. of V.* iii. 2. 78, *M. of V.* v. 1. 80, *Hen. VIII.* iii. 1. 3, etc.

554. *Night-waking.* Awake at night.

556. *Vulture folly.* Cf. *V. and A.* 551 : "vulture thought."

559. *Plaining.* Complaining. Cf. *Lear*, iii. 1. 39; "cause to plain," etc.

560. *Wear with raining.* Cf. 959 below.

565. *His.* Its; as in 532 above. Steevens quotes *M. N. D.* v. 1. 96 : "Make periods in the midst of sentences," etc.

568. *Conjures.* The accent in S. is on either syllable without regard to the sense.

569. *Gentry.* His gentle birth. Cf. *W. T.* i. 2. 393, *Cor.* iii. 1. 144, etc.

574. *Stoop.* Yield. Cf. *M. of V.* ii. 7. 20, *Lear*, i. 1. 51, etc.

576. *Pretended.* Intended; as in *T. G. of V.* ii. 6. 37 : "their pretended flight," etc.

579. *Shoot.* For the noun, cf. *L. L. L.* iv. 1. 10, 12, 26, *2 Hen. IV.* iii. 2. 49, etc. Malone conjectures "suit," with a play on the word, which was then pronounced *shoot.* See *L. L. L.* iv. 1. 110, where is a play on *suitor* and *shooter.*

580. *Woodman.* Huntsman. Cf. *M. W.* v. 5. 30, etc.

581. *Unseasonable.* Cf. *M. W.* iii. 3. 169 : "buck and of the season."

592. *Convert.* For the intransitive use, cf. 691 below. For the rhyme, cf. *Sonn.* 14. 12, 17. 2, 49. 10, 72. 6, etc.

595. *At an iron gate.* Even at the gates of a prison (Steevens).

603. *Seeded.* Matured, full-grown ; used again in *T. and C.* i. 3. 316 : "seeded pride."

607. *Be remember'd.* Remember, bear in mind. Cf. *A. Y. L.* iii. 5. 135 : "now I am remember'd," etc.

609. *In clay.* That is, even in their graves. Their *misdeeds* will live after them. Cf. *Sonn.* 71. 10 : "when I perhaps compounded am with clay," etc.

615, 616. *For princes are the glass, the school, the book,* etc. For the "chiastic" construction, not carried out in the second line, cf. *A. and C.* iv. 15. 25 : —

> "if knife, drugs, serpents have
> Edge, sting, or operation, I am safe."

See also on *L. C.* 265. For the figures, cf. 1 *Hen. IV.* ii. 3. 31.

618. *Lectures.* Lessons. Elsewhere in S. *read lectures* = give lessons, not receive them. Cf. *A. Y. L.* iii. 2. 365, *T. of S.* i. 2. 148, *Cor.* ii. 3. 243, etc.

621. *Privilege.* For the verb, cf. *Sonn.* 58. 10, etc.

622. *Laud.* Cf. 887 below, 2 *Hen. IV.* iv. 5. 236, etc.

637. *Askance.* Turn aside ; the only instance of the verb in S. Schmidt paraphrases the line thus : "who, in consequence of their own misdeeds, look with indifference on the offences of others."

639. *Lust, thy rash relier.* "That is, lust which confides too rashly in thy present disposition and does not foresee its necessary change" (Schmidt). The 5th and following eds. have "reply" for *relier.*

640. *Repeal.* Recall. Cf. *J. C.* iii. 1. 51, *Rich. II.* ii. 2. 49, etc.

643. *Eyne.* See on *V. and A.* 632. The 5th and later eds. have "eies ;" and in 649 "pretty" for *petty.*

646. *Let.* Hindrance ; as in 330 above.

651. *To his.* The reading of the 1st and 2d eds. The 3d has "to the," and the others "to this."

655. *Who.* See on 388 above.

657. *Puddle's.* The reading of 1st, 2d, and 4th eds. ; the others have "puddle." For *hears'd* the 5th and 6th have "bersed," and the 7th "persed." *Hears'd* is found also in *M. of V.* iii. 1. 93 and *Ham.* i. 4. 47.

661. *Thy fouler grave.* Hudson points "thy fouler, grave ;" and adds this strange note : "*Grave* is here a verb, meaning to *bury* or *be* the death of." He seems to take the line to mean, Thou buriest their fair life, and they bury thy fouler life ; but how he would explain the former clause I cannot guess. Of course the meaning is, Thou *art* their fair life — a repetition of the idea in *they basely dignified.*

678. *Controll'd.* See on 448 above.

680. *Nightly.* The 5th and 6th eds. misprint "mighty." *Linen* is not = nightgown (unknown in the time of S.), but a linen cloth about the head. *Nightgown* (in *Macb.* ii. 2. 70, *Much Ado*, iii. 4. 18, *Oth.* iv. 3. 34, etc.) is = *robe de chambre*, or dressing-gown.

684. *Prone.* Headlong. Cf. *M. for M.* i. 2. 188, etc. The 3d, 5th, 6th, and 7th eds. have "proud."

691. *Converts.* Changes. See on 592 above.

696. *Balk.* Disregard, neglect. Cf. Davies, *Scourge of Folly*, 1611 : —

> " Learn'd and judicious lord, if I should balke
> Thyne honor'd name, it being in my way,
> My muse unworthy were of such a walke,
> Where honor's branches make it ever May."

698. *Fares.* The 5th and 6th eds. have "feares," and in 706 " of eine" for *or rein.*

701. *Conceit.* Conception, thought. Cf. 1298 below.

703. *His receipt.* What he has *received;* as in *Cor.* i. 1. 116: —

> " The discontented members, the mutinous parts
> That envied his [the stomach's] receipt."

707. *Till, like a jade,* etc. Steevens aptly quotes *Hen. VIII.* i. 1. 132: —

> " Anger is like
> A full-hot horse, who being allow'd his way.
> Self-mettle tires him."

For *jade* (= a worthless or vicious horse), cf. *V. and A.* 391.

721. *The spotted princess.* The polluted *soul.* For *spotted,* cf. *M. N. D.* i. 1. 110, *Rich. II.* iii. 2. 134, etc.

728. *Forestall.* Prevent; as in *2 Hen. IV.* iv. 5. 141, etc. The 7th ed. has "forest, all ; " as "presence" for *prescience* in 727, and "swearing" for *sweating* in 740.

733. *Perplex'd.* Bewildered, confounded. Cf. *Oth.* v. 2. 346: "Perplex'd in the extreme," etc.

741. *Exclaiming on.* Crying out against. Cf. *V. and A.* 930.

743. *Convertite.* Convert, penitent. The word is found also in *A. Y. L.* v. 4. 190 and *K. John,* v. 1. 19.

747. *Scapes.* Transgressions ; as in *W. T.* iii. 3. 73 : "some scape," etc.

766. *Black stage.* In the time of S. the stage was hung with black when tragedies were performed (Malone). Cf. 1 *Hen. VI.* i. 1. 1 : "Hung be the heavens with black," etc. The upper part of the stage was technically known as the *heavens.* Cf. Sidney, *Arcadia :* "There arose, even with the sunne, a vaile of darke cloudes before his face, which shortly had blacked over all the face of heaven, preparing (as it were) a mournfull stage for a tragedie to be played on."

768. *Defame !* Cf. 817 and 1033 below. These are the only instances of the noun in S.

774. *Proportion'd.* "Regular, orderly" (Schmidt).

780. *Supreme.* For the accent, see on 26 above.

781. *Arrive .* For the transitive use, cf. *J. C.* i. 2. 110, *Cor.* ii. 3, 189, etc. For *prick* = dial-point, cf. *R. and J.* ii. 4. 119 : "The prick of noon," etc.

782. *Misty.* The 1st and 2d eds. have "mustie ; " corrected in the 3d ed., which, however, misprints "vapour" for *vapours.*

783. *In their smoky ranks his smother'd light.* That is, his light smothered in their smoky ranks. The *queen* is of course the moon, the *handmaids* the stars.

786. *Distain.* Stain, defile. The 5th and later eds. have "disdaine."

790. *Fellowship in woe,* etc. "Misery loves company," as the old saw puts it. Cf. 1580 below and *R. and J.* iii. 2. 116 : "sour woe delights in fellowship."

791. *Palmers'.* Pilgrims'. Cf. *A. W.* iii. 5. 38, *R. and J.* i. 5. 102, etc.

792. *Where.* Whereas. See *L. L. L.* ii. 1. 103, etc.

805. *Sepulchred.* S. accents the verb regularly on the penult ;

as he does the noun in *Rich. II.* i. 3. 196, but elsewhere on the first syllable, as in *V. and A.* 622, etc.

807. *Character'd.* S. accents the verb on either the first or second syllable, the noun on the first except in *Rich. III.* iii. 1. 81.

811. *Cipher.* Decipher; used by S. only here and in 207 and 1396 of this poem.

812. *Quote.* Note, observe. Cf. *R. and J.* i. 4. 31, etc. The word is spelled *cote* in the 1st and 2d eds., as it was pronounced.

817. *Feast-finding.* " Our ancient minstrels were the constant attendants on feasts" (Steevens). Their music of course made them welcome.

820. *Senseless.* Not sensible of the wrong done it.

828. *Crest-wounding.* Staining or disgracing the family *crest* or coat of arms — a "blot i' the scutcheon."

830. *Mot.* Motto, or *word*, as it was called in heraldry; used by S. only here.

841. *Guilty.* Malone reads " guiltless." Sewell makes the line a question; but, as Boswell says, Lucrece at first reproaches herself for having received Tarquin's visit, but instantly defends herself by saying that she did it out of respect to her husband.

848. *Intrude.* Invade; not elsewhere transitive in S.

849. *Cuckoos.* For the allusion to the cuckoo's laying its eggs in other birds' nests, cf. 1 *Hen. IV.* iii. 2. 75, v. 1. 60, *A. and C.* ii. 6. 28, etc.

851. *Folly.* " Used, as in Scripture, for *wickedness*" (Malone). Schmidt explains it as " inordinate desire, wantonness," both here and in 556 above. Cf. *Oth.* v. 2. 132: " She turn'd to folly, and she was a whore."

858. *Still-pining.* Ever-longing. Cf. " still-vex'd" (*Temp.* i. 2. 229), " still-closing" (*Id.* iii. 3. 64), etc. For *Tantalus*, see *V. and A.* 599.

859. *Barns.* Stores up; the only instance of the verb in S. The 5th and later eds. have " bannes " or " bans."

864. *Abuse.* Misuse; as in 994 below.

867. *The sweets we wish for*, etc. Cf. *Sonn.* 129, "that greatest of sonnets," as Mr. Verity calls it.

879. *Point'st.* Appointest; but not to be printed "'point'st," as by some editors. Cf. *T. of S.* iii. 1. 19, iii. 2. 1, 15, etc.

884. *Temperance.* Chastity. Cf. *A. and C.* iii. 13. 121; the only other instance of this sense in S.

892. *Smoothing.* Flattering. Cf. *Rich. III.* i. 2. 169, i. 3. 48, etc. The 5th and following eds. have "smothering."

894. *Thy violent vanities*, etc. Cf. *R. and J.* ii. 6. 9: "These violent delights have violent ends."

899. *Sort.* Sort out, select. Cf. *R. and J.* iii. 5. 108, iv. 2. 34, etc.

907. *Advice.* That is, medical advice.

912. *Crosses.* Hindrances, mischances. Cf. 491 above.

914. *Appaid.* Satisfied; used by S. only here.

920. *Shift.* Trickery. Nares (s. v. *Shifter*) quotes *Rich Cabinet furnished with Varietie of Excellent Descriptions*, 1616: "Shifting doth many times incurre the indignitie of reproach, and to be counted a shifter is as if a man would say in plaine tearmes a coosener." Cf. 930 below.

925. *Copesmate.* Companion; used by S. nowhere else.

926. *Grisly.* Grim, terrible. Cf. 1 *Hen. VI.* i. 4. 47, *M. N. D.* v. 1. 140, etc.

928. *Watch of woes.* "Divided and marked only by woes" (Schmidt). Cf. *Macb.* ii. 1. 54: "the wolf, whose howl 's his watch."

930. *Injurious, shifting.* Some editors adopt Walker's conjecture of "injurious-shifting;" but *shifting* may be = cozening, deceitful. See on 920 just above.

936. *Fine.* Explained by Malone as = soften, refine, and by Steevens and Wyndham as = bring to an end. The latter is on the whole to be preferred.

943. *Wrong the wronger.* That is, treat him as he treats others, make him suffer. Farmer would read "wring" for *wrong.*

944. *Ruinate.* Cf. *Sonn.* 10. 7 : " Seeking that beauteous roof to ruinate," etc.

With thy hours. Steevens conjectures " with their bowers," and Malone was at first inclined to read " with his hours."

948. *To blot old books and alter their contents.* As Malone remarks, S. little thought how the fate of his own compositions would come to illustrate this line.

950. *Cherish springs.* That is, young shoots. Cf. *V. and A.* 656. Warburton wanted to read " tarish " (= dry up, from Fr. *tarir*) ; Heath conjectured " sere its ; " and Johnson " perish."

953. *Beldam.* Grandmother ; as in 1458 below.

962. *Retiring.* Returning ; as in *T. and C.* i. 3. 281, etc.

981. *Curled hair.* " A distinguishing characteristic of a person of rank " (Malone). Cf. *Oth.* i. 2. 68 : " wealthy curl'd darlings ; " *A. and C.* v. 2. 304 : " the curled Antony," etc.

985. *Orts.* Scraps, remnants. Cf. *T. and C.* v. 2. 158 and *T. of A.* iv. 3. 400.

993. *Unrecalling.* Not to be recalled. For *crime,* the 4th and following eds. have " time."

1001. *Slanderous.* Disgraceful ; as in *J. C.* iv. 1. 20 : " To ease ourselves of divers slanderous loads." The office of executioner, or *deathsman* (cf. *Lear,* iv. 6. 263), was regarded as ignominious.

1021. *Force not.* Regard not, care not for. Cf. *L. L. L.* v. 2. 440 : " force not to forswear."

1024. *Uncheerful.* The 4th and later eds. have " unsearch-full."

1027. *Helpless.* Unavailing ; as in 1056 below. See on *V. and A.* 604.

1035. *Afeard.* Used by S. interchangeably with *afraid.*

1045. *Mean.* The singular is often used by S., but the plural oftener.

1062. *Graff.* Graft. All the early eds. except the 1st and 2d have " grasse."

1067. *Thy interest.* Thy possession, thy married right to my bed. Cf. 1619 below. See also *Cymb.* i. 3. 90: "my interest and his honour."

1070. *With my trespass never will dispense.* That is, will never excuse it. Cf. 1279 and 1704 below.

1079. *Philomel.* The nightingale. Cf. 1128 below.

1084. *Cloudy.* Cf. *V. and A.* 725. See also 1 *Hen. IV.* iii. 2. 83: "cloudy men," etc. For *shames* = is ashamed, cf. 1143 below.

1092. *Nought to do.* That is, nothing to do with, no concern in.

1094. *Fond.* Foolish ; as in 216 above.

1105. *Sometime.* The 4th and following eds. have "sometimes." The two forms are used indiscriminately.

1109. *Annoy.* See on *V. and A.* 497.

1114. *Ken.* Sight. Cf. 2 *Hen. VI.* iii. 2. 113: "losing ken of Albion's wished coast," etc.

1119. *Who.* See on 388 above.

1124. *Stops.* Referring to the *stops* of musical instruments. Cf. *Ham.* iii. 2. 76, 376, 381, etc.

1126. *Relish your nimble notes to pleasing ears.* Tune your lively notes for those who like to hear them. With *pleasing* cf. *unrecalling* in 993 above.

1127. *Dumps.* Mournful elegies. Cf. *T. G. of V.* iii. 2. 85: "Tune a deploring dump."

1128. *Of ravishment.* Referring to her being ravished by Tereus. See *T. A.* ii. 4. 26 fol. and iv. 1. 48 fol.

1132. *Diapason.* "Deep notes harmoniously accompanying high ones" (Schmidt). Used by S. only here.

1133. *Burden-wise.* As in the *burden* of a song.

1134. *Descant'st.* Singest. For the noun, cf. *T. G. of V.* i. 2. 94. Here the early eds. all have "descants ; " a euphonic contraction of second persons singular of verbs in -*t*, found not infrequently in the early eds. *Skill* must be regarded as the direct object of *descant'st*, not governed by *with* understood, as Malone makes it, pointing "descant'st, better skill." Wyndham says: "S.

here, as ever, exhibits a complete grasp of technical terms. He makes Lucrece contrast her sad, monotonous accompaniment of groans — humming on Tarquin still — with the treble *descant* of the nightingale, complaining in a higher register and with more frequent modulations of the wrong wrought her by Tereus. The one he compares to a single droning bass, chiefly in the *diapason* or lower octave; the other to the *better skill* or more ingenious artifice of a contrapuntal melody scored above it." See Elson (*S. in Music*) on *descant*.

1135. *Against a thorn.* The nightingale was supposed to press her breast against a thorn while singing. Cf. *Two Noble Kinsmen*, iii. 4. 25 : " O for a prick now, like a nightingale, To put my breast against !" See also *P. P.* 379.

1140. *Frets.* The stops that regulated the vibration of the strings in lutes, etc. Cf. *T. of S.* ii. 1. 150, 153.

1142. *And for.* And because.

1143. *Shaming.* Being ashamed ; as in 1084 above.

1144. *Seated from the way.* Situated out of the way.

1149. *At gaze.* Staring about.

1160. *Conclusion.* Experiment. Cf. *A. and C.* v. 2. 358, *Cymb.* i. 5. 18, etc.

1167. *Peel'd.* Here and in 1169 the early eds. have " pil'd," " pild," or " pill'd ; " and this last form might well enough be retained. Cf. *Genesis*, xxx. 37, 38. In *M. of V.* i. 3. 85 the quartos have " pyld " or " pyl'd," and the folios " pil'd."

1186. *Deprive.* Take away ; as in 1752 below.

1202. *Confound.* Ruin ; as in 160 above.

1205. *Oversee.* The *overseer* of a will was one who had a supervision of the executors. The poet, in his will, appoints John Hall and his wife as *executors*, and Thomas Russel and Francis Collins as *overseers*. In some old wills the term *overseer* is used instead of *executor* (Malone).

1206. *Overseen.* Bewitched, as by the " evil eye." Cf. *o'erlooked* in *M. W.* v. 5. 87 and *M. of V.* iii. 2. 15.

1221. *Sorts.* Adapts, as if choosing or selecting. Cf. 899 above.

1222. *For why.* Because; as in *Rich. II.* v. 1. 140, etc.

1227. *Each flower moisten'd,* etc. Cf. *M. N. D.* iii. 1. 204 and *T. and C.* i. 2. 9. The early eds. have "moistned," and Wyndham prints "moist'ned," which he regards as more melodious.

1229. *Eyne.* See on 643 above.

1233. *Pretty.* In this and similar expressions *pretty* may be explained as = "moderately great" (Schmidt), or "suitable, sufficient," as some make it. Cf. *R. and J.* i. 3. 10: "a pretty age." This is still a colloquialism; as in "pretty good," etc.

1241. *And therefore are they,* etc. "Hence do they (women) receive whatever impression their marble-hearted associates (men) choose" (Malone). *Will* = may will (subjunctive).

1242. *Strange kinds.* Alien or foreign natures.

1244. *Then call them not,* etc. Cf. *T. N.* ii. 2. 30: —

> "How easy is it for the proper-false
> In women's waxen hearts to set their forms!
> Alas, our frailty is the cause, not we,
> For such as we are made of, such we be!"

and *M. for M.* ii. 4. 130:

> "Women! Help Heaven! men their creation mar
> In profiting by them. Nay, call us ten times frail,
> For we are soft as our complexions are,
> And credulous to false prints."

1247. *Like a goodly.* The 5th and 6th eds. have simply "like a," and the 7th reads "like unto a."

1254. *No man inveigh.* Let no man inveigh. All the eds. but the 1st have "inveighs."

1257. *Hild.* For *held,* for the sake of the rhyme. The 5th and later eds. have "held." Cf. Spenser, *F. Q.* iv. 11. 17: —

> "How can they all in this so narrow verse
> Contayned be, and in small compasse hild?
> Let them record them that are better skild," etc.

1258. *Fulfill'd.* Filled full. Cf. *T. and C.* prol. 18: "fulfilling bolts." See also *Sonn.* 136. 5.

1261. *Precedent.* Example, illustration.

1263. *Present.* Instant; as in 1307 below.

1269. *Counterfeit.* Likeness, image; as in *M. of V.* iii. 2. 115, *Macb.* ii. 3. 81, etc.

1272. *Of my sustaining.* That I suffer.

1279. *With the fault I thus far can dispense.* See on 1070 above.

1285. *The repetition.* The telling it. Cf. *Macb.* ii. 3. 90, etc.

1298. *Conceit.* Conception, thought; as in 701 above.

1302. *Inventions.* Elsewhere used of thoughts expressed in writing; as in *A. Y. L.* iv. 3. 29, 34, *T. N.* v. 1. 341, etc.

1325. *Interprets.* The figure here is taken from the old *motion*, or dumb-show, which was explained by an *interpreter.* Cf. *T. G. of V.* ii. 1. 101 and *T. of A.* i. 1. 34. Steevens quotes Greene, *Groatsworth of Wit:* "It was I that . . . for seven years' space was absolute interpreter of the puppets."

1329. *Sounds.* That is, waters (which may be *deep*, though not fathomless). Malone conjectured "floods."

1335. *Fowls.* The 6th and 7th eds. have "soules;" an easy misprint when the long *s* was in fashion.

1338. *Villain.* Servant, bondman. Cf. *Lear*, iii. 7. 78: "my villain," etc.

1345. *God wot.* God knows. Cf. *Rich. III.* ii. 3. 18: "no, no, good friends, God wot."

1350. *This pattern.* That is, the groom. On *worn-out age*, cf. *Sonn.* 68. 1: "map of days outworn."

1353. *That.* So that; as in 94 above.

1355. *Wistly.* Wistfully. See on *V. and A.* 343.

1357, 1358. Note the imperfect rhyme.

1368. *The which.* Referring to *Troy*. *Drawn* = drawn up.

1370. *Cloud-kissing Ilion.* Cf. *T. and C.* iv. 5. 220: "Yond towers whose wanton tops do buss the clouds," etc.

1371. *Conceited.* Fanciful, imaginative. Cf. *W. T.* iv. 4. 204 : "an admirable conceited fellow ; " *L. C.* 16 : "conceited characters," etc.

1372. *As.* That ; as in 1420 below. See also *The Phœnix and the Turtle*, 25.

1377. *Strife.* That is, "his art with nature's workmanship at strife" (*V. and A.* 291). Cf. *T. of A.* i. 1. 37.

1378. *And dying eyes*, etc. Cf. *V. and A.* 1127.

1380. *Pioneer.* Sapper. The early eds. have "pyoner" or "pioner." Here the rhyme requires *pioneer*. The early eds. have *pioner* in the four instances in which S. uses the word, except in *Oth.* iii. 3. 146, where the later folios have *pioneer*. Cf. *enginer* and *mutiner.*

1384. *Lust.* Pleasure. Cf. *T. and C.* iv. 4. 134.

1388. *Triumphing.* Accented on the second syllable, as often. Cf. *L. L. L.* iv. 3. 35, 1 *Hen. IV.* v. 4. 14, v. 3. 15, etc.

1400. *Deep regard and smiling government.* "Profound wisdom and the complacency arising from the passions being under the command of reason" (Malone) ; or deep thought and complacent self-control. For *deep regard*, cf. 277 above.

1407. *Purl'd.* "Curl'd" (Steevens's conjecture) ; used by S. only here.

1411. *Mermaid.* Siren. See on *V. and A.* 429.

1417. *Bollen.* Swollen ; used by S. nowhere else. Cf. Chaucer, *Black Knight*, 101 : "Bollen hertes," etc. The later form *bolled* occurs in *Exodus*, ix. 31.

1418. *Pelt.* Probably = throw out angry words, be passionately clamorous ; as Malone, Nares, and Schmidt explain it. Cf. *Wits, Fits, and Fancies:* "all in a pelting chafe," etc. The noun is also sometimes = a great rage ; as in *The Unnatural Brother:* "which put her ladyship into a horrid pelt," etc.

1422. *Imaginary.* Imaginative ; as in *Sonn.* 27. 9 : "my soul's imaginary sight," etc. For *conceit*, see on 701 and 1371 above.

1423. *Kind.* Natural; as often. See *Much Ado,* i. 1. 26, etc.

1436. *Strand.* All the early eds. have "strond;" an old spelling found elsewhere.

1440. *Than.* The old form of *then,* sometimes found in the early eds. (as in *M. of V.* ii. 2. 200, 3 *Hen. VI.* ii. 5. 9, etc.), here used for the sake of the rhyme.

1444. *Stell'd.* Spelled "steld" in all the early eds., and probably = placed, fixed. Cf. *Sonn.* 24. 1 : —

> "Mine eye hath play'd the painter, and hath stell'd
> Thy beauty's form in table of my heart."

In *Lear,* iii. 7. 61, we find "the stelled fires," where *stelled* is commonly explained as derived from *stella,* though probably = fixed, as here. Knight and Hudson suspect that *stell'd* is "simply a poetical form of *styled,* that is, written or depicted as with a *stilus* or *stylus.*"

1449. *Bleeding under Pyrrhus' proud foot.* Cf. *Ham.* ii. 2. 474 fol.

1450. *Anatomiz'd.* "Laid open, shown distinctly" (Schmidt). Cf. *A. Y. L.* i. 1. 162, ii. 7. 56, *A. W.* iv. 3. 37, etc.

1452. *Chaps.* Spelled "chops" in all the early eds. except the 7th. Cf. *chopt* or *chopped* in *A. Y. L.* ii. 4. 50, 2 *Hen. IV.* iii. 2. 294, etc., and *choppy* in *Macb.* i. 3. 44.

1460. *Ban.* Curse; as in *V. and A.* 326.

1479. *Moe?* More; used often, but only with plural or collective nouns.

1486. *Swounds.* Swoons. All the early eds. have "sounds," as the word was often spelled.

1487. *Channel.* Stream; or, as some define it, gutter. Cf. 1 *Hen. IV.* ii. 1. 52.

1488. *Unadvised.* Unintentional, inadvertent. Cf. *T. G. of V.* iv. 4. 127, etc.

1489. *Confounds.* Destroys. See on 160 above.

1494. *On ringing.* A-ringing. This *on* and *a-* (see *a-work* in

1496) are often used interchangeably. Cf. *aboard* and *on board,* etc. *His* = its. Cf. *V. and A.* 159, etc.

1499. *Painting.* All the early eds. except the 1st and 2d have "painted."

1500. *Who.* The reading of all the early eds., changed in some modern ones to "whom." We find *who* even after prepositions.

1504. *Blunt.* Rude, rough. The 5th and later eds. have "these blunt."

1505. *His woes.* "That is, the woes suffered by *Patience*" (Malone). Cf. *T. N.* ii. 4. 117 and *Per.* v. 1. 139.

1507. *The harmless show.* The harmless painted figure.

1511. *Guilty instance.* Token or evidence of guilt. For *instance,* see *Much Ado,* ii. 2. 42, *A. Y. L.* iii. 2. 53, 59, 62, 71, etc.

1521. *Sinon.* Cf. *3 Hen. VI.* iii. 2. 190 and *Cymb.* iii. 4. 61.

1524. *That.* So that. See on 94 above.

1525. *Stars shot from their fixed places.* Cf. *M. N. D.* ii. 1. 153: "And certain stars shot madly from their spheres."

1526. *Their glass,* etc. "Why Priam's palace, however beautiful or magnificent, should be called the mirror in which the fixed stars beheld themselves, I do not see. The image is very quaint and far-fetched" (Malone). The reference is probably to the burnished roof. Boswell cites what Lydgate says of Priam's palace : —

> "That verely when so the sonne shone
> Upon the golde meynt among the stone,
> They gave a lyght withouten any were,
> As doth Apollo in his mid-day sphere."

1527. *Advisedly.* Deliberately, attentively. Cf. *advised* in *V. and A.* 615, and *unadvised,* 1488 above.

1544. *Beguil'd.* Rendered deceptive or guileful. Cf. *guiled* in *M. of V.* iii. 2. 97. The early eds. have " armed to beguild " (or "beguil'd "); corrected by Malone. Wyndham retains " beguild " **as** = *begild,* reading : —

> "To me came Tarquin armed to beguild
> With outward honesty, but yet defiled," etc.

It is true that *gild* is sometimes "guild" in the old eds.; as in 60
above, *Sonn.* 55. 1, etc.; but S. does not use *begild*, and I doubt
whether it was his word here.

1549. *Sheds!* The old eds. have "sheeds" for the rhyme.

1551. *Falls.* Lets fall; as often. Cf. *Temp.* v. 1. 64, *M. N. D.*
v. 1. 143, etc.

1555. *Effects.* Outward manifestations or attributes. Some
make it = efficacies, powers, or faculties.

1565. *Unhappy.* Mischievous, fatal, pernicious; as in *C. of E.*
iv. 4. 127, *Lear*, iv. 6. 232, etc.

1576. *Which all this time.* This (namely, *time*) has passed un-
heeded by her during this interval that she has spent with painted
images; or *which* may perhaps refer to the slow passage of time
just mentioned, and the meaning may be, This she has forgotten
all the while that she has been looking at the pictures. Hudson
says: "*Which* refers to *time* in the preceding stanza, and is the
object of *spent:* Which that she hath spent with painted images,
it hath all this time overslipped her thought." This seems need-
lessly awkward and involved.

1588. *Water-galls.* The word is evidently used here simply as =
rainbows, to avoid the repetition of that word. Nares defines it as
"a watery appearance in the sky, accompanying the rainbow;"
according to others, it means the "secondary bow" of the rainbow
(which Hudson speaks of as being "within" the primary bow).
Halliwell (*Archaic Dict.*) says: "I am told a second rainbow
above the first is called in the Isle of Wight a *watergeal.* Carr has
weather-gall, a secondary or broken rainbow." For *element* = sky,
cf. *J. C.* i. 3. 128: "the complexion of the element," etc.

1589. *To.* In addition to; as not unfrequently.

1592. *Sod.* The participle of *seethe*, used interchangeably with
sodden. Cf. *L. L. L.* iv. 2. 23, *Hen. V.* iii. 5, 18, etc.

1598. *Uncouth.* Strange (literally, unknown). Cf *A. Y. L.* ii.
6. 6: "this uncouth forest," etc.

1600. *Spent?* Consumed, destroyed. Cf. 938 above.

1601. *Attir'd in discontent?* Cf. *Much Ado*, iv. 1. 146: " sc attir'd in wonder," etc.

1604. *Gives her sorrow fire.* The metaphor is taken from the discharge of the old-fashioned firelock musket. Cf. *T. G. of V.* ii. 4. 38: " for you gave the fire."

1606. *Address'd.* Prepared, ready ; as often.

1615. *Moe.* The reading of the first three eds. ; "more " in the rest. See on 1479 above.

Depending. Impending. Cf. *T. and C.* ii. 3. 21, etc.

1619. *Interest.* See on 1067 above.

1632. *Hard-favour'd.* See on *V. and A.* 133.

1645. *Adulterate.* Cf. *C. of E.* ii. 2. 142, *Ham.* i. 5. 42, etc.

1650. *Scarlet.* Dressed in red robes, like a judge.

1661. *Declin'd.* All the eds. except the 1st have "inclin'd."

1662. *Wretched.* Walker plausibly conjectures "wreathed." Cf. *T. G. of V.* ii. 1. 19: " to wreathe your arms."

1667. *As through an arch*, etc. Doubtless suggested by the tide rushing through the arches of Old London Bridge, which greatly obstructed its current. Cf. *Cor.* v. 4. 50.

1671. *Recall'd in rage*, etc. Farmer wished to read " recall'd, the rage being past."

1672. *Make a saw.* The metaphor is quaint, but readily understood from the context. The noun *saw* is used by S. nowhere else, though *handsaw* occurs in 1 *Hen IV.* ii. 4. 187 and *Ham.* ii. 2. 397.

1680. *One woe.* The 1st and 2d eds. have "on " for *one*, a common spelling. In *L. L. L.* iv. 3. 142, for instance, the 1st folio reads: "On [one] her haires were gold, christall the others eyes."

1691. *Venge.* Not *'venge*, as often printed. Cf. *vengeful, vengeance*, etc.

1694. *Knights, by their oaths*, etc. Malone remarks: " Here one of the laws of chivalry is somewhat prematurely introduced."

1698. *Bewray'd.* Exposed, made known. Cf. *Lear*, ii. 1. 109, iii. 6. 118, etc.

1704. *With the foul act dispense.* See on 1070 above.

1705. *Advance?* Raise; opposed to *low-declined.* For *advance* = lift up, cf. ii. 2. 60, etc.

1713. *Carv'd in it.* All the early eds. have "it in" for *in it,* except the 7th, which omits *it.* The correction is Malone's.

1715. *By my excuse,* etc. Livy makes Lucretia say: "Ego me, etsi peccato absolvo, supplicio non libero ; nec ulla deinde impudica exemplo Lucretiae vivet;" which Painter, in his novel (see p. 18 above) translates thus: "As for my part, though I cleare my selfe of the offence, my body shall feel the punishment, for no unchaste or ill woman shall hereafter impute no dishonest act to Lucrece."

1720. *Assays.* Attempts ; as in *T. of A.* iv. 3. 406, *Ham.* iii. 3. 69, etc.

1728. *Sprite.* See on 121 above, where we have *spright.*

1730. *Astonish'd.* Astounded, thunderstruck. Cf. *2 Hen. VI.* v. 1. 146, etc.

1738. *That.* So that; as in 1764 below. See on 94 above.

1740. *Vastly.* "Like a waste" (Steevens); the only instance of the word in S. Cf. *vasty* in *M. of V.* ii. 7. 41: "the vasty wilds of wide Arabia," etc.

1745. *Rigol.* Circle. Cf. *2 Hen. IV.* iv. 5. 36: "the golden rigol" (the royal crown); the only other instance in S.

1752. *Depriv'd.* Taken away; as in 1186 above.

1754. *Unliv'd.* Probably the poet's own coinage, and used by him only here.

1760. *Fair fresh.* Dyce reads "fresh fair," and Staunton and Hudson "fresh-fair."

1765. *Last.* All the early eds. but the 1st and 2d have "hast," and in the next line "thou" for *they.*

1766. *Surcease.* Cease ; as in *Cor.* iii. 2. 121 and *R. and J.* iv. 1. 97.

1774. *Key-cold.* Cf. *Rich. III.* i. 2. 5: "Poor key-cold figure of a holy king ;" the only other instance in S.

1784. *Thick.* Fast. Cf. *thick-coming* in *Macb.* v. 3. 38. See also *Cymb.* i. 6. 67: "thick sighs," etc.

1788. *This windy tempest*, etc. Cf. *T. and C.* iv. 4. 55 : "rain to lay this wind," etc.

1797. *Sorrow's interest.* Tears. Cf. "interest of the dead " in *Sonn.* 31. 7.

1801. *Too late.* Too lately. Cf. 426 above and *V. and A.* 1026.

1803. *I owed her.* She was mine. For *owe* = own, cf. 82 above, *V. and A.* 411, *L. C.* 140, 327, etc.

1805. *Dispers'd.* For the accent, see on 26 above.

1816. *Advisedly.* Deliberately. Cf. 180 and 1527 above. So *advised* = deliberate, in 1849 below.

1819. *Unsounded.* Not *sounded* or understood hitherto. Cf. *2 Hen. VI.* iii. 1. 57.

1822. *Wounds help.* Walker would read "heal" and Staunton "salve" for *help;* but *help* is often = cure. Cf. *Temp.* ii. 2. 97, *A. W.* i. 3. 244, ii. 1. 192, ii. 3. 18, etc.

1829. *Relenting.* The 5th and later eds. have "lamenting."

1832. *Suffer these abominations*, etc. That is, permit these abominable Tarquins *to be* chased, etc.

1839. *Complain'd.* Bewailed. For the transitive use, cf. *Rich. II.* iii. 4. 18. The verb is used reflexively in 845 above and *Rich. II.* i. 2. 42.

1845. *Allow.* Approve. Cf. *2 Hen. IV.* iv. 2. 54.

1851. *Thorough.* Used interchangeably with *through;* so also in *thoroughly* and *thoroughfare.* The 5th ed. has "through out," and the 7th "throughout."

1854. *Plausibly.* With applause or acclamations (Malone and Steevens); or "readily, willingly" (Schmidt). It is the only instance of the adverb in S. *Plausible* occurs only in *M. for M.* iii. 1. 253, where it is = pleased, willing.

A LOVER'S COMPLAINT

For the feminine use of *lover* in the title, cf. *A. Y. L.* iii. 4. 46, *M. for M.* i. 4. 40, *Cymb.* v. 5. 172, etc. We still say "a pair of lovers." The stanza is the same a in *R. and L.*

1. *Re-worded.* Echoed. Cf. *Ham.* iii. 4. 143 : "I the matter will re-word."

2. *Sistering.* Neighbouring. We find the verb in *Per.* v. prol. 7 : "her art sisters the natural roses."

3. *Spirits.* Monosyllabic ; as very often. Cf. 236 below and see on *V. and A.* 181. The *to* is an extra unaccented syllable. *Accorded* = agreed.

4. *Laid.* Malone reads "lay," which is the form elsewhere in S. *Laid* may be a misprint.

5. *Fickle.* Apparently referring to her behaviour at the time.

6. *A-twain.* So in the folio text of *Lear*, ii. 2. 80, where the quartos have "in twain." In *Oth.* v. 2. 206, the 1st quarto has *a-twain*, the other early eds. "in twain."

7. *Her world.* Malone quotes *Lear*, iii. 1. 10 : —

> "Strives in his little world of man to outscorn
> The to-and-fro-conflicting wind and rain."

8. *Hive.* Hat, shaped like a beehive.

11. *Done.* Past, lost. Cf. *V. and A.* 197, 749, and *R. of L.* 23.

14. *Sear'd.* Withered. Hudson has "sere" (also spelt "sear"), which S. uses in *C. of E.* iv. 2. 19 and *Macb.* v. 3. 23, where Schmidt takes *sear* to be a noun.

15. *Heave her napkin.* Lift her handkerchief ; the only meaning of *napkin* in S. For *heave*, cf. *Cymb.* v. 5. 157 : —

> "O, would
> Our viands had been poison'd, or at least
> Those which I heav'd to head !"

and for *napkin* see *Oth.* iii. 3. 287, 290, 321, etc.

16. *Conceited characters*. Fanciful figures. See on *R. of L.* 1371.

17. *Laundering*. Wetting; used by S. only here. Malone calls the verb "obsolete;" but it has come into use again in our day. *Laundress* occurs in *M. W.* iii. 3. 157, 163, and Evans has *laundry* blunderingly in the same sense in *Id.* i. 2. 5.

18. *Season'd*. A favourite figure with S. Cf. *A. W.* i. 1. 55 : "'T is the best brine a maiden can season her praise in;" *T. N.* i. 1. 30 : —

> "all this to season
> A brother's dead love, which she would keep fresh
> And lasting in her sad remembrance ; "

and *R. and J.* ii. 3. 72 : —

> " How much salt water thrown away in waste,
> To season love, that of it doth not taste ! "

See also *Much Ado*, iv. 1. 144. For *pelleted* (= rounded), cf. *A. and C.* iii. 13. 165.

21. *Size*. This use of the word seems peculiar now ; but cf. *Hen. VIII.* v. 1. 136, *A. and C.* iv. 15. 4, v. 2. 97, etc.

22. *Carriage*. The figure is taken from a gun-carriage. *Levell'd* was a technical term for aiming a gun. Cf. *Rich. III.* iv. 4. 202, 2 *Hen. IV.* iii. 2. 286, etc. See also 281 and 309 below.

30. *Careless hand of pride*. That is, hand of careless pride.

31. *Sheav'd*. Straw. Cf. 8 above.

33. *Threaden*. The word is used again in *Hen. V.* iii. chor. 10 : "threaden sails."

36. *Maund*. Hand-basket ; used by S. only here. Cf. Drayton, *Polyolbion*, xiii. : —

> " And in a little maund, being made of oziers small,
> Which serveth him to do full many a thing withall,
> He very choicely sorts his simples got abroad ; "

Herrick, *Poems :* " With maunds of roses for to strew the way," etc. Hence *Maundy Thursday*, from the baskets in which the royal alms were distributed at Whitehall.

37. *Beaded.* The quarto (the 1609 ed. of *Sonnets*, in which the poem first appears) has "bedded ; " corrected by Sewell. Knight and Wyndham retain "bedded" as = imbedded, set.

40. *Applying wet to wet.* A favourite conceit with S. See *A. Y. L.* ii. 1. 48, *R. and J.* i. 1. 138, *3 Hen. VI.* v. 4. 8, *Ham.* iv. 7. 186, etc.

42. *Cries some.* Cries for some. Malone puts *some* in italics (= "cries 'Some'").

45. *Posied.* Inscribed with posies, or mottoes. Cf. *M. of V.* v. 1. 148, 151, and *Ham.* iii. 2. 162. Rings were often made of *bone* and ivory.

47. *Moe.* More. Cf. *R. of L.* 1479, 1615, etc.

48. *Sleided.* Untwisted or unwrought. Cf. *Per.* iv. prol. 21 : "sleided silk." *Feat* = featly, dexterously. Cf. *Temp.* i. 2. 380 and *W. T.* iv. 4. 186.

49. *Enswath'd.* Enwrapped ; used by S. only here. Steevens says : "Anciently the ends of a piece of narrow ribbon were placed under the *seals* of letters to connect them more closely ; " that is, I suppose, the letters were tied with ribbon, and the knot was *sealed* for security — as we might wrap and seal a small package nowadays.

Curious. Careful ; as in *A. W.* i. 2. 20, *Cymb.* i. 6. 191, etc.

50. *Fluxive.* Flowing, weeping ; used by S. only here.

51. *Gan.* The quarto has "gaue," which Knight and Wyndham retain (as "gave") ; corrected by Malone.

53. *Unapproved.* Not *approved*, or proved true ; used by S. only here. *Approve* is often = prove.

55. *In top of rage.* Cf. *3 Hen. VI.* v. 7. 4 : "in tops of all their pride ; " *A. and C.* v. 1. 43 : "in top of all design," etc.

Rents = rends ; an old form of *rend*, found in *M. N. D.* iii. 2. 215, *Rich. III.* i. 2. 126 (*rend* in quartos), *Macb.* iv. 3. 168, etc.

58. *Sometime.* Formerly ; used interchangeably with *sometimes* in this sense. *Ruffle* = bustle, stir ; the only instance of the noun in S.

60. *The swiftest hours.* "The prime of life, when Time appears

to move with his quickest pace" (Malone). *They*, according to Malone, refers to the fragments of the torn-up letters; though he admits that the clause may be connected with *hours*, meaning that "this reverend man, though engaged in the bustle of court and city, had not suffered the busy and gay period of youth to pass by without gaining some knowledge of the world." This latter explanation is doubtless the correct one.

61. *Fancy.* Often = love (see on *R. of L.* 200), and here used concretely for the *lover.* Cf. 197 below. *Fastly* is used by S. only here.

64. *Slides he down,* etc. That is, lets himself down by the aid of his staff, as he seats himself beside her. *Grained* = of rough wood, or showing the *grain* of the wood. Cf. *Cor.* iv. 5. 114 : "My grained ash" (= spear).

69. *Ecstasy.* Passion, excitement. Cf. *V. and A.* 895.

80. *Outwards.* External features ; not elsewhere plural in S. For *Of* the quarto has "O ; " corrected by Malone.

81. *Stuck.* Cf. *M. for M.* iv. 1. 61 : —

> "O place and greatness! millions of false eyes
>   Are stuck upon thee."

88. *What 's sweet to do,* etc. "Things pleasant to be done will easily find people enough to do them" (Steevens).

91. *Sawn.* Explained by some as a form of the participle of *see*, used for the sake of the rhyme ; by others as = *sown*, which Boswell says is still pronounced *sawn* in Scotland. The latter is the more probable.

93. *Phœnix.* Explained by Malone and Schmidt as = "matchless, rare." So *termless* = indescribable. Wyndham makes it = youthful.

95. *Bare.* Bareness ; not elsewhere used substantively by S.

104. *Authoriz'd.* Accented on the second syllable ; as in the other two instances in which S. uses the word (*Sonn.* 35. 6 and *Macb.* iii. 4. 66).

107. *That horse*, etc. Hudson does not include this line in the supposed comment.

112. *Manage.* See on the verb in *V. and A.* 598.

116. *Case.* Dress; as in *M. for M.* ii. 4. 13, etc. It may be = "accessories" (Wyndham).

118. *Came.* The quarto has "Can;" corrected by Sewell. Knight and Wyndham retain "Can" as = "to be effective."

126. *Catching all passions*, etc. Steevens says: "These lines, in which our poet has accidentally delineated his own character, would have been better adapted to his monumental inscription than such as are placed on the scroll in Westminster Abbey." *Craft of will* = "faculty of influencing them" (Wyndham).

127. *That.* So that. See on *V. and A.* 242.

139. *Moe.* Cf. 47 above.

140. *Owe.* Own. See on *R. of L.* 1803.

144. *Was my own fee-simple.* "Had an absolute power over myself" (Malone). Cf. *A. W.* iv. 3. 312: "the fee-simple of his salvation," etc.

153. *Foil.* The background used to set off a *jewel.* Cf. *Rich. III.* i. 3. 266, *Ham.* v. 2. 266, etc.

156. *Assay.* Essay, try. Cf. *V. and A.* 608.

162. *Blood.* Passion. Cf. *Much Ado*, ii. 1. 187, ii. 3. 170, iv. 1. 60, etc.

163. *Proof.* Experience. Cf. *M. of V.* i. 1. 144: "I urge this childhood proof," etc.

164. *Forbod.* Forbidden; an old form of the participle used by S. only here.

170. *The patterns of his foul beguiling.* "The examples of his seduction" (Malone).

171. *Orchards.* Gardens; the usual meaning in S. For the figure, cf. *Sonn.* 16. 6.

173. *Brokers.* Panders, go-betweens. Cf. *Ham.* i. 3. 127: "his vows . . . are brokers," etc.

174. *Thought.* Malone took this to be a noun.

176. *My city.* For the figure, cf. *R. of L.* 469 (see also 1547), *A. W.* i. 1. 137, etc.

182. *Woo.* The quarto has "vow;" corrected by Dyce.

185. *Acture.* Action; not found elsewhere. Cf. *enactures* in *Ham.* iii. 2. 207.

Malone paraphrases the passage thus : " My illicit amours were merely the effect of constitution [or animal passion], and not approved by my reason : pure and genuine love had no share in them, or in their consequences ; for the mere congress of the sexes may produce such fruits, without the affections of the parties being at all engaged."

192. *Teen.* Trouble, pain. See on *V. and A.* 808.

193. *Leisures.* Moments of leisure. Schmidt makes it = " affections, inclinations," which it *implies.*

197. *Fancies.* See on 61 above.

198. *Paled.* The quarto has " palyd," and Sewell reads " pallid," which may be right. *Paled* is due to Malone.

204. *These talents,* etc. " These *lockets,* consisting of hair platted and set in *gold* " (Malone). Wyndham thinks it may mean " precious possessions," or gifts.

205. *Impleach'd.* Interwoven. Cf. *pleached* in *Much Ado,* iii. 1. 7, and *thick-pleach'd* in *Id.* i. 2. 8.

207. *Beseech'd.* Cf. the past tense in *Ham.* iii. 1. 22.

208. *Annexions.* Additions ; used by S. only here, as *annexment* only in *Ham.* iii. 3. 21.

210. *Quality.* " In the age of S. peculiar virtues were imputed to every species of precious stone " (Steevens).

212. *Invis'd.* " Invisible " (Malone); or, " perhaps = inspected, investigated, tried " (Schmidt). No other example of the word is known.

214. *Weak sights,* etc. Eye-glasses of emerald were much esteemed by the ancients ; and the near-sighted Nero is said to have used them in watching the shows of gladiators.

215. *Blend.* Walker makes this a participle = blended. He

adds : "The expression is perhaps somewhat confused, but it refers to the ever-varying hue of the opal."

217. *Blazon'd.* Interpreted, explained. Cf. the noun in *Much Ado*, ii. 1. 307.

219. *Pensiv'd.* Found only here. *Pensive* occurs in 3 *Hen. VI.* iv. 1. 10 and *R. and J.* iv. 1. 39. Hudson adopts Lettsom's conjecture of "pensive" here ; but the "pensiu'd" of the quarto could hardly be a misprint.

223. *Of force.* Perforce, of necessity. Cf. *L. L. L.* i. 1. 148, *M. N. D.* iii. 2. 40, etc.

224. *Enpatron me.* Are my patron saint. The verb is used by S. only here.

225. *Phraseless.* Probably = indescribable, like *termless* in 94 above. Schmidt thinks it may possibly be = silent, like *speechless* (hand) in *Cor.* v. 1. 67 S. uses it only here.

229. *What me,* etc. Whatever obeys me, your minister, for (or instead of) you, etc.

231. *Distract.* Disjoined, separate. For the accent, see on *R. of L.* 26.

233. *A sister.* The quarto has "Or sister ; " corrected by Malone.

Note. Notoriety, distinction. Cf. *Cymb.* i. 4. 2 : "of crescent note," etc.

234. *Which late,* etc. Who lately withdrew from her noble suitors.

235. *Whose rarest havings,* etc. "Whose accomplishments were so extraordinary that the flower of the young nobility were passionately enamoured of her" (Malone).

236. *Spirits.* Monosyllabic, as in 3 above. *Coat* may be = coat-of-arms (Malone), or dress as indicative of rank, as some explain it.

240. *Have not.* Hudson adopts Barron Field's conjecture of "love not" — a needless if not an injurious change.

241. *Paling the place,* etc. The quarto has "Playing the place,"

etc.; for which no really satisfactory emendation has been proposed. *Paling*, which is as tolerable as any, is due to Malone, who explains the line thus : "Securing within the pale of a cloister that heart which had never received the impression of love." Lettsom conjectures " Salving the place which did no harm receive." Staunton proposes " Filling the place," etc. *Paling* is adopted by most of the editors. For *pale* = enclose, cf. *A. and C.* ii. 7. 74, 3 *Hen. VI.* i. 4. 103, etc.

243. *Contrives.* Some make this = wear away, spend; as in *T. of S.* i. 2. 278.

250. *Eye.* The rhyme of *eye* and *eye* is apparently an oversight, no misprint being probable.

251. *Immur'd.* The quarto has " enur'd " and " procure ; " both corrected by Gildon. S. may have written " emur'd " (= *immur'd*), as Wyndham suggests.

252. *To tempt, all.* Most eds. join *all* to *tempt*, which, to my thinking, mars both the antithesis and the rhythm.

258. *Congest.* Gather in one ; used by S. only here.

260. *Nun.* The quarto has " Sunne." The correction was suggested by Malone, and first adopted by Dyce. Wyndham retains " sun," as " a metaphor not far-fetched."

261. *Ay, dieted.* The quarto has " I dieted," not " I died," as Malone (who reads " and dieted ") states.

262. *Believ'd her eyes*, etc. " Believed or yielded to her eyes when they, captivated by the external appearance of her wooer, began to assail her chastity" (Malone). "When I the assail " was an anonymous conjecture which Malone was at first inclined to adopt.

265. *Sting.* Stimulus, incitement. Cf. *Oth.* i. 3. 335 : " our carnal stings." Note the " chiastic " construction. See on *R. of L.* 616, 617.

271. *Love's arms are proof*, etc. Another perplexing line. The quarto has " peace" for *proof*, which was suggested by Malone. Steevens conjectures " Love aims at peace," Dyce " Love arms our

peace," and Lettsom "Love charms our peace." Wyndham retains the old text without question or comment. The meaning might possibly be : Love's warfare is peaceful (though arbitrary and persistent) rather than hostile ; which may be favoured by the *sweetens* that follows. The passage, however, is probably corrupt.

272. *And sweetens.* And *it* (*Love*) sweetens.

273. *Aloes.* The only mention of the bitter drug in S.

276. *Supplicant.* Not found elsewhere in S.

279. *Credent.* Credulous. Cf. *Ham.* i. 3. 30 : "too credent ear," etc.

280. *Prefer and undertake.* Recommend (cf. *M. of V.* ii. 2. 155) and guarantee, or answer for (see 1 *Hen. VI.* v. 3. 158, *Hen. VIII.* prol. 12, etc.).

281. *Dismount.* "The allusion is to the old English fire-arms, which were supported on what was called a rest " (Malone). For *levell'd* = aimed, see on 22 above. Cf. the noun in 309 below.

286. *Who glaz'd with crystal gate*, etc. Malone points thus : "Who, glaz'd with crystal, gate ; " making *gate* "the ancient perfect tense of the verb *to get*." *Flame* he took to be the object of *gate.*

290. *But with.* With but, or only.

293. *O cleft effect!* The quarto has "Or" for *O;* corrected by Gildon.

294. *Extincture.* Extinction ; used by S. only here.

297. *Daff'd.* Doffed, put off. Cf. *Much Ado*, ii. 3. 176, v. 1. 78, etc. *Stole* (= robe) is not found elsewhere in S.

298. *Civil.* Decorous ; as in *Oth.* ii. 1. 243 : "civil and humane seeming," etc.

303. *Cautels.* Deceits. Cf. *Ham.* i. 3. 15 ; the only other instance in S. *Cautelous* (= false, deceitful) occurs in *J. C.* ii. 1. 129 and *Cor.* iv. 1. 33.

305. *Swooning.* The quarto has "sounding," and "sound" in 308 below. See on *R. of L.* 1486.

309. *Level.* See on 281 above.

314. *Luxury.* Lust, lasciviousness ; the only meaning of the word in S. Cf. *Hen. V.* iii. 5. 6, *Ham.* i. 7. 83, etc.

315. *Preach'd pure maid.* Cf. *A. Y. L.* iii. 2. 227 : "speak sad brow and true maid."

318. *Unexperient.* Used by S. only here, as *unexperienced* only in *T. of S.* iv. 1. 86.

319. *Cherubin.* Used by S. ten times. *Cherub* he has only in *Ham.* iv. 3. 50, *cherubim* not at all.

327. *Owed.* That is, owned, or his own. See on 140 above. *Borrow'd motion* = counterfeit expression of feeling.

THE PASSIONATE PILGRIM

Swinburne remarks : "What Coleridge said of Ben Jonson's epithet for ' turtle-footed peace,' we may say of the label affixed to this rag-picker's bag of stolen goods : *The Passionate Pilgrim* is a pretty title, a very pretty title ; pray what may it mean ? In all the larcenous little bundle of verse there is neither a poem which bears that name nor a poem by which that name would be bearable. The publisher of the booklet was like ' one Ragozine, a most notorious pirate ; ' and the method no less than the motive of his rascality in the present instance is palpable and simple enough. Fired by the immediate and instantly proverbial popularity of Shakespeare's *Venus and Adonis,* he hired, we may suppose, some ready hack of unclean hand to supply him with three doggerel sonnets on the same subject, noticeable only for the porcine quality of prurience ; he procured by some means a rough copy or an incorrect transcript of two genuine and unpublished sonnets by Shakespeare, which with the acute instinct of a felonious tradesman he laid atop of his worthless wares by way of gilding to their base metal ; he stole from the two years published text of *Love's Labour's Lost,* and reproduced, with more or less mutilation or corruption, the sonnet of Longaville, the ' canzonet ' of Biron, and the

far lovelier love-song of Dumain. The rest of the ragman's gath-
erings, with three most notable exceptions, is little better for the
most part than dry rubbish or disgusting refuse ; unless a plea may
haply be put in for the pretty commonplaces of the lines on a
'sweet rose, fair flower,' and so forth ; for the couple of thin and
pallid if tender and tolerable copies of verse on 'Beauty' and
'Good Night,' or the passably light and lively stray of song on
'crabbed age and youth.' I need not say that those three exceptions are the stolen and garbled work of Marlowe and of Barnfield,
our elder Shelley and our first-born Keats : the singer of Cynthia
in verse well worthy of Endymion, who would seem to have died
as a poet in the same fatal year of his age that Keats died as a
man ; the first adequate English laureate of the nightingale, to be
supplanted or equalled by none until the advent of his mightier
brother."

The contents of Jaggard's piratical collection, stated more in detail, were as follows (the order being that of the "Globe" ed.) : —

I., II. Shakespeare's *Sonnets* 138 and 144, with some early or
corrupt readings (noted in my ed. of the *Sonnets*).

III. Longaville's sonnet to Maria in *L. L. L.* iv. 3. 60 fol.: "Did
not the heavenly rhetoric of thine eye," etc. The verbal variations
in the two versions (as in V. and XVI.) are few and slight.

IV. (I. of the present ed.).

V. The sonnet in *L. L. L.* iv. 2. 109 fol.: "If love make me
forsworn," etc.

VI., VII. (II. and IV. of this ed.).

VIII. The following sonnet, probably by Richard Barnfield, in
whose *Poems : In diuers humors*, 1598 (appended, with a separate
title-page, to a small volume containing *The Encomion of Lady Pecunia* and *The Complaint of Poetrie, for the Death of Liberalitie*),
it had first appeared, with this heading : "To his friend Maister
R. L. In praise of Musique and Poetrie :" —

> "If music and sweet poetry agree,
>   As they must needs, the sister and the brother,

> Then must the love be great 'twixt thee and me,
> Because thou lov'st the one, and I the other.
> Dowland [1] to thee is dear, whose heavenly touch
> Upon the lute doth ravish human sense ;
> Spenser to me, whose deep conceit is such
> As, passing all conceit, needs no defence.
> Thou lov'st to hear the sweet melodious sound
> That Phœbus' lute, the queen of music, makes;
> And I in deep delight am chiefly drown'd
> Whenas himself to singing he betakes.
>> One god is god of both, as poets feign :
>> One knight loves both, and both in thee remain."

Barnfield terms these poems " fruits of unriper years," and expressly claims their authorship. The above sonnet is the first in the collection. Both this and XX. are omitted in the second edition of *Lady Pecunia*, 1605 ; but so also are nearly all of the " Poems in Divers Humors," so that no substantial argument can rest upon the absence of the two *P. P.* sonnets from that edition (Halliwell-Phillipps).

IX., X. (III. and V. of this ed.).

XI. The following sonnet, probably by Bartholomew Griffin, in whose *Fidessa more Chaste than Kinde*, 1596, it had appeared with some variations : [2] —

[1] John Dowland (1563–1625) was the most famous musician of his day. He published several collections of *Songs or Airs*, and is often referred to by contemporary dramatists. He is here the representative of *music*, as *Spenser* of *poetry*. In line 14 there may be an allusion to Sir George Carey, to whom Dowland dedicated his first book. Carey's wife was an intimate friend of Spenser.

[2] Instead of lines 9–14, the following are given in the *Fidessa* : —

> " But he a wayward boy refusde her offer,
>> And ran away, the beautious Queene neglecting :
> Shewing both folly to abuse her proffer,
>> And all his sex of cowardise detecting.
> Oh that I had my mistris at that bay
> To kisse and clippe me till I ranne away ! "

"Venus, with young Adonis sitting by her
 Under a myrtle shade, began to woo him ;
 She told the youngling how god Mars did try her,
 And as he fell to her, so fell she to him.
 ' Even thus,' quoth she, ' the warlike god embrac'd me,'
 And then she clipp'd Adonis in her arms ;
 ' Even thus,' quoth she, ' the warlike god unlac'd me,'
 As if the boy should use like loving charms ;
 ' Even thus,' quoth she, ' he seized on my lips,'
 And with her lips on his did act the seizure ;
 And as she fetched breath, away he skips,
 And would not take her meaning nor her pleasure.
   Ah, that I had my lady at this bay,
   To kiss and clip me till I run away ! "

XII., XIII., XIV. (VI., VII., and VIII. of this ed.).

XV. Here begin the "Sonnets To sundry notes of Musicke"
(see p. 13 above) with the following, which is certainly not Shakespeare's, though it is not found elsewhere : —

"It was a lording's daughter, the fairest one of three,
 That liked of her master as well as well might be,
 Till looking on an Englishman, the fair'st that eye could see,
   Her fancy fell a-turning.
 Long was the combat doubtful that love with love did fight,
 To leave the master loveless, or kill the gallant knight ;
 To put in practice either, alas, it was a spite
   Unto the silly damsel !
 But one must be refused ; more mickle was the pain
 That nothing could be used to turn them both to gain,
 For of the two the trusty knight was wounded with disdain ;
   Alas, she could not help it !
 Thus art with arms contending was victor of the day,
 Which by a gift of learning did bear the maid away.
 Then, lullaby, the learned man hath got the lady gay ;
   For now my song is ended."

XVI. Dumain's poem to Kate, in *L. L. L.* iv. 3. 101 fol.: "On
a day — alack, the day ! " etc.

XVII. The following, from Thomas Weelkes's *Madrigals*, 1597, certainly not Shakespeare's : [1] —

> " My flocks feed not,
> 　My ewes breed not,
> 　My rams speed not,
> 　　All is amiss ;
> 　Love's denying,
> 　Faith's defying,
> 　Heart's renying,
> 　　Causer of this.
> All my merry jigs are quite forgot,
> All my lady's love is lost, God wot ;
> Where her faith was firmly fix'd in love,
> There a nay is plac'd without remove.
> 　One silly cross
> 　Wrought all my loss.
> 　　O frowning Fortune, cursed, fickle dame !
> 　For now I see
> 　Inconstancy
> 　　More in women than in men remain.
>
> 　In black mourn I,
> 　All fears scorn I,
> 　Love hath forlorn me,
> 　　Living in thrall ;
> 　Heart is bleeding,
> 　All help needing,
> 　O cruel speeding,
> 　　Fraughted with gall.
> My shepherd's pipe can sound no deal ;
> My wether's bell rings doleful knell ;
> My curtal dog, that wont to have play'd,
> Plays not at all, but seems afraid.

[1] Weelkes was the composer of the music, but not necessarily the author of the words. The poem is found also in *England's Helicon* 1600, with the title "The Unknown Sheepheard's Complaint," and subscribed "Ignoto."

My sighs so deep
Procure to weep,
   In howling wise, to see my doleful plight.
How sighs resound
Through heartless ground,
   Like a thousand vanquish'd men in bloody fight!

Clear wells spring not,
Sweet birds sing not,
Green plants bring not
   Forth their dye;
Herds stand weeping,
Flocks all sleeping,
Nymphs back peeping
   Fearfully.
All our pleasure known to us poor swains,
All our merry meetings on the plains,
All our evening sport from us is fled,
All our love is lost, for Love is dead.
Farewell, sweet lass,
Thy like ne'er was
   For a sweet content, the cause of all my moan.
Poor Corydon
Must live alone;
   Other help for him I see that there is none."

XVIII. (IX. of this ed.).

XIX. The following imperfect version of Marlowe's " Come, live
with me," etc., with *Love's Answer* (a mere fragment), attributed
to Sir Walter Raleigh : —

      " Live with me, and be my love,
         And we will all the pleasures prove
         That hills and valleys, dales and fields,
         And all the craggy mountains yields.

      There will we sit upon the rocks,
         And see the shepherds feed their flocks,
         By shallow rivers, by whose falls
         Melodious birds sing madrigals.

There will I make thee a bed of roses,
With a thousand fragrant posies,
A cap of flowers, and a kirtle
Embroider'd all with leaves of myrtle,

A belt of straw and ivy buds,
With coral clasps and amber studs;
And if these pleasures may thee move,
Then live with me and be my love.

LOVE'S ANSWER

If that the world and love were young,
And truth in every shepherd's tongue,
These pretty pleasures might me move
To live with thee and be thy love."

XX. The following (except lines 27, 28) from Richard Barnfield's *Poems: In diuers humors*, 1598 (the first 28 lines also found
in *England's Helicon*, 1600, where it is subscribed "Ignoto") : —

" As it fell upon a day
In the merry month of May,
Sitting in a pleasant shade
Which a grove of myrtles made,
Beasts did leap, and birds did sing,
Trees did grow, and plants did spring.
Every thing did banish moan,
Save the nightingale alone ;
She, poor bird, as all forlorn,
Lean'd her breast up-till a thorn,
And there sung the dolefull'st ditty,
That to hear it was great pity :
' Fie, fie, fie,' now would she cry;
' Tereu, tereu ! ' by and by;
That to hear her so complain,
Scarce I could from tears refrain,
For her griefs, so lively shown,
Made me think upon mine own.

Ah, thought I, thou mourn'st in vain!
None takes pity on thy pain.
Senseless trees they cannot hear thee;
Ruthless beasts they will not cheer thee;
King Pandion he is dead;
All thy friends are lapp'd in lead;
All thy fellow birds do sing,
Careless of thy sorrowing.
Even so, poor bird, like thee,
None alive will pity me.
Whilst as fickle Fortune smil'd,
Thou and I were both beguil'd.

   Every one that flatters thee
Is no friend in misery.
Words are easy, like the wind;
Faithful friends are hard to find.
Every man will be thy friend
Whilst thou hast wherewith to spend;
But if store of crowns be scant,
No man will supply thy want.
If that one be prodigal,
Bountiful they will him call,
And with such-like flattering,
' Pity but he were a king!'
If he be addict to vice,
Quickly him they will entice;
If to women he be bent,
They have at commandement;
But if Fortune once do frown,
Then farewell his great renown;
They that fawn'd on him before
Use his company no more.
He that is thy friend indeed,
He will help thee in thy need.
If thou sorrow, he will weep;
If thou wake, he cannot sleep;
Thus of every grief in heart
He with thee doth bear a part.

> These are certain signs to know
> Faithful friend from flattering foe."

Some editors have divided the above poem, making the first 28 lines (or the portion printed in *England's Helicon*) a separate piece ; but the whole (except lines 27, 28) forms a continuous "Ode" in Barnfield's book, and there is no real division in the 1599 ed. of the *P. P.* The editors have been misled by the printer's arrangement of his matter in that little book, where each page has an ornamental head-piece and tail-piece, with unequal portions of text between. The first 14 lines of this poem are on one page, the next 12 on the next page (27 and 28 wanting), the next 14 on the next, and the last 16 on the next. As there is something like a break in the piece between the 2d and 3d pages as thus arranged, it might appear at first sight that it was a division between poems rather than *in* a poem ; but, as Mr. Edmonds has pointed out, " the poet's object being to show the similarity of his griefs to those of the nightingale, he devotes the lines ending with *sorrowing* to the bird," and then "takes up all his own woes with the line *Whilst as fickle fortune smil'd,* and enlarges upon them to the end of the ode." For typographical proof that it should not be divided (as I was the first to point out), see on viii. below.

The editor of *England's Helicon* seems to have taken the first two pages from the *P. P.,* supposing them to be a compl_te poem ; but feeling that it ended too abruptly, he added the couplet,

> " Even so, poore bird like thee,
> None a-live will pitty mee,"

to round it off.

It may be added that his signing the poem " Ignoto " shows that he was not aware it was Barnfield's, and did not consider that its appearance in the *P. P.* proved it to be Shakespeare's ; and the same may be said of XVII., the *Helicon* copy of which is evidently from the *P. P.,* not from Weelkes. On the other hand, XVI. of the *P. P.* (" On a day, alack the day," etc.), taken from *L. L. L.,* is given in the *Helicon* with Shakespeare's name attached to it. Furnivall says : "Mr. Grosart has shown in his prefaces to his editions of Barnfield's *Poems* and Griffin's *Fidessa* that there is no reason to take from the first his Ode (XX.) and his Sonnet (VIII.), or from the second his Venus and Adonis Sonnet (XI.), many of whose readings the *Passionate Pilgrim* print spoils." See also Mr. Edmonds's able plea in behalf of Barnfield's title to VIII. and XX. in the preface to his reprint (London, 1870) of the 1599 ed. of the *P. P.* p. xiv. fol.

I

1. *Cytherea.* Cf. *T. of S.* ind. 2. 53, *W. T.* iv. 4. 122, and *Cymb.* ii. 2. 14.

9. *Conceit.* Understanding. Cf. *2 Hen. IV.* ii. 4. 263, etc.

10. *Figur'd.* Expressed by signs.

14. *Ah, fool,* etc. See p. 31 above.

II

4. *Tarriance.* The word occurs again in *T. G. of V.* ii. 7. 90.

6. *Spleen.* Heat; as often in a figurative sense. Cf. *V. and A.* 907.

12. *Wistly.* Wistfully. See on *V. and A.* 343.

13. *Whereas.* Where. Cf. *2 Hen. VI.* i. 2. 58 and *Per.* i. 4. 70.

III

The 2d line is wanting in all the editions, the omission being first marked by Malone.

3. *Dove.* See on *V. and A.* 153.

5. *Steep-up.* Cf. *Sonn.* 7. 5 : "the steep-up heavenly hill." We find *steep-down* in *Oth.* v. 2. 280.

11. *Ruth.* Pity. Cf. *Rich. II.* iii. 4. 106, *Sonn.* 132. 4, etc.

IV

This may possibly be Shakespeare's, but I think it extremely improbable. Cf. *Sonn.* 138.

3. *Brighter than glass*, etc.   Steevens quotes the following lines "written under a lady's name on an inn window : " —

> " Quam digna inscribi vitro, cum lubrica, laevis,
>   Pellucens, fragilis, vitrea tota nites ! "

For *brittle* the old *brickle* (which means the same) might well be substituted for the rhyme.

8. *Between each kiss*.   I think that S. is never guilty of *between each*.

14. *Out-burneth*.   Sewell has " out burning."

V

This is probably not Shakespeare's.

1. *Vaded*.   Faded.   Cf. vii. 2. below.   See also *Rich. II*. i. 2. 20, where the folios have *vaded*, the quartos *faded*.

3. *Timely*.   Early.   Cf. *A. and C.* ii. 6. 52, etc.

8. *For why*.   Because.   See on *R. of L.* 1222.   The old eds. have "lefts" for *left'st* in both 8 and 9 ; a common contraction of such harsh second persons.   See on *R. of L.* 1134.

VI

Possibly Shakespeare's.   In the eds. of 1599 and 1612 it is printed, as here, in twelve lines.   Malone and others make twenty of it.

2. *Pleasance*.   Pleasure.   Cf. *Oth.* ii. 3. 293 ; the only other instance in S.

4. *Brave*.   Fair, beautiful ; as very often.

11. *Defy*.   Despise, spurn.   Cf. *K. John*, iii. 4. 23 : "I defy all counsel, all redress ; " 1 *Hen. IV*. i. 3. 228 : "All studies here I solemnly defy," etc.

VII

Probably not Shakespeare's ; perhaps by the same author as V.

1. *Doubtful*.   A copy of this poem, said to be from an ancient

MS. and published in the *Gentleman's Magazine*, vol. xxii. p. 521, has "fleeting" for *doubtful* both here and in 5 below. In 3 it has "almost in the bud" for *first it gins to bud;* in 4, "that breaketh" for *that's broken;* in 7, "As goods, when lost, are wond'rous seldom found;" in 8 "can excite" for *will refresh,* and in 10 "unite" for *redress;* in 11 "once, is ever" for *once's forever;* and in 12 "pains" for *pain.*

A second copy, "from a corrected MS.," appeared in the same magazine, vol. xxx. p. 39. The readings are the same as in the other copy, except that it has "a fleeting" for "and fleeting" in 1, and "fading" for *vaded* in 8.

7. *Seld.* Seldom. Cf. *T. and C.* iv. 5. 150 : "As seld I have the chance." We find "seld-shown" in *Cor.* ii. 1. 229.

11. *Once's.* This is the reading generally adopted; but it is very harsh. The eds. of 1599 and 1612 have "once, forever," which might well enough be retained. Verity suggests "once for ever 's lost."

VIII

Probably not Shakespeare's. All recent eds. make the last three stanzas a separate poem; but this is unquestionably a mistake. Dowden (in his introduction to the "Griggs" fac-simile of the 1599 ed. of *P. P.*) gives good reasons for not dividing this poem, but neither he nor any other critic has seen that the 1599 ed. proves its unity beyond a doubt. The first two stanzas are on one page, the next two on another, and the last stanza on a third; but the third stanza does *not* begin with the *large initial letter,* which elsewhere in the book is used to mark the beginning of a poem. I may add that there is similar typographical evidence in the 1599 ed. that XX. (cf. p. 272 above) should not be divided.

Dowden notes that in the 1640 ed. of the *Poems,* the five stanzas of VIII. appear as one poem (see p. 284 below). Malone (in his *Supplement,* 1780) seems to have been the first editor to divide it.

3. *Daff'd me.* Put me off, sent me away. See on *L. C.* 297.

4. *Descant.* Comment; as in *Rich. III.* i. 1. 27. Cf. *R. of L.* 1134.

6. *Fare well.* There is a play on *fare* = feed; as in *T. of S.* ind. 2. 103.

8. *Nill.* Will not. Cf. *T. of S.* ii. 1. 273 : "will you, will you;" *Ham.* v. 1. 19 : "will he, will he," etc.

9. *'T may be.* Steevens says : "I will never believe any poet could begin two lines together with such offensive elisions. They may both be omitted without injury to sense or metre." I cannot imagine S. guilty of them, or of sundry other metrical faults in the poem.

12. *As take.* That take. Cf. *R. of L.* 1372, 1420.

14. *Charge the watch.* Probably = accuse or blame the watch (for marking the time so slowly).

17. *Philomela.* The nightingale. See on *R. of L.* 1079. The Cambridge editors conjecture that *sits and* should be omitted; and they are probably right.

20. *Dismal-dreaming.* The old eds. have "darke dreaming night;" corrected by Malone.

21. *Pack'd.* Sent packing, gone. Cf. *Rich. III.* i. 1. 146 : "Till George be pack'd with post-horse up to heaven." See also 29 below.

23. *Solace, solace.* The old eds. have "solace and solace;" corrected by Malone.

24. *For why.* See on *R. of L.* 1222, and cf. v. 8 above.

27. *Moon.* The old eds. have "houre;" corrected by Malone.

30. *Short, night, to-night.* Shorten to-night, O night. For the antithesis, cf. *Cymb.* i. 6. 200 : —

> "I shall short my word
> By lengthening my return."

IX

This may possibly be Shakespeare's, but I seriously doubt it. Furnivall says : "That 'to sin and never for to saint,' and the whole

of the poem, are by some strong man of the Shakspere breed."
But the whole tone and spirit of it are unlike S. himself.

1. *Whenas.* When. See on *V. and A.* 999.

2. *Stall'd.* Got as in a *stall*, secured. Cf. *Cymb.* iii. 4. 111 : —

> "when thou hast ta'en thy stand,
> The elected deer before thee."

4. *Partial fancy like.* For *fancy* = love, see on *R. of L.* 200. The early eds. have "fancy (party all might)." Malone gave in 1780 "fancy, partial tike," but later from an ancient MS. "fancy, partial like." Staunton conjectures "fancy martial might ; " the Cambridge editors read "fancy, martial wight" (a conjecture of Malone's); and White "fancy's partial might." The text is from a manuscript in the possession of Collier. As Schmidt notes, *like* is "almost = love ; " as in *A. Y. L.* iii. 2. 431, *K. John,* ii. 1. 511, *R. and J.* i. 3. 97, etc.

8. *Filed talk.* "Studied or polished language" (Malone). Cf. *L. L. L.* v. 1. 12 : "his tongue filed." See also *Sonn.* 85. 4.

12. *Sell.* The early eds. have "sale; " corrected by Malone, from his old manuscript, which also has "thy" for *her.* The editors have generally adopted "thy," but the other reading may be = "praise her person highly, as a salesman praises his wares" (White). Cf. *T. and C.* iv. 1. 78 : "We 'll but commend what we intend to sell;" *L. L. L.* iv. 3. 240 : "To things of sale a seller's praise belongs; " *Sonn.* 21. 14 : "I will not praise that purpose not to sell," etc.

14. *Clear ere.* The reading of Malone's manuscript, for the "calme yer" of the old eds.

20. *Ban.* Curse. See on *V. and A.* 326.

28. *In thy lady's ear.* Malone reads "always in her ear."

32. *Humble-true.* First hyphened by Staunton.

42. *Nought ?* The rhyme with *oft* is peculiar. In *Rich. III.* iii. 6. 13 and *Macb.* iv. 1. 70, *nought* rhymes with *thought.* On the

passage, cf. *T. G. of V.* i. **2.** 55. There was an old proverb, " Maids say nay, and take it."

43–46. *Think women still*, etc. Expect women always, etc. Malone reads from the old manuscript thus : —

> " Think, women love to match with men,
>   And not to live so like a saint:
>   Here is no heaven : they holy then
>   Begin, when age doth them attaint."

The early eds. have in 45, 46 : —

> " There is no heaven (by holy then)
>   When time with age shall them attaint."

The reading in the text is due to White, and gives a clear meaning with very slight changes in the old text. In a passage so corrupt, emendation is but guesswork at best ; but this seems to me a happier guess than that of the writer of Malone's manuscript. I do not, however, think it necessary to put " seek " for *still* in 43, as White does.

50. *Lest that.* The early eds. have " Least that." Malone reads " For if " from his manuscript, connecting the line with what follows.

51. *To round me i' the ear.* To whisper in my ear. Cf. *K. John*, ii. 1. 566 and *W. T.* i. 2. 217, the only instances in S. The early eds. have " on th' are " and " on th' ere." Malone changed " on " to *i'* in 1780; but in 1790 he read " ring mine ear." Collier has " warm my ear " (from his old manuscript). White reads " She 'll not stick to round me i' th' ear."

54. *Bewray'd.* Disclosed, exposed. See on *R. of L.* 1698.

THE PHŒNIX AND THE TURTLE

The title-page of Chester's *Loves Martyr*, after referring at some length to that poem and " the true legend of famous King *Arthur*," which follows it, continues thus : " *To these are added some new*

*compositions, of seuerall moderne Writers whose names are sub-
scribed to their seuerall workes, upon the first subiect: viz. the*
Phœnix *and* Turtle."

The part of the book containing these "compositions" has
a separate title-page, as follows:—

HEREAFTER | FOLLOVV DIVERSE | Poeticall Essaies on
the former Sub- | iect; viz: the *Turtle* and *Phœnix.* | *Done by the
best and chiefest of our* | moderne writers, with their names sub- |
scribed to their 'particular workes: | *neuer before extant.* | And
(now first) consecrared by them all generally, | *to the loue and
merite of the true-noble Knight,* | Sir Iohn Salisburie. | *Dignum
laude virum Musa vetat mori.* | [wood-cut of anchor] *Anchora
Spei* | MDCI.

Among these poems are some by Marston, Chapman, and Ben
Jonson.

Malone has no doubt of the genuineness of *The Phœnix and the
Turtle.* White says: "There is no other external evidence that
these verses are Shakespeare's than their appearance with his signature in a collection of poems published in London while he was
living there in the height of his reputation. The style, however, is
at least a happy imitation of his, especially in the bold and original
use of epithet." Dowden writes me that he has now no doubt that
the poem is Shakespeare's (cf. his *Primer,* ed. 1878, p. 112); and
Furnivall also believes it to be genuine. All the recent editors
and commentators, so far as I am aware, take the same view of it,
though most of them agree that the allegory has not been satis-
factorily explained. Sidney Lee remarks: "Happily Shakespeare
wrote nothing else of like character."

Dr. Grosart (see his introduction to the New Shaks. Soc. ed.
of Chester's *Loves Martyr*) sees a hidden meaning in this poem
and those associated with it in Chester's book. "The *Phœnix* is a
person and a woman, and the *Turtle-dove* a person and a male;
and while, as the title-page puts it, the poet is 'Allegorically shad-
owing the truth of Love,' it is a genuine story of human love and

martyrdom (*Love's Martyr*). . . . No one at all acquainted with what was the *mode* of speaking of Queen Elizabeth to the very last, will hesitate in recognizing her as the *Rosalin* and *Phœnix* of Robert Chester, and the 'moderne writers' of this book. . . . So with the *Turtle-dove*, epithet and circumstance and the whole bearing of the Poems make us think of but one pre-eminent man in the Court of Elizabeth . . . and it will be felt that only of the brilliant but impetuous, the greatly-dowered but rash, the illustrious but unhappy Robert Devereux, second Earl of Essex, could such splendid things have been thought." See, however, on line 67 below. Dr. Grosart believes *The Phœnix and the Turtle* to be Shakespeare's, and calls it "priceless and *unique*."

For a recent and very thorough study of the poem by Mr. Arthur H. R. Fairchild, see *Englische Studien* (Leipzig), xxxiii. 3. 337–384.

1. *The bird of loudest lay.* As Dr. Grosart remarks, this is *not* the *Phœnix*, as has generally been assumed, as "it were absurd to imagine it could be called on to 'sing' its own death," and besides it is nowhere represented as gifted with song.

2. *The sole Arabian tree.* Malone cites *Temp.* iii. 3. 22 : —

> "Now I will believe
> That there are unicorns ; that in Arabia
> There is one tree, the phœnix' throne ; one phœnix
> At this hour reigning there."

He adds : "This singular coincidence likewise serves to authenticate the present poem." The *tree* is probably the *palm*, the Greek name of which is the same as that of the phœnix (φοινιξ).

3. *Trumpet.* Trumpeter. Cf. *Ham.* i. 1. 150, *Hen. V.* iv. 2. 61, etc.

4. *To.* For its use with *obey*, cf. *T. and C.* iii. 1. 165. We now say "obedience to."

Dr. Grosart, who takes the *bird* to be the nightingale, says : "I have myself often watched the lifting and tremulous motion of the singing nightingale's wings, and *chaste* was the exquisitely chosen word to describe the nightingale, in reminiscence of the classical story."

5. *Shrieking harbinger.* The screech-owl (Steevens). Cf. *M. N. D.* v. 1. 383 : —

> " Whilst the screech-owl, screeching loud,
>   Puts the wretch that lies in woe
>   In remembrance of a shroud."

The *fever's end* is of course death.

13. *Surplice.* The old reading is " Surples." S. uses the word only here and in *A. W.* i. 3. 99.

14. *That defunctive music can.* That understands funereal music, or can perform it. For this absolute use of *can*, cf. Chaucer, *C. T.* 5638 (ed. Tyrwhitt) : —

> " I wot wel Abraham was an holy man,
>   And Jacob eke, as fer as ever I can," etc.

See also *Ham.* iv. 7. 85 : " they can well on horseback ; " where *can* = are skilful.

16. *His.* Its. See on *V. and A.* 359.

17. *Treble-dated.* Living thrice as long as man. Steevens quotes Lucretius, v. 1053 : —

> " Ter tres aetates humanas garrula vincit
>   Cornix."

18. *That thy sable gender mak'st,* etc. " Thou crow that makest [change in] thy sable gender with the mere exhalation and inhalation of thy breath " (E. W. Gosse). It was a popular belief that the crow could change its sex at will.

25. *As.* That. Cf. *R. of L.* 1372 and 1420.

32. *But in them it were a wonder.* " So extraordinary a phenomenon as *hearts remote, yet not asunder,* etc., would have excited admiration, had it been found anywhere else *except in these* two birds. In them it was not wonderful " (Malone).

34. *Saw his right*, etc. "It is merely a variant mode of expressing seeing love-babies (or one's self imaged) in the other's eyes. This gives the true sense to *mine* in 36" (Grosart).

37. *Property.* Property in self, individuality.

43. *To themselves.* Grosart suggests that these words should be joined to what precedes.

44. *Simple were so well compounded.* That is, were so well blended into one.

45. *That.* So that. Cf. *V. and A.* 242.

49. *Threne.* Threnody, funeral song. It is the Anglicized *threnos* (θρῆνος), with which the following stanzas are headed. Malone quotes Kendal's *Poems*, 1577 : —

> "Of verses, threnes, and epitaphs,
>   Full fraught with tears of teene."

A book entitled *David's Threanes* was published in 1620, and reprinted two years later as *David's Tears.*

67. *These dead birds.* That these *birds* are not Elizabeth and Essex has been shown clearly in Dr. F. J. Furnivall's paper "On Chester's *Love's Martyr*" in *Trans. of New Shak. Soc.* 1877–79, p. 451 fol.

APPENDIX

The 1640 Edition of the Poems

The contents of this book (see p. 14 above) are not described accurately by any editor or bibliographer that I have been able to consult. They are as follows : —

1. Poems by Leon. Digges[1] and John Warren[2] in eulogy of Shakespeare.

2. All the *Sonnets* (except Nos. 18, 19, 43, 56, 75, 76, 96, and 126) arranged under various titles. The first group, for instance, includes 67, 68, and 69, with the heading "The glory of beautie," and the second puts together 60, 63, 64, 65, and 66 under the title "Injurious Time." From one to five sonnets appear under a title. When two or more are grouped they are printed as a continuous piece, with no space between the sonnets.[3]

3. *All* the poems of *The Passionate Pilgrim* of 1599 (not "some," as the "Cambridge" ed. says (not corrected in the revised ed.), or "the greater part," as Knight and others give it), mostly interspersed among the Sonnets and furnished with titles. For instance, No. 4 ("Sweet Cytherea," etc.) is headed "A sweet provocation ; " No. 8 ("If music," etc.), "Friendly concord ; " No. 10 ("Sweet rose," etc.), "Loves Losse ; " No. 12 ("Crabbed age," etc.),

---

[1] Not the verses prefixed to the folio of 1623, but a much longer piece, beginning "Poets are borne not made, when I would prove," etc. See Ingleby's *Centurie of Praise*, 2d ed., p. 231 fol.

[2] A sonnet, beginning "What, lofty *Shakespeare*, art again reviv'd ? " See *Centurie of Praise*, p. 235.

[3] For a full list of the groups with their titles, see Knight's *Pictorial Shakspere*, vol. ii. of Tragedies, etc., p. 487 fol., or Dowden's larger ed. of the *Sonnets*, p. 47 fol.

"Ancient Antipothy;" No. 15 ("It was a lording's daughter," etc.), "A Duell;" and so on. The five stanzas of "Good night, good rest," are printed as one poem with the title "Loath to depart." "As it fell upon a day" also appears without division, and is entitled "Sympathizing love."

4. The following translations from Ovid, and other poems :—

"The Tale of Cephalus and Procris" (inserted *before* Sonnets 153 and 154).

"That Menelaus was cause of his owne wrongs."

"Vulcan was Iupiters Smith, an excellent workeman, on whom the Poets father many rare Workes, among which, I find this one. Mars and Venus."

"The History how the Mynotaure was begot."

"This Mynotaure, when he came to growth, was inclosed in the Laborinth, which was made by the curious Arts-master Dedalus, whose Tale likewise we thus pursue."

"Achilles his concealment of his Sex in the Court of Lycomedes."
A Lover's Complaint (Shakespeare's).

"The amorous Epistle of Paris to Hellen."

"Hellen to Paris."

"The Passionate Shepheard to his Love" (the complete text of Marlowe's poem, given imperfectly in *P. P.*).

"The Nimphs reply to the Shepheard" (the six stanzas, of which only one is given in *P. P.*).

"Another of the same Nature" (a poem of 44 lines, beginning :—

> "Come live with me and be my deare,
> And vve will revill all the yeare,
> In plaines and groves, on hills and dales,
> Where fragrant ayre breeds sweetest gales.
> There shall you have the beautious Pine,
> The Ceder and the spreading Vine,
> And all the vvoods to be a skrene,
> Least *Phœbus* kisse my Summers Queene."

And ending thus :—

"If these may serve for to intice,
    Your presence to Loves Paradise,
    Then come vvith me and be my deare,
    And we will straight begin the yeare.").

"Take, O take those lips away" (the stanza in *M. for M.* iv. 1.
1 fol., with the additional stanza, ascribed to Fletcher; the song
appearing here without a title).

"Let the bird of lowest [*sic*] lay" (*The Phœnix and the Turtle*,
without a title, except for the *Threnos*, which is headed "*Threnes*").

"Why should this Desart be" (the lines from *A. Y. L.* iii. 2.
133 fol., without a title).

"An Epitaph on the admirable Dramaticke Poet, William
Sheakespeare" (signed "I. M.," that is, John Milton).

"On the death of William Shakespeare, who died in Aprill,
Anno Dom. 1616" (the lines, "Renowned Spenser, lie a thought
more nigh," etc., signed here "W. B.," that is, William Basse, who
probably wrote them, though they have been ascribed to Dr. Donne
and others).

"An Elegie on the death of that famous Writer and Actor, M.
William Shakspeare" ("I dare not do thy memory that wrong,"
etc., unsigned and not traced to any author).

5. After the "FINIS" that follows the above poems there is an
appendix, with the heading: "An Addition of some Excellent |
Poems, to those precedent, of | Renowned *Shakespeare*, | By other
Gentlemen."

The poems are as follows: —

"His Mistresse Drawne" (signed "B. L." — evidently intended
for "B. I.," or Ben Jonson, in whose works the lines are printed).

"Her minde" (signed "B. I.," and also printed as his).

"His Mistris Shade."

"Lavinia walking in a frosty Morning."

"A Sigh sent to his Mistresse."

"An Allegorical allusion of melancholy thoughts to Bees"
(signed "I. G.").

"The Primrose."

"A Sigh."

"A Blush."

"Am I dispis'd because you say," etc. (no title)

"Vpon a Gentlewoman walking on the Grasse."

"On his Love going to Sea."

"Aske me no more where *Ioue* bestovves," etc. (no title).

A second "FINIS" ends the volume.

EARLY ALLUSIONS TO THE POEMS

THE earliest allusion to any of the *Poems*, according to Ingleby's *Shakespeare's Centurie of Prayse* (1879) is to *Lucrece* in 1594, in an *Epicedium* (or *Funerall Song*) ascribed to Sir William Harbert:—

> "You that have writ of chaste Lucretia,
> Whose death was witnesse of her spotlesse life."

Drayton, in his *Matilda* (1594), has a reference to Lucretia, but it seems to imply a dramatic representation rather than a poem:—

> "Lucrece of whom proude Rome hath boasted long,
> Lately reviv'd to live another age,
> And here ariv'd to tell of *Tarquins* wrong,
> Her chast denial, and the Tyrants rage,
> Acting her passions on our stately stage."

Robert Southwell, in the poetical preface to his *Saint Peter's Complaint*, etc. (1595), says:—

> "Still finest wits are 'stilling Venus rose,
> In Paynim toyes the sweetest vaines are spent;
> To Christian workes few have their talents lent."

As Southwell was executed Feb. 20, 1594-5, this may have been written as early as the references quoted above.

In John Weever's apostrophe to Shakespeare, which is supposed to have been first published in 1595, though the earliest extant edition is of 1599, we have allusions to both *Venus and Adonis* and *Lucrece :* —

> " Honie-tong'd *Shakespeare*, when I saw thine issue,
> I swore *Apollo* got them and none other,
> Their rosie-tainted [tinted] features cloth'd in tissue,
> Some heaven born goddesse said to be their mother :
> Rose-checkt [cheek'd] *Adonis* with his amber tresses
> Faire fire-hot *Venus* charming him to love her,
> Chaste *Lucretia* virgine-like her dresses,
> Prowd lust-stung *Tarquine* seeking still to prove her," etc.

Thomas Edwardes, in 1595, in the *Envoy* to his *Cephalus and Procris*, referring to certain poets under the names of their best-known works, alludes to Shakespeare thus : —

> " *Adon* deafly masking thro,
> Stately troupes rich conceited
> Shew'd he well deserved to
> Loves delight on him to gaze
> And had not love herselfe intreated,
> Other nymphs had sent him baies."

The next reference to the *Poems* that has been noted is the familiar one in Meres's *Palladis Tamia* (see p. 15 above), where both the *Venus and Adonis* and *Lucrece*, as well as the "sugred Sonnets," are mentioned.

In the same year both poems are referred to in "A Remembrance of some English Poets," the fourth tract in a volume called *Poems : in diuers humors*, of which the first tract bears Richard Barnfield's name (see p. 265 above) : —

> " And *Shakespeare* thou, whose hony-flowing Vaine,
> (Pleasing the World) thy Praises doth obtaine ;
> Whose *Venus*, and whose *Lucrece* (sweete and chaste).
> Thy Name in fame's immortall Booke have plac't.
> Liue ever you ! at least, in Fame liue ever !
> Well may the Bodye dye ; but Fame dies neuer."

In 1598 also, as Furnivall remarks, "the Satirist, John Marston, published 'the first heir of his invention,' which he called 'the first bloomes of my poesie,' *The Metamorphosis of Pigmalion's Image. And Certaine Satyres;* and in it, says Mr. Minto (*Characteristics of English Poets*, 1874), reviving an old theory, 'Shakspere's *Venus and Adonis* was singled out as the type of dangerously voluptuous poetry, and unmercifully parodied; the acts of the goddess to win over the cold youth being coarsely paralleled in mad mockery by the acts of Pygmalion to bring his beloved statue to life.' Now the fact is, that there is no trace of 'mad mockery' or parody in Marston's poem, though there are echoes in it of *Venus*, as there are of *Richard III., Hamlet,* etc., in Marston's *Scourge of Villanie,* his *Fawn,* etc.; and the far more probable view of the case is that put forward by Dr. Brinsley Nicholson: that Marston, being young, and of a warm temperament and licentious disposition, followed the lead of a poem then in everybody's mouth [1] (Shakspere's *Venus*), and produced his *Pigmalion's Image;* but being able only to heighten the *Venus's* sensuality, and leave out its poetry and bright outdoor life, he disgusted his readers, had his poem suppressed by Whitgift and Bancroft's order, and then tried to get out of the scrape by saying that he had written his nastiness only to condemn other poets for writing theirs! A likely story indeed! But let him tell it himself. In his 'Satyre VI.' of his *Scourge of Villanie,* 1598 (completed in 1599), he says: —

'Curio! know'st my sprite;
Yet deem'st that in sad seriousness I write

[1] See *The Fair Maid of the Exchange:* —

"*Crip[ple].* But heare you sir? reading so much as you haue done,
Doe you not remember one pretty phrase,
To scale the walles of a faire wenches loue?
    Bow[dler]. I never read any thing but *Venus* and *Adonis.*
    Crip. Why that's the very quintessence of loue;
If you remember but a verse or two,
Ile pawne my head, goods, lands, and all, 't will doe."

Such nasty stuffe as is *Pigmalion* ?
Such maggot-tainted, lewd corruption ! . . .
Think'st thou that I, which was create to whip
Incarnate fiends . . .
Think'st thou that I in melting poesie
Will pamper itching sensualitie,
That in the bodies scumme, all fatally
Intombes the soules most sacred faculty ?
   Hence, thou misjudging censor ! know, I wroi
Those idle rimes to note the odious spot
And blemish that deformes the lineaments
Of moderne poesies habiliments.
Oh that the beauties of invention
For want of judgements disposition,
Should all be spoil'd ! ' . . .

Then, after describing seven types of poets — of whom the fifth *may be* Shakspere,[1] and the sixth Ben Jonson — Marston goes on to satirize the readers of his and other writers' loose poems, for whom he 'slubber'd up that chaos indigest' of his *Pigmalion*. This epithet is certainly not consistent with the dedication of his poem to Good Opinion and his Mistress ; and his excuse for his failure in it is plainly an after-thought. But whatever we determine as to Marston's motives and honesty, we shall all join in regretting the 'want of judgements disposition' that let Shakspere choose Venus for an early place in his glorious gallery of women — forms whose radiant purity and innocence have won all hearts ; though we will remember this fault only as the low level from which he rose on stepping-stones of his dead self to higher things. He who put Venus near

[1] Yon 's one whose straines haue flowne so high a pitch,
   That straight he flags, and tumbles in a ditch.
   His sprightly hot high-soring poesie
   Is like that dream'd-of imagery,
   Whose head was gold, brest silver, brassie thigh,
   Lead leggs, clay feete : O faire fram'd poesie ! "

That Shakspere's subject was clay, and his verse gold, is certainly true.

the beginning of his career, ended with Miranda, Perdita, Imogen, and Queen Katherine.   Let *them* make atonement for *her !*"

John Lane, in *Tom Tel-Troths Message*, 1600, says : —

> " When chast *Adonis* came to mans estate,
>   *Venus* straight courted him with many a wile;
>   *Lucrece* once seene, straight *Tarquine* laid a baite,
>   With foule incest her bodie to defile:
>   Thus men by women, women wrongde by men,
>   Give matter still unto my plaintife pen."

It was probably between 1600 and 1603 that Gabriel Harvey wrote the following manuscript note in a copy of Speght's *Chaucer* (1598), now lost : "The younger sort take much delight in Shake-speare's Venus and Adonis ; but his Lucrece, and his tragedy of Hamlet, Prince of Denmarke, have it in them to please the wiser sort."

In 1601, Robert Chester, in the introduction of his *Loves Martyr* (see p. 278 above), has the following lines : —

> " To the Kind Reader.
>   Of bloody warres, nor of the sacke of *Troy*,
>   Of *Pryams* murdred sonnes, nor *Didoes* fall,
>   Of *Hellens* rape, by *Paris Troian* boy,
>   Of *Cæsars* victories, nor *Pompeys* thrall,
>   Of *Lucrece* rape, being ravisht by a King,
>   Of none of these, of sweete Conceit I sing."

In *The Returne from Parnassus* (1601–2) Judicio says : —

> " Who loves *Adonis* love or *Lucre's* rape,
>   His sweeter verse containes hart robbing life,
>   Could but a graver subject him content,
>   Without loves foolish lazy languishment."

In *Saint Marie Magdalens Conversion*, by "I. C." (1603) we find the following : —

> " Of *Helens* rape and *Troyes* beseiged *Towne*,
>   Of *Troylus* faith, and *Cressids* falsitie,

> Of *Rychards* stratagems for the english crowne,
> Of *Tarquins* lust, and lucrece [*sic*] chastitie,
> Of these, of none of these my muse nowe treates,
> Of greater conquests, warres, and loves she speakes."

William Drummond of Hawthornden, in his list of "Bookes red by me, anno 1606," mentions *The Passionate Pilgrime* and *The Rape of Lucrece;* and among those under "anno 1611," *Venus and Adon. by Schaksp.* and *The Rap of Lucrece.*

George Peele, in his *Merrie Conceited Jests* (earliest known ed. 1607), refers to a certain tapster as "much given to poetry," and mentions *Venus and Adonis* among the books which he "had collected together."

In 1609 the *Venus and Adonis* was alluded to in the publisher's Address prefixed to some copies of the first edition of *Troilus and Cressida* and reprinted in the standard modern editions of that play.

Thomas Freeman, in a poetical address "To Master W. Shake-speare," 1614, says : —

> "Vertues or vices theame to thee all one is:
> Who loves chaste life there's *Lucrece* for a teacher:
> Who list read lust there's *Venus* and *Adonis*,
> True model of a most lascivious leatcher" [lecher].

Richard Brathwaite, in *The Civill Devill* (1615) has the following passage : —

> "Ile be thy *Venus*, pretty Ducke I will,
> And though lesse faire, yet I have farre more skill,
> In Loves affaires: for if I *Adon* had,
> As *Venus* had: I could have taught the lad
> To have been farre more forward than he was,
> And not have dallied with so apt a lasse."

These are specimens (in addition to those given in the introduction pp. 15 and 32 fol.) of the more important allusions to the two poems between their first appearance and the death of Shakespeare in 1616. For others, between that date and 1693, the reader may be referred to *Shakespeare's Centurie of Prayse*, to which I have been mainly indebted in making these selections.

The only allusions to *The Passionate Pilgrim* cited in that book are the mention of it by Drummond above, and Thomas Heywood's protest in his *Apology for Actors* (1612) against the insertion of two of his poems under Shakespeare's name in the second edition of the *Pilgrim*, printed the same year. He says : " I must necessarily insert a manifest injury done me . . . by taking the two Epistles of *Paris* to *Helen*, and printing them in a lesse volume under the name of another. . . . As I must acknowledge my lines not worthy his patronage, under whom he hath publisht them, so the Author [Shakespeare] I know much offended with M. Jaggard that (altogether unknowne to him) presumed to make so bold with his name." This led Jaggard to insert a new title-page, omitting Shakespeare's name (see p. 13 above).

INDEX OF WORDS AND PHRASES EXPLAINED